Your Band Sucks

SUCKS

WHAT I SAW AT INDIE ROCK'S FAILED REVOLUTION

(BUT CAN NO LONGER HEAR)

JON FINE

VIKING

VIKING
Published by the Penguin Group
Penguin Group (USA) LLC
375 Hudson Street
New York, New York 10014

USA | Canada | UK | Ireland | Australia | New Zealand | India | South Africa | China
penguin.com
A Penguin Random House Company

First published by Viking Penguin, a member of Penguin Group (USA) LLC, 2015

Excerpt from "Louder Than Hell," performed by NME. © 1985 Dezeezed Music / NME.
Used with permission.

ISBN 978-0-670-02659-3

Printed in the United States of America
10 9 8 7 6 5 4 3 2 1

Set in Scala OT with DINk
Designed by Daniel Lagin

For the guys I've toured with the most:

Orestes Morfín
Sooyoung Park
Fred Weaver
and for Jerry Fuchs.

We are ugly, but we have the music.

Leonard Cohen

Contents

CONTENTS

Preface

A toddler, still small enough to strap into an infant's car seat in his father's white Plymouth Fury II, a vehicle so huge that, when he was a newborn, his parents fit his crib in the backseat.

He is a jumpy child, easily bored, always seeking new stimulation, and his parents have been murmuring to each other for many miles before noticing he's unusually quiet on this rainy and dreary day.

The father's head tilts up as he glances in the rearview mirror. Flashing a big movie star grin, he waggles his eyebrows and calls out, "How are you doing back there?"

But the boy is oblivious, eyes vacant, lost and dreaming. He did not hear the reassuring rumble of his father's voice. All he knows is the sound of the wipers as they squeak and rub across the slick windshield, chasing each other across the glass in an endless, perfect rhythm above the drone of the sighing motor and tires on wet pavement:

Kkwssh—nn—a—gaah—kknnn.

Kkwssh—nn—a—gaah—kknnn.

Kkwssh—nn—a—gaah—kknnn . . .

Melody, drone, and percussion, entrancing in their repetition, onto which he fixates this rainy day, staring, stupefied and in absolute fascination, at the windshield, hearing a song that blocks out everything else.

Kkwssh—nn—a—gaah—kknnn . . .

Foreword

Despite everything I'll say in the next few hundred pages, I really liked this stuff. Still do, even.

My first real band, formed in late 1986, was Bitch Magnet. It's always kind of gross to have to characterize your own band, but: we started out playing loud, noisy punk rock, then soon started stretching out song lengths and playing in odd time signatures. We were steeped in the American independent rock underground of that time, we released three critically acclaimed records, we enjoyed a dedicated but not particularly sizable fan base, we toured Europe and America, and at no point were we threatened, even distantly, by actual fame. Though a video we made in 1990 for about $100 on expired black-and-white film made it onto MTV once, in the ghetto at the end of *120 Minutes*, where they played short snippets of weirder and more aggressive stuff. To varying degrees, my other bands—among them Coptic Light and Vineland—share that same story. Books like this generally tell stories by or about the luminaries. This book isn't that.

Anyway, massive record sales and videos on MTV and whether or not your uncool cousins would have known us are the wrong yardsticks.

Bands like ours didn't give a shit about any of that, because we all understood immediately that most of it was out of reach. An incredibly liberating realization, one that went hand in hand with our general instinct to play only what we wanted, leave all edges unsanded, and never modify anything in a bid for a bigger audience. We were lucky to be teenagers in the eighties, futzing around with instruments we didn't quite know how to play, during a rare and oddly open moment when a scruffy crowd of like-minded souls gathered, far from the gloss and waste of the big-time music business, and an underground network arose that spanned the globe: venues, bands, zines, fans, record labels, record stores, college radio stations. It seems accidental and frankly miraculous that we all ended up in the same rooms at the same time, but we did, and in those rooms a culture was built, by hand and often from the barest of raw materials. On tour, our bands crashed on fans' floors, not in hotels, and rode in rattling vans, not fancy buses. We loaded and unloaded these vans by ourselves each night. We rarely had managers or other middlemen; we often dealt directly with club owners and labels. Or we released our records on our own, selling them to the companies that distributed them to record stores, hand-packing promotional copies into cardboard boxes to mail them to the hundred or so college radio stations that cared and all the fanzines we knew.

We built this thing—our own circuit—because we had to, because otherwise it wouldn't have existed, and because it felt like a life-and-death matter that our favorite bands and our own bands got heard. Just enough people erected just enough of an infrastructure to make possible the foundation of a parallel music industry—one that also entailed three-record deals and international tours—while still remaining a tight and (mostly) welcoming community. It was a swimming hole small enough, and secret enough, for you to know everyone in it. It wasn't hard to float atop its surface for a couple of records and tours if your band was good, and sometimes even if it wasn't.

There was always something provisional and flimsy about all this, before the likes of Pavement and Nirvana started selling records in greater than five-figure quantities, and even afterward. Labels and distributors and clubs and promoters were always going out of business, so money that was owed frequently disappeared outright. (As I write, Sub Pop Records is still around, twenty-eight years after releasing its first records. Congrats! It has also almost gone under at least four times, and—who knows?—may well be gone by the time you read this.) All this happened long before the Internet was anything, which meant that while we lacked a key communications channel for tightly knit outsider communities, our generations weren't distracted by a mythology of getting filthy rich young in a sort of cool and Web-by way. If you got out of college in the post-Reagan economic doldrums, as I did—well, why wouldn't you play in a band and live off temp jobs?

So, beginning in my late teens, many of my most cherished experiences took place in dusty practice spaces crammed with barely functioning equipment, inside cramped and overfull vans, and in small clubs that stank of cigarette smoke and yeast from old spilled beer and featured absolutely horrifying bathrooms. (You learned, eventually, to bring soap and toilet paper with you on tour: you couldn't count on either being there when you arrived at the venue.) Once I found this world, I found my home. The people who remain my closest friends to this day. My tribe. Or, rather, *our* tribe, because I was not the only one looking for these people and the small patch of land that was ours and ours alone. I threw myself upon it with a great and almost tearful relief. And, above all, I loved the music. I loved it so much it made my whole body hurt. (It also fried my ears and left them ringing, but sometimes love extracts a price.) The bands I most liked—the bands I was in— were guitar-based; quite loud; aggressive; eager to explore varying degrees of complexity and compositional ambitiousness; and instrumentally oriented, even though most had vocalists. I mention many in this book, but some of my favorites are Scratch Acid, Slovenly, Gore, the Ex, Meat Puppets, Slint, Swans, Mission of Burma, and Bastro. The best known among them are probably Black Flag and Sonic Youth. None would exist were it not for punk rock, but none were *just* punk rock; apart from that distinction, allow me to give up right now on trying to classify this stuff. Many times in this book I just say something like "weird bands," which is somewhat imprecise and insulting—but they *were* all a bit off-center, in one way or another, and often that was why I loved them.

Some guys lunge toward cultural moments to meet girls and drinking and drugging buddies. Not me and my friends. If you're looking for recitations of rock depravity, let me say right now I saw cocaine exactly once before I turned thirty, spent a great deal of my adult life working in cubicles, and can count on one hand the number of times I had sex as a direct consequence of being in a band—and still have fingers left over. Kurt Andersen once wrote that the eighties were America's manic episode; if so, indie rock was its depressive phase. But that was fine, because for me and many of my friends, the music pretty much blocked out everything else. It was shocking how much better this music, and its antecedents, were than any current music on the radio—than most of anything ever recorded, even. Realer, more visceral, and more direct. Smarter and more adventurous, too. It clearly expressed the emotional extremes all outsiders know. And, since the musicians and fans in our underground weren't exactly high school football stars, these extremes were especially keenly felt. This music was unafraid to color outside the lines unimaginative people thought defined what was acceptable in rock music. Because there were so many things you could do with rock music, once you started ignoring all the rules: *What if a song had only one part? What if a song had only one chord? Why do we need choruses? Why not write songs where no parts repeat? What if we never play in 4/4 again? What if we distorted the bass and made it the lead instrument? Why do we need vocals? Everyone's playing really fast, so why don't we play really slow?* I thought this music

was the most important thing in the world. I probably would have died
for it.

Sometimes I try to explain playing in such a band to people unfamiliar with this era, and, in trying to understand it, they grope for
words and say something like "Oh, so you had a *cult following*." That
awkward term—which I will not use again—makes me think of musicians and bands that never had a big hit and never will but still have
enough fans to eke out a living. Someone like Richard Thompson.
Bands like Bitch Magnet weren't even that. Nor were we the kind of
band whose name my less obsessive co-workers might know, like
Arcade Fire or Yo La Tengo or Dinosaur Jr., the ones that attain what
Ted Leo likes to call "indie tenure." The diehards of this culture encompassed a couple hundred thousand people scattered across the globe—
and "diehard" does not overstate the case, as its adherents generally
organized their lives around the music. Our fans were a significantly
smaller subset of that crowd. We were beloved by ten or fifteen thousand people worldwide, more or less. As to our record sales, that's probably a good guess, too. (I'm not being coy: thanks to how disorganized
our early labels were, we really don't know the numbers.) Not many
people cared—but a good chunk of those who did care were *really* into
it. They cared enough to make Bitch Magnet reunion tours possible in
Asia and Europe and America twenty-one years after our final album
was released. They drove several hours or got on planes to attend those
shows, even if they were often as fortysomething as we were, and as
worn out from the demands of parenthood and careers, and also had
to be at work the next morning.

Back when he was a writer, the baseball executive Bill James came
up with a fantastic sentence: "It is a wonderful thing to know that you
are right and the world is wrong; would God that I might have that
feeling again before I die." In the eighties and early nineties I was certain we were participating in something important. Something that

would change the world, or the world of culture, at least. I was, of course, completely wrong, and neglecting to consider how the world would eventually change the music and the people who made it, but that's a common mistake of youth. I also didn't know at the time that all your bands would eventually break your heart, albeit in slightly different ways, or how the insularity of this world would eventually make you insane. But there was great power in being young and not knowing those things. As there was in being certain that if you pointed your van or car toward any city or college town, you could find the people who didn't know those things, either.

And, despite my complicated relationship with this time and its many aftermaths, what I'd do to have that feeling again before I die.

BOOK 1

Thank You, New Jersey. Good Fucking Night

In the woodsy New Jersey suburb where I went to high school in the early eighties, the idea of a band as a unit that writes and performs its own material did not exist. The term "cover band" wasn't used, because that's what all bands effectively *were*, playing some version of the hits, and their names generally signaled the ground they plowed. Rapid Fire was metal, and ambitious, which meant they sometimes rented a lighting rig. They wore denim and black leather and played songs by Judas Priest. Leather Nun, who apparently didn't know the Swedish band that first used the name, was a more poorly accessorized version of the same idea. Scufl (pronounced "scuffle") wore bright colors and lots of hair mousse. You know: new wave. Some of the guys in Scufl and Rapid Fire ended up in a band called Fossil that had a blink-and-you-missed-it moment on Sire in the early nineties. General Public—which wasn't the dull English Beat offshoot that had a minor hit with "Tenderness"—probably had the highest percentage of honor roll members. One guitarist was even a class president. The one time I saw them, he carefully applied a pair of Ray-Bans just before going onstage with his new-looking Strat. General Public played songs by Genesis and Men

3

at Work, and, to paraphrase Raymond Carver quoting Charles Bukowski, here I am, insulting them already.

Other bands had headache-inducing early-eighties names like Feedback and Steeler, and a few of them actually wrote a song—like *one* song. The only punk rock band in our school was the Pukes. (Could I make up that name? No.) Their singer had spiky hair—still a novelty in the suburbs back then—a rubber face built for bugging eyes and bared teeth, and a stick figure's physique. I thought they played extraordinarily fast, but I saw them before I'd heard much hardcore. They, alone, may have written their own material, since I can't imagine that the song titles I think I remember—"Puke Now," "Mercenary Life for Me"—were covers.

The idea of making your own record was completely inconceivable to us, even though, by the mid-eighties, it was a reality rampant throughout the world. How did you even do it? No one knew. Teenage bands in our stretch of suburban New Jersey didn't even have a place to play. There were no rock clubs near us. Bars were out, since the state drinking age was raised to twenty-one in 1983, and, as far as I knew, you had to go to a city for any all-ages hardcore shows. But once a year local high schools staged a battle of the bands, and bands crossed town lines for them, to perform for other students amid humid atmospheres consisting of hair mousse and longing and hormones. Our school hosted its battles of the bands on a Friday night in late fall, when the days were cooler but not yet cold, and dark arrived in the late afternoon. Under inky skies parents' cars nudged through the parking lot, brake lights flashing on and off, disgorging clots of teens. Returning to school after hours made you think that the normal rules were somehow suspended. Everyone searched for someone to fumble with in a dark corner, or for some small bit of contraband to make the evening.

Yeah, those nights. Even outcasts like me were susceptible to whatever hung in the air.

All the girls in makeup, in skimpy tops, in short skirts, in leg warmers, and doused in perfume; the scent they trailed was unbearable. A girl from French class showed up in skintight satiny black pants made more remarkable by the big chunky zipper traversing the entirety of her crotch, belly button to spine. MTV was now widely disseminating bad-hair ideas, so I urge you to visualize the horror show atop this crowd's heads. Parachute pants, loud colors, and geometric striped-and-gridded shirts and skinny ties for the Scufl fans. The more fashion-forward dudes among them wore white Capezios—jazz oxfords—which, somehow, no one found hilarious. The guys who didn't particularly fit in wore Members Only. (I was one of them, dividing my time among the pocket-protector crowd, the most droolingly unregenerate dope smokers, and a few smart outsiders orbiting around art and music.) The boys identifying as heavy metal all had spandex pants and faded-denim vests emblazoned with Iron Maiden and Judas Priest and Ozzy patches. These vests had been denim jackets before their arms were ripped off, leaving behind dangling fringes of white cotton fabric, which you burned off with a lighter. If you weren't careful while you did this, you set your vest on fire, though it was kind of fun when it happened. Only the stoners had a look that still holds up today: lank-haired, sleepy-eyed, jeans and faded tees. They were totally onto something, and they *didn't even know it!*

The cafeteria was briefly remade into something else—the lunch tables hauled away and a couple of makeshift stages quickly assembled at opposite ends of the room. In a major concession to atmosphere the blazing fluorescent overhead lights were turned off. If you squinted, it kind of looked like a club. It would do. It had to, anyway. Then the bands nervously took the stage and played other bands' songs. Oftentimes the *same* other bands' songs. One night, during that odd interval when Quiet Riot was briefly the biggest band in the world, three different bands covered "Metal Health."

Rapid Fire impressed me. Or at least their guitar solos did. The witless commercial-metal version: finger sprints, really, dashing up and down blues scales as fast and as smoothly as possible. The sheer speed lit up something in my brain. As much as I professed to detest metal, at home I'd shut the door to my room, plug my lousy Peavey guitar into my lousy Peavey amp—both bought with bar mitzvah money—and see how quickly I could run through scales, too. (In sum: not fast enough.) Then Scufl would play the Cars' "Touch and Go," and suddenly everyone in the room was singing along and reaching up to mime the "I touched your star" part, as if that lyric was about a star in the sky and not, you know, a vagina. I joined in while secretly glancing at the preposterously hot girl I was crushing on, wholly without hope, who was nice enough to befriend me, though nothing more. Michelle was half-Asian, half-Italian, absolutely *Jesus Christ she's beautiful.* I wore oversized glasses with lenses so thick they distorted my face, a halfhearted Jew-fro, and braces. I cringed when I looked into mirrors and was mutely grateful for our long phone calls. For any flakes of her attention, really. At this battle of the bands, she was all tarted up, hotter than a heartache, and, unlike everyone else, she didn't sing along, just nodded her head and languidly chewed gum in time with the music, a hand on her hip. Grown men have gone to jail for less. I looked at her and thought, as overwrought as any teen, *She does not know this entire moment is about her,* even though girls that pretty usually do.

Everything about these nights was totally Tinkertoys, and I knew it even then. But knowing it didn't stop how crazy and excited and bottled-up and absolutely unable to express it I felt, so uncomfortable in my skin it may as well have itched, crazy from the crowd and the guitars and the amps and the drums and the girls and *that* girl especially. I thought, maybe I could start a band to impress her. No. Wait. This is better. Maybe I could start a band *with* her. I'd see her a lot more then, right? We actually tried this, though she wanted to sing a bunch of Pat Benatar songs for which I couldn't even feign interest, and in any event I couldn't play the solos fast enough. And I hadn't yet realized that you started a band not to get the girl but because you *couldn't* get the girl. To channel all the horrible churning, surging feelings—the goddamned unmanageable desire and anger and other emotions you couldn't name, you could never understand, and that nonetheless never left you alone. A band might make them into something other than what you seethed over endlessly, or what you whacked off to behind a locked bathroom door.

* * *

I DID MOST OF MY GROWING UP IN WARREN, NEW JERSEY, about an hour west of Manhattan, in the kind of development common to comfortable suburbs erected in the late sixties and seventies, and the one good thing I can say about my hometown is that it gave you time and space to dream. The houses kept a respectful distance from one another. There were woods with tall trees, and great expanses of lawns. We lived well off any main road, and the surrounding streets were very lightly trafficked. Cars floated by slowly, gently, kids wriggling and bouncing in the backseat. You could ride your bike for hours, dazed and drifting, seeing no other humans, utterly and gloriously alone. The gears on your ten-speed made a nasal, narcotic clicking when you stopped pedaling, and there was a song in that sound. You achieved a minor cinematography coasting down the street, a slow pan past the trees through which you glimpsed your neighbors' houses. Though no one would want to make a movie out of this.

Other boys my age lived in the neighborhood, and though we sometimes played endless games of two-on-two baseball during the longest days of summer, I spent a lot of time alone, riding my bike on the quiet roads or reading and poring over baseball statistics in my room. Middle-class American childhood was not yet a relentlessly scheduled sequence of commitments, and you had lots of time for idle dreaming. So much stillness and quiet. So little around that you could spend all day inside yourself, as confused and whimpering as it may have been in there. You had no sense of a "we"—the thought that people like you did, in fact, exist and you hadn't spun off, alone, into some solitary and forgotten corner of the cosmos—but you knew where the "I" was.

We moved into that neighborhood when I was four and my older brother, Neil, was ten. After we had our housewarming party, I remember asking my dad if we were really going to live here, because it was so much bigger than the downstairs rental in which we'd lived before. There was a two-car garage and an acre and a half of tall trees. Neil and I now had our own bedrooms. The low-ceilinged basement had more square footage than our entire old apartment, and down there Neil and I somehow managed to play baseball and basketball. It was a big leap for my dad, an only child whose father repaired watches and whose mother ground out ridiculously long workweeks as a back-office clerk on Wall Street to put him through Columbia and med school. For years the three of them lived with my dad's maternal grandparents in a one-bedroom, one-bathroom apartment in the Flatbush section of Brooklyn, but when he was thirty-six, he was able to move his pretty wife and two smart sons into the kind of house every Jewish mother wishes for her son the doctor, and my grandmother is a Jewish mother right down to the homemade chicken soup.

My mom grew up in the Inwood section of Manhattan, on a hilly and cobblestoned street near Isham Park, in a top-floor three-bedroom duplex that, if it's been left untouched, is someone's dream apartment today. Her dad ended a long career with the city's Board of Education as the assistant superintendent overseeing all of Brooklyn's high schools. That may scan as "hack," but that wasn't my grandfather: the squib the *New York Times* ran when he died in 1993 said, accurately, that he was known for developing interesting educational programs. My mom's mother, to whom she was closer, died of leukemia when my mom was sixteen and away at summer camp. (Typing that sentence brings home, again, the horror she surely felt.) She and my dad started dating at that camp. Their courtship survived those summers, as well as the commute once the two of them were back home—Flatbush to the north end of Manhattan is a ninety-minute subway ride, if you're lucky. She ended up at Barnard and he at Columbia, and they got married just before she turned twenty. After graduating from Barnard, and before my parents moved to New Jersey, she taught fifth grade at Manhattan's PS 122. Today it's a famous performance space, but her stories made the East Village of the early sixties sound like wartime Beirut with worse parenting. She gave up teaching to raise my brother and me and became a librarian once I started grade school. She was the family disciplinarian and had a temper that terrified me whenever it blew. I'm sometimes a hothead, too. Hi, Mom!

Everyone in my house was so much older and talked so fast about things I didn't understand that at the dinner table I felt several crucial seconds behind each exchange, head-swiveling as the conversation bounced between my parents and my big brother, a few beats too slow to follow the ball in some Ping-Pong competition. Like a lot of youngest children, I craved much more attention than I got. James Murphy of LCD Soundsystem—the baby of his family, too—once told me that being the youngest and feeling ignored or left to your own devices can leave you with a tight core of stubbornness about whatever you wanted to do: *All those years you abandoned me to dream this up in my room, and now you're telling me I can't? Fuck you.* I knew exactly what he meant.

My brother is one of my best friends today, but the six years between us is a huge gap when you're children, something I learned over and over again when I would galumph after Neil and his friends to be rejected, or grudgingly tolerated. Like a lot of Jewish kids from the Northeast, Neil and I went to summer camp for two months each summer, amid hills and trees and soccer and softball fields and basketball and tennis courts semicircling a mile-wide lake. Neil had gone to that camp for years and was kind of a big deal there when I arrived for my first summer. The annoying thing about him was that, early on, he mastered never looking like he was trying very hard, and he possessed the remove and equilibrium older siblings sometimes have. Whereas I always felt like I was belly flopping around school and camp and our hometown, socially leprous, barely getting by. (He did especially well with girls at camp, unlike me, about which I remain incredibly bitter.) Sometimes when grown-ups who knew him—teachers, coaches, counselors at camp—made the connection between us, they would light up, and I'd stupidly stew on this, feeling too insubstantial to cast a shadow, visible only as an adjunct to someone more memorable who'd passed through before. My mom's response was, better that than dread flashing across their faces, a sentiment with which I didn't necessarily agree.

Then, when I was eleven, in 1979, Neil went off to college, and suddenly it was only me and my parents in that big suburban house, and the seventies turned into the eighties just as I started getting bored with Little League and youth soccer and baseball cards and, restless, started searching *Creem* and *Rolling Stone* and *High Times* for some new excitement. There was a symphony of crickets' and cicadas' drones on summer nights—when I go back to visit my parents now, I'm surprised how loud it gets—but nothing else going on after dark, which was the whole problem. There was no culture that didn't come from a television, a radio, or the malls' movie theaters and record stores, and they all had such narrow ideas of what they could present.

I mean, if I'd grown up in an earlier era, maybe I could sing some paean to radio, the magic appliance through which you received secret transmissions from your true home planet, the best friend with whom you huddled in the dark, etc., but good God was radio awful in the eighties. Tears for Fears. Debbie Gibson. Billy Idol. George Thorogood. Genesis, after Peter Gabriel left, and Phil Collins's entire solo career. Corey Hart, the poor man's Bryan Adams in new wave sunglasses, while Bryan Adams was a poor man's John Cougar Mellencamp, as if just being John Cougar Mellencamp weren't brutal enough. Things were so bad we tried to get excited about John Fogerty's first album in like ten years, even though any chemistry textbook was more exciting and contained no writing as horrendous as the lyrics to "Centerfield." Survivor. Fucking *Starship*. Journey played on an endless loop, and no one acted like it was funny or weird. Howard Jones had a huge hit with

"Things Can Only Get Better," and no one called him out for lying. During one surpassingly strange fifteen or eighteen months, the ghastly and bouncy Men at Work was the biggest band in the world. Even the "quality" rock bands—those adored by critical consensus, like Bruce Springsteen and U2—were as wearying as algebra. Dog-faced with sincerity. Groaning with sanctimony. Their endless, applause-seeking urge to *do the right thing.* The great secret history of music, the stuff with some substance to it—Stooges, Suicide, Leonard Cohen, Can and Guru Guru and NEU! and the entirety of krautrock, Funkadelic, Blue Cheer, Albert Ayler, Magma, Wire, King Crimson, Joy Division, all the great mutant offshoots of disco, punk, hardcore, and psych—was so far out of reach in my suburb it might as well have been buried on Mars. Before breaking up in 1983, Mission of Burma had been desperately setting off signal flares up in Boston, where they practically invented the template for brainy and aggressive underground bands that's still followed today: unusual song structures; melodic and powerful bass; distorted guitar serving more as sonic sculpture than mere notes and chords; relentless off-center drumming. But the local college radio playlists were still choked with synthy new wave and British imports, so, as with everything else going on with an entire founding generation of American punk rock, we had no way of knowing.

Nor did anyone at any of our battles of the bands in 1983 know about a few oddballs in rural Washington who toggled between hardcore and slowed-down Sabbath riffs and called themselves Melvins. Nor that, in Minneapolis, Hüsker Dü was readying *Zen Arcade*, the double album that would win them the maximum attention the mainstream could bestow upon a super fast, super distorted punk rock band. (Of course they'd eventually end up in *Rolling Stone*: their buried pop hooks made them the one noisy and aggressive band R.E.M. fans could like.) Wipers had been playing in Portland, Oregon, for years, ditto the Meat Puppets in Phoenix and Naked Raygun in Chicago. An unstable agglomeration of smart kids and party-jock types in Louisville, Kentucky, were playing in a band called Squirrelbait Youth—they hadn't yet chopped off the last word in their name, or recorded the two albums that are still rightly cherished today. Sonic Youth lived and practiced thirty-five miles from my high school. They'd released two EPs and a full-length album by the end of my junior year, but no one around me had any idea. Metal was huge in my hometown, but only the weak and flashy kind—Judas Priest and Quiet Riot. Slayer and Metallica and Voivod and a zillion others were already reordering the entire genre, but no one I sold pot to knew anything about them. Things weren't necessarily better for those lucky enough to grow up in cities, where many key people in bands were still considered complete weirdos. Sometimes even to the *other* weirdos. "I always thought [Wipers front man] Greg Sage was a cancer patient," Joe Carducci, a former co-owner of the label SST, told me. "He had tufts of hair missing, and what was there was white. He was too old to look like a punk rocker. So you assumed he was a patient."

In 1983, when I was fifteen, a friend's older brother brought a cassette to summer camp with Sex Pistols' *Never Mind the Bollocks* on one side and Dead Kennedys' *Fresh Fruit for Rotting Vegetables* on the other. I grabbed it and never gave it back, and it pretty much got me through the following year. It took me forever to find the first New York Dolls album. Once I did, I played the hell out of it. Over time it grew less interesting, especially once that band became the model for a junkie-Stonesy subgenre that still really annoys me. But I'd heard them described as being a generation too early for punk rock, and in high school I was desperate for any kind of different. I didn't hear any Stooges songs other than "I Wanna Be Your Dog" until college. All their records were out of print everywhere, and if Iggy was far from deification in the early eighties, no one in the world cared the tiniest bit about Ron and Scott Asheton. In the absence of any guidance, you developed your own strategies. Growing up in Peoria, Illinois, years before he formed Tortoise, Doug McCombs would go to the local record store and buy the albums with the weirdest covers. In that way, he explained, he quickly found records by Wire, the Stranglers, Television, and X. Then again, he also bought the first Pearl Harbor and the Explosions record, so, you know, crapshoot. It could have been worse. In Manchester, Iowa, where Thinking Fellers Union Local 282 bassist Anne Eickelberg grew up, the record store was a couple of bins in the hardware store.

* * *

THERE WAS ONLY ONE OTHER LOCAL VENUE BESIDES THE BAT- tles of the bands. Every June my hometown held a fair called Expo Warren, with carnival games and rides, all trucked in and assembled on the fields where the Little League played, and an outdoor stage. Expo Warren brought a lovely boardwalk seediness to our town. Greasy trav- eling carnies collected tickets and thunked rides into life—and they really were greasy, since futzing with their machinery smeared their hands with oily black gunk, which came off when they thoughtlessly wiped sweat off their faces or slapped away mosquitoes. The midway was full of bad fried food and games with cheap stuffed-animal prizes. Entire stalls sold nothing but those small rectangular mirrors with band logos emblazoned on them. (It took me fifteen years to realize you were supposed to chop up coke on them.) School was finally out. Night came on slowly, swollen with summertime. One year I snuck into the woods past the Tilt-A-Whirl and the Roundup with a bunch of other kids to smoke joints rolled in strawberry-flavored rolling papers. That and the cotton candy dust drifting in the air—I can taste it all right now.

When it came to music, though, Expo Warren couldn't even match a battle of the bands' after-hours-at-the-mall atmosphere. And we couldn't help but notice, even through the fog of adolescence and what- ever cigarettes and bad weed and cheap, sweet booze we scrounged. One evening the band consisted of one guy with a guitar and a practice amp struggling through some Kiss songs. (To steal the old joke: He played "Rock and Roll All Nite," and "Rock and Roll All Nite" lost.) Another time some chubby guys with mustaches came onstage, looking like accountants and seemingly much older than us, which probably meant they were thirty. The lead mustache stepped up to the microphone and announced, "Hello, everyone. We're the Electrons!" and the band launched into "White Wedding." They got through the introduction, but when the first verse began, that guy moved back to the mike and sang, "White Weddinnnnnnggggggg! I don't know the lyrics!" Why none of us watching ever got the urge already common in places near and far to say, "Fuck them, we can do it better"—well, I have no idea.

Some of this is hard to remember. I smoked a great deal of pot back then, but that's not why I don't remember, because I have very clear memories of being extraordinarily stoned through many gorgeous and horrific events. Rather, hormones and throbbing teenage anxieties created their own amnesia. Simple interactions and conversations often, and out of nowhere, transformed into hostility and sometimes even violence and the blurring, yappy chaos of an overcrowded dog run, albeit one with fists and flung bottles. One night my best friends, Andy and Mike, and I were driving around aimlessly, Mike kept his bright lights on a little too long, and a guy we drove behind went white hot with rage. He trailed us all the way to Andy's house—into which Andy quickly disappeared—and charged out of his car, looking for a fight. Mike stood absolutely silent and motionless while this guy screamed and shoved and fake-lunged at him. Mike didn't talk or fight back, which completely baffled this guy. Finally he screamed that if Mike ever wanted to fight, Mike knew what car he drove, and stomped off. (People actually said things like "If you wanna fight, you know my car!") I watched, stoned and paranoid, from the backseat, bewildered and overmatched, as always, by aggressive male display. No fucking way was *I* getting out.

Adolescent hostility, that hot and insensible anger, was everywhere. Testosterone flooded bodies that couldn't handle it. It's understandable to me now as another generation of boys imperfectly body-slamming their way toward adulthood, but had any grown-up tried to explain it at the time, I wouldn't have listened. It wouldn't have made sense, because very little made sense. Close friends turned on you. Bullies shocked you with moments of tenderness. Conversations at parties would turn on a dime, and then you'd have to flee—from parties! Where for a moment you thought you'd found a temporary détente!

As a very scrawny freshman, I knew a hulking upperclassman. "Hulking," meaning his neck was roughly as thick as my waist. He alternated between subjecting me to grotesque cruelties—once, in one of our school's legendarily gross and doorless bathroom stalls, he held me by my legs and dangled me over the toilet until my collar rubbed the dried piss on its rim—and speaking to me candidly, in a way I wondered if he did with anyone else. He'd played varsity football and certainly had the build and violence for it. But, as he explained to me once, he couldn't take knowing that he could fuck up someone forever with one hit, and this knowledge made him quit. Was this bullshit? The way he delivered it, I didn't think so. Another guy, wiry and entirely overwired, eventually stopped punching me in gym class and instead started pulling me aside to confess that he worried he did too much coke, or how it bothered him to watch a friend drink beer for breakfast. He was an admitted racist, but I spent a lot of time with him talking fairly seriously about politics. He could do that, though he was deeply ignorant—I mean this in a certain Southern sense, where "ignorant" can carry a racial valence—and lacked even a brain cell's worth of impulse control and common sense. I was learning that the bond between the bullied and the bully is strikingly intimate: odd, deeply sexual, confusing. But listening patiently to either of these guys was better than getting punched in the stomach.

Sometime in junior or senior year I got my hands on a bag of magic mushrooms, and one Friday or Saturday night I felt what-the-fuck enough to eat about half of it. Maybe more. I'd never tripped before, but I was curious. I was going out that night with Andy and Mike, but I didn't tell them what I'd done, which was probably a big mistake, although not as big a mistake as having no sense of "enough" or "too much" when it came to mushrooms. They started to kick in at a party we crashed, where I ducked outside to smoke a joint with our class president. My heart was pounding, and my general sense of reality was buckling and fractalizing even before we lit up, but that didn't stop me. Soon enough I became somewhat subverbal and was no longer seeing properly, but I still swear he told me which girl he planned to make out with at the party *exactly* as he put on his pair of douchebag Vuarnet sunglasses before walking back inside. (DEAR GOD, WHAT WAS IT WITH CLASS PRESIDENTS AND SUNGLASSES?) I stumbled through the front door for the tail end of a conversation in which Andy and Mike managed to piss off everyone so badly we had to leave very quickly. There may have been some threats made toward us. I don't really remember, because by now I was totally tripping my balls off.

Then I was in the backseat of Mike's car as he drove somewhere. Ten minutes passed, then fifteen. No one spoke. Mike stopped the car on the edge of a giant marshland preserve called the Great Swamp, without explanation, and I lurched outside to pee.

Then the car quietly drove off.

There were no lights anywhere nearby, and the night was absolutely black. The swamp gurgled, stirred, breathed, belched, grunted, sighed, bubbled. Sounds piled atop sounds. Things thrashed in the muck. It was impossible to know what was real and what was not. I peered into the dark and saw patterns and flickers. Anything could be lurking in the enormous soup that began a few yards in front of me, though I was already sort of unable to discern where I stopped and the swamp started. Miles from home, in a remote nature preserve, late at night. I could reasonably expect to see no cars till morning. Maybe I was just together enough to walk home, if I knew the way. But I didn't.

Time, too, distorted, so I don't know how long I stood there, but at some point the car pulled up again, and the back door swung open. No one said anything. Andy and Mike stared straight ahead in the front seats, unsmiling, and had no explanation when I asked why, other than to say: "Because."

These guys, I remind you, were my best friends.

* * *

THERE HAD TO BE SOMETHING ELSE. BUT WHAT?

In junior high school I'd failed to convince one of the few guys even less cool than me to start playing bass, but prospects seemed better in high school. For one thing: I could now play bar chords. Andy was another smart underachiever (short version: I smoked pot daily and sold it ineptly; he had far worse grades), and he and I had similar taste. He had a Telecaster—even then I hated Teles, but whatever—and, like me, a lousy solid-state Peavey amp. We tried playing together, but whether we worked from sheet music or attempted to play by ear, it didn't work. A song as simple as R.E.M.'s "7 Chinese Brothers" completely eluded us. It wasn't until after I got to college that I learned about drone strings: playing two strings together, leaving one open, and working your way up and down the fretboard on the other. Once you know that, you can play "7 Chinese Brothers" in five minutes. But as with everything else, learning that in the suburbs in the eighties was a matter of groping blindly in the dark. I know, I know, it's a total cliché to even bother pointing this out, but it's still true: life was much lonelier and more isolated without any entrée to interesting music and the people who flocked to it, without a band, and without any band culture. If you were surrounded by assholes hostile to the fact of your existence, it was easy to assume that everyone everywhere would be like that, for the rest of your life. *I* assumed that. No one could point me to a control group that proved that life could be different. No one like me knew it wasn't our fault. Or that there were even enough of *us* somewhere to create a bigger *our*, one that encompassed more people than the few freaks we hung out with.

But there were ten or fifteen or fifty kids like us in most high schools. There were a few hundred in every small city and thousands in each state. There were a hundred thousand or more in America and a few hundred thousand more worldwide. There was plenty of kindling. Something was about to happen.

The Importance
of a Tiny Stage

Pictures from the early days of any rock or art movement always display discordant details. No style has been codified, everyone looks too young, and a kind of aesthetic baby fat blurs many edges. Photos from Sex Pistols gigs show dudes in the crowd with mustaches and seventies hair. In shots from the early hippie days, there's always at least one guy with hair that wouldn't be out of place at IBM. So it was with indie rock when I first really discovered it upon arriving at Oberlin College in August 1985. What ultimately became a blend of hippie, punk, and hobo still had jarring touches of eighties MTV here and there: mushroom-shaped or asymmetric hair, boys in tight black shirts buttoned to the throat, boys who looked like they wanted really badly to be in the Cure. It wasn't even called "indie rock" back then. We generally stuck to "punk rock," since it was hard to use a more common term du jour—"alternative"—with anything like a straight face.

Oberlin is a small, reasonably pretty college town situated within a landscape so featureless that a hill is an event. The closest major city is a forty-five-minute drive, and since that city is Cleveland, you kept your expectations low. The skies over the college were almost always gray as you passed the old stone buildings and crisscrossed the quad, shoulders hunched against the wind, hurrying down brick paths to get to the two-street town. (Oberlin has a unique microclimate, which is a polite way to say it rained all the time and stayed cold until early May.) Among us music freaks, the boys wore flannels and ripped jeans and plain white T-shirts—they were cheap, and available everywhere. Quite a few of the girls dressed like that, too, though those with good thrift-store instincts opted for secondhand dresses or skirts with dark tights. It was acceptable, and even desirable, for everything to be oversized and slouchy—a terrible idea today, but a common one when no manufacturer made jeans that actually fit. We were also big on discarded classic-rock concert T-shirts, picked up secondhand for a buck or less, decades before they went on sale at places like Barneys for hundreds of dollars. (The bassist in one campus band sometimes wore a perfectly faded black Pink Floyd tee, the one with the pig from *Animals* on the front. Today he could practically make a mortgage payment with it.) We all wore sneakers or combat boots or motorcycle boots. Long coats for most, and faded denim or army surplus jackets for the stonier types. The boys let their hair get shaggy or cut it very short, and never used any kind of product. The girls made more of an effort, dyeing theirs blond or black or burgundy. Many of us smoked. Cigarettes occupied your hands during those twenty years until smartphones were invented. That all this became a look, in the fashion sense, a few years later, after some Seattle bands got big—well, we found that hilarious. We dressed that way to *avoid* having a look.

Nestled outside a third-floor window in the student union building, a clock radio tuned to the campus station was almost always on. The sound cascaded down the building's sandstone front, beamed across an adjacent lawn, and bounced off the other nearby buildings, creating an unusual amplifying effect: from fifty or even a hundred yards away, you heard it loud and clear, as if it came through a set of speakers far bigger and better than any the station owned.

Steam clouds hung in the air over the campus power plant. Spring would come one day, we were sure of it.

Left to our own devices far from anywhere, with no adults around, none of us had any idea what we were doing. But there was also no one to say you were doing it wrong. Anyway, what were you supposed to take cues from in 1985? Commercial radio and MTV were wastelands. Many college radio stations were still content to play the overproduced and underwhelming major-label "alternative" bands of the time, like the Woodentops and China Crisis and Aztec Camera, bands no one liked then and no one remembers now. Once a year *Rolling Stone* would cover some other going-nowhere, penny-ante sort-of-subculture and the bands it spawned—the Paisley Underground and the Three O'Clock! Roots rockers like the BoDeans and the Del Fuegos! (The Del Fuegos got started at Oberlin; their frontman, Dan Zanes, now writes songs for well-bred toddlers.) *Those* records you could find everywhere. But you had to strain so hard to get even the teeniest buzz from them.

A very strong hippie streak persisted on campus. Deadheads and tie-dye were everywhere, as were men with ass-length hair, whom you'd see playing hacky sack on the quad. Hideous scarves and ponchos hand-knit by the oppressed indigenous peoples of Nicaragua, etc., passed for fashion statements, and people showed off by pronouncing "Nicaragua" with the correctly rolled "r." I was still at an age when any hardcore band yapping about how much Reagan sucked sounded pretty good, but at Oberlin I got disgusted with lefty politics almost immediately. Still, I lucked out by ending up there, and one big reason was my freshman-year roommate, Linc, an extremely skinny, short-haired, pale-skinned music autodidact from suburban L.A. He was wearing a Meat Puppets T-shirt the day we moved in. He was clearly much cooler than me, but more important, he was much more *knowing* than me. He owned every record SST put out—I barely knew Black Flag; he was already over them—back when that signified something. Linc had heard everything I'd heard, everything I wanted to hear, and everything

I didn't know I wanted to hear, had answers for almost every musical question I posed, and brought a few hundred carefully annotated cassettes with him to school.

The second reason I lucked out by attending Oberlin was its radio station, WOBC, staffed by music nuts and, in the classic sense of college radio, unformatted. (Too many college radio stations back then mimicked commercial radio, with programmers insisting that DJs choose among songs placed in "rotation." That would *never* fly with the freaks of WOBC.) At station headquarters in the student union building, entire walk-in closets were stuffed floor to ceiling with old records—you could get lost in them for hours, and I often did—and a few mail crates overflowing with telltale square cardboard packages arrived each day. The college was continually pissed off at the radio station, because the collective weight of those records made the old floors sag, requiring regular reinforcement. I graduated in 1989, and I'm not sure the station even owned a CD player by the time I left.

WOBC's office had all the institutional charm of a military recruiting center, albeit with more smokers and fewer ashtrays. Everything in the control room appeared to be government-surplus gear from the fifties, if not earlier. The occasional giveaway poster from random bands like the Raunch Hands or the Reducers passed for decoration. Ceiling tiles were past yellowing and getting well into brown. Couches sagged and groaned when you sat on them, and smelled like an old man's flannel shirt. DJs coughed their colds into the decaying gray foam covering the on-air mike and made one another sick. A crescent of metal protruded from the giant black speaker in the lounge, on which someone had scrawled in white wax pencil: THIS IS NOT AN ASHTRAY YOU ASSHOLE. I adored it all, spent every minute there I could, and, like everyone else, started with a weeknight 2 a.m. to 5 a.m. show.

WOBC was also a link, however tenuous, to the occasional concert in Cleveland. Early in my freshman year I won free tickets from the station to see the jangly Austin band Zeitgeist. It was a weeknight, and there were maybe twenty people at the club. But forget the music, which was mildly interesting at best. A friend, who earned my plus-one by borrowing a station wagon for the trip there, spent much of the night at the bar, hanging out with the woman who played second guitar for Zeitgeist, because here it wasn't arenas, backstage passes, and limousines, and there was hardly any barrier between performer and fan. You could know these people. A really important thing about this world, because your real influences were ultimately the people you *knew*: the friends with whom you hung out, went to shows, traded tapes, and talked endlessly about music.

Oberlin was just a few thousand kids, but it midwifed a shocking number of real bands that wrote and played their own material every weekend at dorm lounge parties and in off-campus living rooms amid the cornfields in our nowheresville. Flyers advertising upcoming shows fluttered from the overfilled bulletin boards in every public space. These bands got airplay on WOBC, on a kind of 8-track tape that DJs called "carts," and they were the most important fact about this time and place, which is why I'm going to talk about one you've never heard of, called Pay the Man.

No one outside Oberlin knows about Pay the Man, because ultimately they never did anything. They moved to Boston at the end of my freshman year, but then the drummer left, and they couldn't replace him. Nothing they recorded was ever released. (They were supposed to do a four-song EP, "Gettin' the Juke," on the long-defunct Cleveland label St. Valentine Records, but it never happened.) But they were genuinely good, and not "good" as in "acceptable to hear in a friend's basement" or "there's a halfway decent song on the cassette they guilt-sold to their friends." "Good" as in, you would listen to them if they were from San Francisco or Spokane or Madison or Amsterdam, because their songs stuck with you and got bigger with repeated listening. You looked forward to their shows. I've been carrying a bunch of their songs for decades, first on cassettes, now on a computer, and those songs hold up, beyond the way they scratch an old itch. Each of the guys in Pay the Man played better than he needed to and was smarter than necessary. Most crucially, their drummer, Orestes Delatorre, was a *lot* better than he needed to be. Mike Billingsley wrote the tougher and darker songs and played a fretless bass. The guitarist, Chris Brokaw, played actual solos, and played them well. (Chris went on to a long career in music, playing with everyone from Thalia Zedek to Steve Wynn to Bedhead to Thurston Moore.) By the time I was at Oberlin they'd been together for three years, and though they still played some of their early, ultrafast songs, it was clear they had grown beyond them. Like a lot of bands from the mid-eighties, they had commonalities with Hüsker Dü and early Soul Asylum without sounding like either—that is, another band that started out playing hardcore, then grew out of it without totally forsaking it.

Aside from being really good, the guys in Pay the Man were also just *there*: walking to class, eating at the dining hall, hanging out at parties. I was generally too chickenshit to talk to any of them, though Chris went out of his way to be nice to me. He and Mike were as skinny as scarecrows, with long, straight high school stoner hair trailing down to the middle of their backs. Chris was a senior and an English major. I'd see him out and about, a bottle of Boone's Farm sometimes dangling from a pocket of his army jacket, and something about the whole literate stoner-rocker vibe made me think, *Jesus. Too cool.*

I didn't have much going on that freshman year. No girlfriend, quite shy, absolutely virginal. I slept through my morning classes, shared delivery pizzas each night with friends in my dorm, listened to WOBC nonstop, and spent all the money I'd saved from the previous summer and then some on records. I went to parties only if bands played, and I drank keg beer while waiting for Pay the Man or the Full Bodied Gents or What Fell? to start their set, then jumped and thrashed around when they did. It was a release. Also easier than trying to talk to girls.

Every local music culture needs a Pay the Man, the big-brother band that shows the way, the tentpole that holds everything up. It doesn't have to be a band everyone likes, but it has to be sturdy and compelling enough to be the main organizing principle and have enough going on to warrant being the center of attention. Fall became winter, and murmurs started among the music obsessives that Pay the Man were good enough to crack the national circuit. We could invite our normal pals out to see them, and they could like the band, too, even if for them seeing Pay the Man wasn't as huge as it was for me and my closest friends, those stalwarts at every show who could handle the crucial duty of holding my glasses when I went into the mosh pit.

But understand this: no one outside Oberlin knew Pay the Man. Maybe a hundred people—at most—on campus cared deeply about them. The campus cover band that played faithful versions of current hits routinely drew more people. But any touring musician who ever had an unexpectedly great Tuesday night in Champaign, Illinois, or Lawrence, Kansas, or Morgantown, West Virginia, knows that forty excited people is more than enough to make a show memorable, and a local circle of a hundred fans can easily sustain a band. My first spring at Oberlin, Pay the Man had a hit on WOBC, a song Chris wrote called "When We Were Young." (At the time, the band's average age was twenty-one.) One warm night a few weeks before the school year ended, a few hundred beered-up college kids came to see Pay the Man play a party held in a sprawling sixties-era institutional dorm lounge. Winter was finally over, women were showing bare arms and legs again, and the crowd was rowdy and loud and enormously appreciative. At one point between songs Chris looked over to Mike and mouthed a delirious *WOW!* They played a long time that night.

I still have the set list from that show hanging in my bedroom at my parents' house, and sprinkled among the scrawled song titles are four oblique entries: C-1, C-2, C-3, and C-4—"C" as in "cover." Near the end of the set, they began repeating the opening groove to "Hot Child in the City." Mike struggled to sing the first verse and chorus, realized he didn't know the lyrics, and, still thumping out the bassline, stepped to the mike and asked if anyone else did.

Had it been an actual club with an actual stage, I wouldn't have. Had there been even a couple of monitors in front of the band, or something—anything—to delineate where *we* were supposed to stand and where *they* were, I wouldn't have. But I was only three feet away, stepped toward the band, grabbed the mike, and:

> *So young*
> *To be loose*
> *And on her own*

I wasn't born to sing, but I could carry a tune. Chris and I did the male-bonding back-to-back onstage thing, which we briefly considered, for some reason, to be the *ne plus ultra* of performance. Like the band, the crowd played along, as if they found it plausible, and that was more than enough.

> *Come on down*
> *To my place*
> *Woman . . .*

I finished the song and stepped offstage, back into the crowd, glowing and flushed with adrenaline. Even now, more than a quarter-century later, I can still feel it. A needle finding a vein, and something new coursing through my bloodstream: the first rush of performance, the first hint of being in a band onstage. This was just a Saturday night party at a small college. Nothing remotely rock about the setting: a bulbous seventies TV suspended from the ceiling just behind the band, cinder-block walls painted beige, dull gray ceramic tile floors, truly horrible blue and green polyester curtain partially obscured by the dimmed lights. But a moment like this doesn't have to happen at a stadium. Or in a bigger club in a bigger city, where famous punk rock bands played. Or in a legendary, beloved tiny shithole like CBGB or the Exit or the Rat. It could happen in your own backyard. No. The *whole point* was for the epiphany and the enlightenment to happen in your own backyard, among friends and the faces that you knew. This thing was spreading, and when it reached your town and you saw bands being bands, writing their own material, driving tired-looking generic vans from show to show, you realized: *I can do this, too.* No matter where you were. Everything else followed from that dawning.

I'd spent much of that year trying to talk my friends into starting a band, but now I was as hot and desperate as a high schooler who's been dry-humping his girlfriend all night. I had to do this.

Much more important: I now knew anyone could.

This Is Not the Way to Start a Band

It made sense, our starting a band. Linc and I got geeky about the same music and had similar suburban upbringings. Above all, Linc was my best friend, and in my late teens I still hadn't gotten over what I took to be the mythology surrounding the Replacements: a band is your gang, your drinking buddies, your best friends. (It wasn't until much later that I tired of Paul Westerberg's sappiness and learned that the Replacements weren't best friends. Not even close.) But Linc didn't play an instrument, so I spent most of freshman year talking him into learning to play drums. Finding the drummer is always the biggest problem. Demand far exceeds supply, because a drum set is a much bigger commitment than a guitar, and because parents prefer living with instruments that don't sound like a car crash. Drums are also the hardest instrument to master, since drummers generally always have both hands and both feet going, often doing vastly different things with each.

I had it all worked out: I'd play guitar and sing. Linc on drums, once he learned how. My other best friend, Roger, a classically trained pianist from Newt Gingrich's congressional district in Georgia, who got me into AC/DC and was still parting his shaggy brown hair in the middle, would also play guitar. Doug, an earnest and strapping hardcore kid with a soft spot for Dylan, who neatly rolled up the sleeves of the flannel shirts he wore each day, would play bass, because he owned one, along with the saddest and weakest bass amp I ever heard.

Everyone agreed. Sometimes that happens. We also agreed on a name, which, unfortunately, was Ribbons of Flesh. That summer between our freshman and sophomore years, Linc bought a drum set and started practicing. Doug, who lived twenty minutes from me in New Jersey, claimed he'd been practicing, too, though after we played in his parents' basement I had a hard time believing him. Roger promised to bring his guitar and amp with him when school started. We'd already played together a bit, so I wasn't worried about him. When I returned to Oberlin in late August, I brought along my lousy Peavey T-60 guitar and lousy Peavey Bandit amp, and presto: a band.

But we didn't have songs. Or a songwriter. I contributed one surf instrumental and one deeply embarrassing attempt at heartfelt guitar pop, which hinged on the brutally overused open D–to–open G chord change. (You gotta be Malcolm Young to make that sound good.) None of us knew how to start a band. None of us knew that a tentative, underpracticed rhythm section wouldn't work in a loud rock band, for the same reason that structural engineers advise against building houses on unstable ground. None of us knew how to meld two guitars into a coherent-sounding whole. And we believed that the correct way to practice was (a) on a weekend night, (b) after plenty of pizza and beer, and (c) as loudly as humanly possible. On a good night, given a running start and a strong push downhill, we could make it through Judas Priest's "Living After Midnight" before collapsing in a spent heap. Though I couldn't play the guitar solo. Or any other guitar solo.

There is no easy alchemy that just creates a credible rock band, and credible rock songs, once you throw together four friends, some gear, and a lot of cheap beer. We knew rock didn't require virtuosity—that's straight from Punk Rock 101—but we didn't know the crucial corollary: you still needed to do something interesting with your instruments. Volume was great and powerful and necessary, but it made communicating during our practices hard, and we needed to communicate a lot, since we generally couldn't play the same parts at the same time.

At least we understood what we were trying to do: be in a loud, sloppy punk rock band. In many places in the mid-eighties you'd suffer through desperately trying to get this across to someone who wanted to play Springsteen or Poison covers. And at least some of us knew how to play our instruments. Previous generations started bands before they knew how. Or before they owned any equipment. David Yow, the singer for Scratch Acid and the Jesus Lizard, formed his first band, Toxic Shock, with his best friend in Austin around 1980. "We saw in the paper there was this syndrome called Toxic Shock," he told me. "And immediately we said, 'That's the name of our band. Now all we gotta do is find somebody who can play instruments.'" For about a year Toxic Shock existed as a name on a series of confrontational flyers, some of which showed up years later in art books. "We would just make posters that said, TOXIC SHOCK: FUCK YOU, and draw a picture of a woman pulling a tampon out of her pussy, and plaster them all over campus," Yow recalled, so a local publication referred to them as a "poster band." Mr. Epp and the Calculations was another poster band, formed by a teenage Mark Arm in 1980, years before Green River and Mudhoney. Since they were, you know, in a band, Arm and another member split the cost of a cheap pawnshop guitar. "We didn't know how to tune it," Arm admitted and then corrected himself: "We didn't know what tuning *was*."

We knew what tuning was. But we didn't have a tuner. Ever been at a show where the guitarist starts checking his tuning at full volume? Add a lot of cluelessness, multiply that guitarist by two, and you have a pretty good idea of what our rehearsals sounded like.

* * *

LATE IN MY FRESHMAN YEAR I STARTED NOTICING AN ASIAN guy around campus. He was skinny, had big, round wire-rimmed glasses, and generally wore oversized white T-shirts, jeans, and black Chuck Taylors. Even before I saw him with Hüsker Dü's first album tucked under his arm, something about him registered on my punk rock sonar. He knew some of my friends—Oberlin is a small place—and eventually Sooyoung Park and I met and started bonding over music. He was a math major, had a show on WOBC, played bass in a campus pop band called Tall Neighbors. Like me, he was very nerdy, but he seemed to know what he was doing. Sooyoung also had a hard-core band called Easter Trauma back home in Charleston, West Virginia, and one of their songs, which he wrote and I loved, got some airplay on WOBC. He was writing others, too, but when he showed them to Tall Neighbors, they plainly didn't fit.

Tall Neighbors fell apart in the fall of our sophomore year, an event that seemed to throw Sooyoung and me together. He found me in the campus library soon afterward, and though we weren't saying much, both of us grinned foolishly, and he was sitting there like he'd already moved in, because—I don't think we even needed to say it out loud—*we were starting a band*. One that already had a bunch of songs, written by someone who had been in a real band that played real shows opening for bands whose names I recognized. (Albeit ones no one listens to today, like DOA and Social Unrest.)

Not until I wrote that paragraph did I realize that Sooyoung effectively poached me from my own band, and yet I was happy about it.

It was incredibly important to me that Sooyoung had been in a hard-core band, because I desperately wanted to play really fast. So I was disappointed when, at our first practice, I met Sooyoung's drummer friend, Jay, a brilliant political science major who was sleeping with the high-strung politica who ran WOBC, a tough chick with long brown hair and a doll's giant blue eyes. I quickly learned to steer clear of arguing with him, not just because he made mincemeat of any opposing view but because great mounds of spit bubbled from the corners of his mouth when he got worked up, and he got very worked up over politics. The bigger problems were that he was a hippie and a Deadhead and smoked pot. I hated pot with a convert's zeal, having quit at college, and despised the Dead. Worse, Jay couldn't play fast. But there were barely any other drummers on campus. Also, that WOBC connection couldn't hurt.

Sooyoung had a set's worth of songs, so all we had to do was learn them and rehearse. Which we did. To the chagrin of Ribbons of Flesh, I started channeling all my ardor into this new band, and Linc and Doug, sensing that I thought they needed summer school, started practicing on their own. But by then I was already gone. I don't remember if we ever had a real conversation about my leaving, and it's possible we never did. (Already I was learning the finer points of indie rock passive aggression.)

We named our new band while Sooyoung and I sat at the radio station with a few friends contemplating a flyer announcing our first show, which lay on a table amid a bunch of discarded paste-on letters. The flyer was finished, except for the blank space where the band name belonged. But no matter how long we stared at it, nothing appeared. Someone started talking about a particularly good-looking DJ at the station, a guy who had fabulous success with women. I mumbled a bad attempt at a joke that involved calling him a bitch magnet, a bit of some Southern slang I'd learned. Sooyoung started cracking up and gasped, "That's it!" and then he was pasting letters on the flyer.

We got shit *forever* for that name. When our records were reissued in 2011, a couple of reviewers claimed that it was a key reason we never got the recognition they thought we deserved. I know now that it's a bad idea to choose a name that lets people easily dismiss you as not being serious, or that makes them laugh or do a spit-take. (Vomit Launch's second album, *Exiled Sandwich*, is pretty great—a lovely, all-over-the-place artifact from people who'd just learned to play together—but good luck explaining that to someone who doesn't already know that.) All I can say in our defense is that Sooyoung and I were *teenagers*. We weren't really thinking about the long term.

* * *

IF YOU WERE IN A BAND AT OBERLIN AND BURNING TO PER-form, you spent the beginning of each week searching for someone planning a party that weekend and then worked on them to let your band play it. Then you tried to rent one of the few PAs on campus, for vocals. That part was politically tricky, since the guys who did have PAs generally played in bands that you didn't want playing at your party, so often you borrowed one or (ideally) two bass amps and ran the vocal mikes through those instead. Before each gig Sooyoung and I would spend hours constructing and copying flyers and taping them up all over campus. He was very good with X-ACTO knives and photocopiers, both necessary tools in 1986. He knew that Oberlin's art library had the best copy machine in town, and that the town copy shop stocked multiple colors of copier ink, and you could swap out these different colors and rerun flyers through the machine for interesting effects. My favorite early Bitch Magnet flyer has an image copied in blue and then red ink, on green paper, with a blown-up black typewriter font announcing the particulars.

My other favorite flyer—which totally cracked me up when Sooyoung showed it to me—was a brilliant deadpan joke, and spelled out, over and over again, in white block lettering against a jet-black background, a song title from the Thrown Ups' most recent single. Being disgusted that everyone around you was doing it wrong—as I was in high school— was always a good reason to start a band. But it was still hilarious to see it expressed as baldly as this:

YOUR BAND SUCKS

You set up and played in living rooms. You set up and played in dorm lounges. You set up and played in spare bedrooms. You set up and played in actual bedrooms. I sent my mom a photo of Bitch Magnet playing in a kitchen, crammed in alongside the refrigerator and stove. What Fell? appeared with us that night and thought through that setting more carefully: before they started performing, they put freshly mixed batter in the oven, and after their last song, they served warm cake.

I cannot sufficiently thank the people who, after the barest introductions, helped us become a less-bad band by letting us play in their homes, and tolerated us—well, me—flinging their way full cups of beer, or, on the night Sooyoung and I suddenly decided in mid-song to strip down to our underwear, articles of clothing. (We each arrived at that decision spontaneously, or, rather, it just sort of happened, but perhaps presciently Sooyoung kicked off our set that night by cheerfully informing everyone they'd be really sorry they stuck around to see us.) If I were them and they were me, I doubt I'd have been as generous.

I'd get as cranky as a quitting smoker if a couple of weekends went by without a show, because, really, what else was there to do? *Study?* Days were better spent daydreaming about the next party we'd play, or cueing up tapes Sooyoung made of his newest song sketches and working on them until they were ready to play live. There was the crackle of possibility in each new cassette Sooyoung shared, in each new step forward every song suggested, and when you're just getting started, each morsel of progress rocks you like a revelation. Hunched up against a hallway wall in Sooyoung's dorm, squinting in that awful institutional combination of fluorescent light and deep shadow, we sat chatting while Sooyoung noodled on his bass and suddenly started to repeat a riff that made me whip my head around. "What's that?" I demanded. The part to a new song, he explained, and repeated it over and over again, looking away, nodding in time, eyes half open, bass slung low: cool but quietly pleased with himself.

I remember listening to a tape of an early show at the library with

Jay, passing one set of headphones back and forth, flashing teeth at each other like Cheshire cats, alit with the joy of playback. But Jay, it was clear, wasn't obsessed like Sooyoung and me. He was also playing in another band at Oberlin with two of his best friends. They were all long-haired, unabashedly hippie, and jammed onstage a lot, so I hated them. Named, for some unfathomable reason, Boo Boo Kitty, they once got a gig on the same night as a Bitch Magnet show. When Jay opted to play with Boo Boo Kitty, Sooyoung and I borrowed What Fell?'s drummer, Noah.

Shortly afterward Sooyoung dropped by where I lived and, on his way out, paused to ask, "Do you think Jay is holding us back?"

Yes, I agreed, but in the end our slutting around with other drummers made the decision for us. Sooyoung and I had also recorded a ten-song Bitch Magnet cassette—our first—with a seriously good drummer he knew in West Virginia, who played in an actual hardcore band. (He could play fast.) Jay was pissed about the recording and pissed about the show we had played without him, and during an outraged lunch at a campus dining hall, he quit.

We were, we figured, screwed. Except that while Pay the Man was no longer around—Chris had graduated the previous spring, and Mike left with him—Orestes was back at school and wanted to play with us. What can I say about him? He looked, and drank, like a jock. He was the captain of the rugby team. You could easily mistake him for a meathead—because he *was* kind of a meathead—but then he'd start reciting long, dirty passages from *The Canterbury Tales* in the original Middle English, or conversing in one of the seven languages he knew, or rattling off incredibly baroque insults in Mandarin involving filthy chickens and your grandmother's most private parts. He was serious about his drumming in a way I hadn't really seen before—he was far more dedicated to his art than 90 percent of the art majors at a particularly artsy school. He was also a huge Zappa fan, but I didn't hold it against him.

Our early shows toggled between scraggly hardcore and a few sore-thumb pop songs. Even with Orestes we were still the annoying little brother band among our peers—too loud, still inept—and the fifteen people who saw us every other week started rolling their eyes when I ripped the strings off my guitar, one by one, to conclude each set. I needed those theatrics, because I was a terrible guitarist. There was a huge gap between what I heard in my head and what I could actually coax from my instrument, a gap I sometimes tried to bridge by throwing my guitar at the amp. Also, I couldn't keep in tune for more than half a song. But it was also becoming clear that Sooyoung had bass and songwriting chops far beyond what a scraggly hardcore band required and that Orestes was by far the best drummer on campus and, honestly, one of the best drummers in the world. (I have played with a lot of great drummers and seen many more, and I do not throw that superlative around lightly.) His explanation for what he was even doing in Bitch Magnet was that he wanted to play in a loud and weird band and of all local contenders we best fit the bill. We were also well-behaved. Orestes was only twenty-one, but already he'd been in a band with someone who liked heroin too much. Orestes only had to take one look at Sooyoung and me to know that would never be a problem. (All this four-eyed nerdiness was finally good for something.) During my worst moments onstage, with the crowd and the sound and my gear and my hands all working against me, I'd sometimes look back at him and think, *We can't be* that *bad if he's there.*

Christ. I'm just getting started, and already this is getting sentimental. Don't get the wrong idea. We were three extremely different individuals who shared one specific and important interest. I was in the midst of transitioning from *shy* to *angry, hormonal chatterbox* and *frankly obnoxious music geek.* Orestes was laconic and something of a loner. He was an only child whose father, whom he adored, was a percussionist. His earliest musical memory—one of his first memories, period—is sitting on his dad's lap while his dad played congas with friends in an impromptu living room band. Then: cancer, and his father was gone at thirty-eight, when Orestes was only ten. Once you knew this, it confirmed what you thought you knew about Orestes, because there was always something slightly orphaned and apart about him. But he was destined to have a hard time fitting in anyway: part Mexican, part French, part Native American, part Turkish, part Greek, seriously built, a geology and French lit major, a drum and language savant.

Sooyoung was the child of two driven Korean immigrants, the first-born son from a culture in which that status carries significant weight. Five foot nine and punk-rock skinny, he was, like me, nearsighted almost to the point of requiring a seeing-eye dog. His aptitude for math and academics in general—for a shocking array of topics and skills, really—coexisted, often uneasily, with an equivalent facility for music. He started writing songs in high school, and more than once I heard him say, "It's not that hard to write a song" or "It's easy to start a band." Despite being Bitch Magnet's front man, he often was the most ambivalent member because of his kinky, conflicted, stop-and-start relationship with music and the role it would play in his life. Since before we could even drink legally, he always seemed one tour or one record away from quitting music forever, and often said so outright. But he ended up playing in touring bands far longer than Orestes or I did. Over the years I've shared beds with Sooyoung—each of us in our own sleeping bag, but such intimacies came with the territory—spent long hours driving all night with him, and traveled through thirteen countries with him. I can recite a litany of his attributes—even-keeled, relentlessly logical, a long fuse but a big bomb, proud, quiet—and still feel like I'm fumfering around when I try to describe him accurately. I always thought I was the angrier one, but some of his early lyrics were full of guts and nuts, pissed and reeking from frustrated desire ("I could split your head in two," "Each thrust out of love," "A brick across the bean"). Then, on the last song of the record, he'd often slip in stuff full of longing for a girlfriend and a home. I'd see his ideas in his note-book, jotted in his precise geometric handwriting, and marvel at how he translated a stray observation or an overheard snippet into the lyrics of a song, like the plainly insane homeless woman cops at Port Author-ity led away while her pants were still pulled down to her ankles, who turned up in the first verse of "Americruiser."

All this may make him seem grim and overly serious, but his dead-pan humor could tie you up in knots if you weren't careful. Once a gleeful Sooyoung told me about yanking Linc's chain for an entire con-versation by insisting that the best new record at the radio station was that of Metal Church, the dire Northwestern speed-metal band. As Linc lathered himself into a full-on righteous indie rock frenzy tinged with dumbfounded disbelief, Sooyoung demanded, with a pitch-perfect blend of impatience and indignation, "Linc, have you even *heard* the new Metal Church record?"

A Korean, a Mexican, and a Jew walk into a band . . . Orestes's run-ning joke was that no country club in the world would have us. The common thread running through our backgrounds, I think now, was an otherness and loneliness. Part of it was ethnic: on a certain level, all of us were outsiders in America. Then there was Sooyoung's tension over which world he'd occupy, Orestes's fatherlessness, and my sad-boy suburban yadayada at having being ignored or overlooked at home and at school and at camp and the subsequent determination to wreak revenge on my hometown and those there who had methodically kicked my ass year after year. We never admitted any of this to each other, of course, and even if we had, I doubt it would have been enough to unite us. Some bands are touchy-feely, huggy, always talking. Not us. But we didn't have to talk much, because, when it came to music, we under-stood each other intuitively and absolutely, in a way that none of my other bands ever replicated. Sooyoung would write a song, and I'd prac-tically see the guitar part appear and fall into place with perfect seam-less logic. At practice we'd show Orestes a couple of parts and, nodding his head, he would instantly play the *exact* thing that pulled the song together and made it better. As with great sex, there was no need for discussion. No need for anything, really, other than a nod and a muttered "yeah." Every band has a creation myth that ends with the right musicians finding one another and bursting out into daffy grins—it's our equivalent of a shared orgasm. Clint Conley once told me that meeting his Mission of Burma co-founder Roger Miller, who thirty-five years later remains the most important musical collaborator of his life, was "not unlike falling in love. It's so rare. And it's very powerful. I just thought, *Wow. This is the guy I want to be with.*" I wanted to be with Sooyoung and Orestes. My secret was that I kept waiting for both of them to realize I had no business being in their band. But maybe if I put up a brash enough front, no one would ever find out.

* * *

ONCE ORESTES JOINED BITCH MAGNET, THE MUSIC FELT BETTER and stronger. Like we were suddenly seeing everything in 3-D. The songs no longer seemed as if they were made from toothpicks and could be knocked over by doubt or a strong wind. It all felt *correct*. Songs are problems you set up and try to solve, and with Orestes a new and better logic snapped into place. Though we still had a long way to go. We recorded four songs just a few weeks after he joined—a terrible and thin-sounding recording that the world is better for never having heard, but underneath it all, Orestes was there. Making everything on that sad tape better. The best drummers always do.

Atlanta, ABBA, and Agnostic Front

Because I had nothing worth doing at home, and since both Sooyoung and I knew you hang on to a great drummer with all you've got, Bitch Magnet spent the summer of 1987 in Atlanta, where Orestes was living with his girlfriend. Absolutely no one knew us in Atlanta, but since maybe two hundred people anywhere knew us at this point, one place seemed as good as another. The prior summer I lived with my parents and made $4.88 an hour working in a Dun & Bradstreet print room. Anything was better than that.

My parents opposed everything about our plans, but I'd hit that crucial age when even slightly overbearing Jewish parents realize they can't stop their children. We had one of those heartbreaking, nascent-adult conversations in which your parents try to convince you to do something or not do something and you stand firm and watch them—slowly, with sadness, the full weight of their age and then some pressing down upon them—give in. Sooyoung's parents were against the entire idea, too, although I didn't know that until I drove down to pick him up at their house in North Carolina, in suburban Charlotte. I arrived as his report card did. Atypically for him, some of his grades that last semester of sophomore year weren't great, though they were still probably much better than mine, and this set off a huge conflagration. His dad—a compact, capable, and tightly wound man, an ex-smoker who was always chewing gum with real intensity and purpose—invited me to stay for a while, presumably to give them time to work on Sooyoung, but I politely cast my lot with Sooyoung, and he wanted to leave. As I pulled the car out I saw his Dad slump, as if with some huge, exhausting weight on his shoulders, running a hand over his face and forehead as if he were trying to mop off some trouble. Later Sooyoung told me that his parents were starting a business, and there were expectations that he'd stick around and pitch in. He felt guilty about splitting, but like me, he had to do it. The band had become that important, rickety and uncertain though it was.

It rained very hard on the drive to Georgia, a Southern summer storm that doesn't let up or blow over for a long time. As Sooyoung drove and the car slopped through the downpour, I said to him, "Remember this lyric: *Swimming to Atlanta*." He glanced over at me but said nothing. He was kind enough not to point out that I hadn't mastered writing songs or lyrics yet.

Sooyoung and I found rooms in a house in Decatur, run by the kind of itinerant management consultant who names his dog after a favorite baseball player. Shortly after we arrived, we heard about a loft space downtown run by a guy who spelled his name Jhymn, a hippieish Butthole Surfers freak with long red hair and deep-set blue eyes. He put on a hardcore show one of the first nights we were in town featuring Porn Orchard, Dead Elvis, and General Revolt. (Which we thought would be the coolest name ever if they'd only change it to *Joe* Revolt.) We gave him a cassette, and he agreed to put us on an upcoming show and—even better—let us practice in the loft for cheap, or free, I don't remember which.

Atlanta's exurbs were exploding with zillions of housing developments, and we landed jobs on a landscaping crew that sodded fresh lawns at new houses that cost $70,000, $40,000, sometimes less. Around those still-unpopulated subdivisions it was just construction guys and us. The guy who ran our crew, Merritt, moved slowly and didn't talk much. He had red-brown hair, a full beard, ruddy skin from spending so much time in the sun, and the kind of physical presence that makes people say "a mountain of a man": at least six four, and while he was well over three hundred pounds, easy, his build wouldn't have looked fat if he'd weighed two-fifty. He insisted on steak for lunch every day, at whichever chain restaurant was closest. You could definitely picture Merritt in a pair of extra-extra-large overalls, but he wore a polo shirt with a collar every day, and this detail gave him a certain authority. The only physical work Merritt did was driving his tractor, and each day we followed behind it, raking out the stones and smoothing the broken sunbaked red clay dirt. When the ground was ready, you picked up coils of sod and rolled them out to form a tight carpet of new grass; dark gray sandlike soil drizzled onto your shorts and shirt as you did. There was a trick, using a shovel, to chomp down on adjoining sod strips so they'd grow together to form an instalawn. Then you turned on sprinklers and moved on to the next house. Or, after plowing and raking, you'd strap something resembling a large flour sifter to your chest like an infant in a harness, then turn a crank to fling grass seed over the newly turned dirt. Afterward you spread wheat straw over the seed. I once asked Larry, a taciturn and tight-lipped man who appeared to be Merritt's right-hand man, what the wheat straw did. He said it helped fertilize what we laid down. "Like with a man and a woman," he said, and cracked a rare grin at his joke—unnaturally, like someone twisted his arm to force it out of him. When he did, I saw a mouth full of empty space and tiny rotting teeth. I understood then why I never saw him smile.

I learned to be Southern on that job, if being Southern means moving slowly in the sun, and during those long, steamy days it was easy to drift off while we hauled sod or dug holes and think about riffs and songs and the next round of shows. Sometimes a summer falls into an easy, simple rhythm. I ate cereal for breakfast and fast food for lunch and dinner. I learned why drinking Coke for breakfast was a thing in the South, because when we awoke at seven for a day of working out-doors, it was already 93 degrees and hot coffee sounded like a bad joke. We woke, drove, worked. We practiced at Jhymn's and afterward went to Krispy Kreme—then a novelty found in only a few states—and suf-fered intense sugar rushes and crashes from splitting a dozen hot doughnuts chased with water because we didn't want to spend money on milk. We didn't make new friends. We didn't go to any shows after the one we saw at Jhymn's loft. We called clubs from pay phones during our lunch break, trying to line up gigs. I found Wuxtry, the one good record store near where we lived, where I bought the first two records by the growling, grimy, and hazy-sounding Australian trio feedtime, which I still listen to. I slept deeply each night, exhausted from all the work in the sun.

Practicing was all we really needed. A few evenings each week we rolled up to Jhymn's un-air-conditioned loft as a dirty summer sun set slowly over the deserted downtown and pleasantly streamed through the front window while we played. The evenings were still so hot that you sweated just walking up the one flight of creaky wooden stairs, so we stripped off our shirts upon arriving before switching on fans and dragging our gear out from the alcoves and niches where we'd stashed it all. I carried my boombox to the middle of the long loft, pushed RECORD, and scurried back so we could start playing. What had been skeletal and stumbly was finally starting to sound like something. We learned to slow songs down. Jhymn's loft had really high ceilings, and their height and the length of the room produced a natural reverb that made everything sound bigger on tape, and you wanted to make sure the notes hung in all that air.

Between practice and work, Sooyoung and I probably spent more hours shirtless than shirted. Apart from Orestes's girlfriend, I don't know if either of us had a real one-on-one conversation with a woman the entire summer. I did send a few postcards to Martha, a curvy blond freshwoman with striking blue eyes. She was quiet and had a very dramatic way of blushing that made me think she was shy, but I liked her even more when I found out she wasn't and got to know her loud, throaty laugh. I'd spent spring semester at school trying to overcome her ambivalence, with mixed success at best, but I couldn't stop thinking about her. She was back home in Seattle for the summer. She had a history of ending up with rock guys, and in 1987 it was clear there were lots of them in her hometown, but I tried not to think about that too much.

Some days, at quitting time, Merritt drove off in his pickup to go get the cash he'd pay us after counting out our wages on his fingers, and one of us would head to the nearest gas station convenience store for a twelve-pack of cheap beer. One guy in Merritt's crew said "cold beer" as a kind of one-and-a-half-syllable whoop. Like this: "Col'beer! Col'beer!" Dirt from the sod and new yards clung to our arms and chafed our skin, but the sun sank while we drank something that could give you a brain freeze if you gulped it down too quickly. That sweet, soft blow booze delivers to a hot, tired head. It was more than okay that it barely tasted like anything, because you just wanted that prickle of cold bubbles, the tiny hint of bitterness in each swallow. It made us feel worse on our long slog home in Atlanta's rush-hour traffic, but in the moment it was pure pleasure. I suspected that the guy packed so much joy into col'beer because he didn't get much happiness elsewhere. Sooyoung and I had guitars waiting for us in our rented bedrooms, still children of the comfortable class, only passing through where these guys lived.

* * *

WE TRIED TO PROMOTE THAT ONE SHOW AT JHYMN'S BY sending cassettes to *Creative Loafing*—the *Village Voice* of Atlanta, back when such a status mattered and such papers were the only outlets writing about bands like us—and spending a few nights pasting up flyers all over Five Points and other neighborhoods where people who might be interested gathered.

It didn't work. A punk rock band called Rotten Gimmick—they were as generic as their name—opened for us, and then we played to an entirely empty room. Every band has a story of a show that no one attends, but they rarely really mean it. There's always a soundman, the bartender, the guys in the opening bands, someone asleep with his head on the bar, maybe a few confused tourists who are too shy to leave. But when I say "empty room," I mean: *no one*. No bartender. No sound guy. Everyone in Rotten Gimmick moved onto the sidewalk, along with their friends. Jhymn was outside, too.

Jhymn's dog, Sid? Nope. He'd also fled.

Really and truly no one, besides us, so we all kind of grinned and shrugged and treated it like another rehearsal. (Though Sid—named, in the tedious and predictable fashion of a million punkers' dogs, for Sid Vicious—usually stuck around when we practiced.) We sounded pretty good that night, I think. We often did, in that space. Afterward we finished the single pint of Wild Irish Rose we had bought before the show.

Sooyoung left town a few weeks before me, and I moved into Jhymn's place. He had a band with his girlfriend that tried to sound like Sonic Youth, but then they broke up—both the couple and the band, as often happens—and she moved out, so it was just the two of us, in a few thousand square feet. Every evening I would shower in the makeshift bathroom, dry myself off, and stand naked in a window, towel around my neck, the freeway rushing by in the distance. A breeze, or what passed for one, would curl up my crotch and chest. No one was around for miles. Nothing nearby but a grim-looking Church's Fried Chicken. God knows what that apartment would be worth today.

I don't really remember what we did on the weekends, except for the one night when Jhymn and a couple of his friends were tripping. I wasn't, so I drove. Jhymn's idea was to go where skinheads hung out and spray-paint ABBA all over the place. Then someone else had to one-up him somehow, flashed on a terrible New York band huge among the more hammerheaded precincts of Hardcore USA, searched for a long stretch of unmarked concrete wall, looked in both directions for skinheads, and quickly sprayed I BUTTFUCKED AGNOSTIC FRONT in letters three feet high.

That's how crazy things got in Atlanta.

There were moments of horrible loneliness that summer, especially after Sooyoung left. One night, as I was calling home from a pay phone in a deserted strip mall, the line went dead, and suddenly my head was in my arms, hard up against the brick wall, and I found myself sobbing so loudly that it echoed. When I returned to the loft, Jhymn poked his head from the curtains cordoning off his room, then quickly withdrew it.

Huh. He'd never done that before.

Then certain noises started, which gradually assumed a rhythm, sometimes accompanied by mumbling, and a different voice, one in a higher register, began its own mumbling and sighing, too.

After a long, bad day, after blubbering loudly and wiping off snot onto the back of my hand and steadying myself just enough to drive home and get upstairs to the hot, dog-smelling loft to bury myself under the sheet atop my mattress on the floor, there's my roommate sucking and fucking twenty yards away in a loft that lacked any walls.

It lasted a very long time, and she went into baby talk right as it ended. After that—and only then—was there silence. I looked up into the dark and thought, *Well, at least tomorrow won't be worse.*

I left Atlanta with a terrific tan, since this was before anyone wore sunscreen, and with my arms and chest ropy with muscle from all that physical work. Back at school, Martha finally gave in, and she and I stayed together, off and on, for three years. Bitch Magnet outgrew most of the songs from that summer pretty quickly. But down there in a city where we didn't fit in and where no one was paying any attention, we became a real band. We sounded, and acted, like a real band, and started to think of ourselves as one, too. In Atlanta there was nothing else on which to base an identity—no other friends, no classes, no jobs worth talking about. It was the first part of the answer, if anyone asked us what we were doing there. We were finally a band, and being in a band was central to how I saw myself and my place in the world. This is a chapter with a happy ending.

Life Is Painful.
Love, Bitch Magnet

Sooyoung drove and I rode shotgun, sneakers on the dashboard, my seat reclined as far as it could against the wall of guitars and amps in the backseat of my mom's blue Toyota Camry, as we listened to a tape I'd made from a bunch of new 7's and compilation tracks: Green River, Rapeman, Honor Role, and Spacemen 3's seventeen-minute-long cover of the 13th Floor Elevators' "Rollercoaster," which no one else in Bitch Magnet liked at all. It was late August of 1988. We were on our way to our first show in Boston and savoring the last dregs of that lovely summer between junior and senior year. Orestes, who'd already graduated, was now living in Boston, working at a store that sold maps. Our first record, *Star Booty*, which we were putting out ourselves, would come out in a couple of weeks. In six months I'd turn twenty-one. Few things are as grand as being a young American male road-tripping on a glorious day in August, and I may even have realized this at the time.

A few hastily dubbed cassettes of *Star Booty* had drummed up enough interest to get us a gig and some college radio airplay in Boston. A DJ from Harvard's station wanted to interview us once we arrived. It wasn't that we were excited by these first tendrils of attention reaching our way because we thought they meant that untold treasures awaited—that we'd soon sell tons of records and that fleshpots were quivering and ready, throughout the nation, across the world. That wasn't it at all. We were excited because the fact of anyone, anywhere, listening was amazing. That we'd been invited to play in Boston, by some guy we didn't know and had never met, felt like someone had found our message in a bottle. And in a sense he had, given the crates of demo tapes and records that every big-city booking agent watched their weary mailman haul in each day.

In 1988 only a few mainstream outlets paid attention to our culture. (Robert Hilburn of the *Los Angeles Times* was a rare perceptive observer at a major newspaper.) To most of the world this music was still hidden under rocks. But the biggest bands among us routinely drew several hundred people to their big-city shows and sold lots of records, too, though how many remained unknown, since virtually every indie label was fly-by-night, crooked, or mysterious about such data. (It was rumored that Hüsker Dü sold more than fifty thousand copies of *Zen Arcade*, which, pre-Nirvana, was a decent guess at what number represented the outer limits of the possible.) We were millions of miles from any of that, of course. But there were record labels interested in us. We'd turned down offers from a few after being warned off them, but getting a deal with one of the half-dozen half-decent independent labels was now thinkable. When we signed to one, we'd be advanced a couple thousand dollars, paid up front against future royalties, to make a record. Then the label would take over the scut work of getting it manufactured and distributed and promoting it to college radio stations, fanzines, and the college-radio trade outlets *CMJ* and *Rockpool*. Such minor forms of assistance sounded incredible, as did the fact that they seemed within reach. What I most wanted was to be known and respected—no, *adored*, I was far too hungry to settle for respect—by Fanzine USA and college radio and the people I most wanted to impress.

My circle of friends, basically, times a few thousand. The people who loved music so much that they let it destroy their lives. And capacity crowds at the small clubs where we all gathered. Those were the most important stages in the world. To me, anyway.

No music freak from an analog generation really gets over the bond formed with the records they listened to over and over again, but this was when listening to this music always involved a series of physical and intimate transactions. The thrill of entering the record store that most people overlooked, the tactile sensation of carrying a fresh stack of records home, tucked under your arm, in crinkled square brown paper bags. In your room you slit the plastic wrap and inhaled the new-vinyl-and-cardboard smell before slipping the record from its sleeve—gently, bracing the hole in the center with your middle finger—and carefully laying it onto your turntable. All that time we all spent crouched and kneeling in front of tiny stereos, doing nothing but *listening*, and maybe staring at the album cover. Looking back, it seems so premillennial it may as well have been the Middle Ages, and all of us supplicants from another epoch. Knowing Bitch Magnet had even a chance to enter bloodstreams this way was deeply gratifying.

We had no idea whether anyone would come see us in Boston, though I sensed some minor excitement stirring, a hint or a tingle that the show wouldn't be like playing to five people in Youngstown, Ohio, or an empty room in Atlanta. But not even that mattered. Boston was a new city to us, and, new to the whole experience, we thrilled to each microdevelopment. Much later I asked Rose Marshack, the bassist in Poster Children, if she ever got dispirited by lousy shows or tiny audiences, and she got indignant at the very suggestion, insisting, "Every single show was exciting." (Bear in mind that Poster Children toured nonstop for years and played close to a thousand shows.) It was an honor, she said, just to be able to throw your amps and drums and instruments in a van, drive for hours, and play, for any number of people, anywhere. In 1988 I believed this, too.

I looked out the window at the shimmer of a late-summer afternoon, the sun lighting each leaf while we sped through some placeless place in Connecticut or central Massachusetts. I probably lit a cigarette. We still smoked. That, too, was fun, that summer.

* * *

I'D LEARNED BY THEN HOW BEING IN A BAND ENTERED YOU into a conspiracy against the rest of the world. Sooyoung and I would search for each other among the carrels where everyone studied in Oberlin's giant Brutalist library and motion each other into the badly lit stairways, all dark tile and raw concrete, to strategize our next moves: the next show, the next time we'd record, the flyers we needed to make, the gag Valentine's Day cards we sent out one year (a badly drawn heart crudely colored with a green or brown crayon on the front, the inside inscribed "Life is painful. Love, Bitch Magnet"), the insert designs for the cassettes we sold for a few bucks and sent out to labels, and our worries that Orestes might not be in as deep as we were. Whenever we called him, he always insisted he was, but he also made clear how much he hated talking on the phone, so often we were left only with his absence and his word. But if you were as desperate as I was for any sort of rock to stand on, that was good enough. Sooyoung spent spring semester of our junior year away from Oberlin in North Carolina, working for his family's business—the one he'd felt guilty leaving when we went to Atlanta—and we stayed in touch, mostly by letter. He wrote about the band, about being bored and lonely, made mordant jokes about the girls he had no luck with. The sort of stuff we didn't really talk about much and that came out more easily for him in lyrics and letters.

In June of '88, after junior year ended, we all drove to Chicago and spent two or three days remixing *Star Booty* with Steve Albini at a place in Evanston called Studiomedia—roughly the same amount of time a studio down the hall from ours took to finish the voiceovers for a single radio commercial for an obscure Midwestern pizza chain called

Edwardo's. We recorded and mixed that record in three days that January at Oberlin's antiquated 8-track studio, for the grand total of three hundred bucks. One guitar track was recorded so ineptly it was barely audible over the tape hiss. Even after remixing, *Star Booty* is a very strange aural experience. The guitar tone is probably best described as "phlegmy," and Orestes sounds as if he's hammering on a toy drum kit situated somewhere down the block, if not in an adjacent zip code. But it took a lot of work to get it even to that point.

While in Chicago we played our first show there, at Batteries Not Included—the long-shuttered club, not the more-recently-shuttered dildo-and-lubricant shop—with a forgettable band still suffering from major new-wave damage, called Birds at the End of the Road. Chicago was only about twenty minutes from becoming the epicenter of all indie culture and had already spawned a few generations of punk and post-hardcore bands, but its every practice space and studio was still thronged with asymmetric-haired hordes chasing implausible MTV-sized success. Their cluelessness was sort of heartbreaking, if you knew that their music was going out and another was coming in. Albini brought one or two pals to see us that night, so Batteries wasn't entirely empty. At one point during the show I tried to shit-talk some jokes about a local fanzine editor—one of the few who'd written about us so far—as if there were even enough of a crowd there to rile. Real rock-star stuff.

After we finished mixing, I drove to my parents' house in New Jersey and worked for a construction company, where I was the most despised member of a broadly disrespected cleanup crew. One day I was instructed to dig a sizable hole, roughly four feet square and about as deep. I finished the following afternoon and stood wiping off sweat and guzzling water while some slightly-higher-ups eyed what I'd done, conferred amongst themselves, then told me to refill the hole. But each night I came home to a to-do list for getting *Star Booty* pressed and released: shipping artwork to printers, listening to test pressings, sending cassettes to distributors to drum up orders, and taking out a bank loan of three thousand bucks to finance all the above. Back then I was programmed for overexcitement even more than I am now, and each day's progress and minor victories that Sooyoung and I reported to each other—One hundred records presold to a distributor in Chicago! Two hundred sold to another in Europe!—often left me revved too high to sleep, making me draggier and even more useless for the next day of work.

In July the band reconvened at a studio close to a very pre-Disney Times Square called Sound on Sound. Friends worked there, and we recorded some newer songs for free. Well, not quite free. If those songs ever turned up on a record, we would owe the studio its standard hourly fee. Sound on Sound's rates were industry standard—not at all cheap, in other words—and very soon we racked up some absolutely preposterous sum, probably over $5,000, which was more than we'd be advanced by any record company that might sign us. But we figured it was worth it to hear our newest songs in a more realized and recorded form. We were pretty excited about them.

Generally no band I've ever been in has had enough money to record. Which means there isn't nearly enough time in the studio, which means you eventually cave in to the reality of camping out there for several consecutive days to kamikaze straight through it, staying up as long as possible, sleeping only when absolutely unavoidable. Luckily if you provided Sound on Sound's head engineer, Mike McMackin—a beefy redhead with a curly mullet and a mustache at least a decade out of date—with a steady supply of forty-ouncers of Bud, he had an absolutely heroic ability to transcend human fatigue, even while calmly negotiating the peculiar dynamics of a young band made up of very disparate personalities: the skilled and unflappable rhythm section, and the marginally skilled and quite flappable guitarist, who was in meltdown mode because his crappy amp and cheap distortion pedals sounded cloudy and diffuse and lacked any impact whatsoever when recorded in such a pro and pristine setting.

Like a hospital, a recording studio is an artificially quiet and antiseptic environment. But its raison d'être is that of a casino: to insulate its inhabitants from any outside noise, light, or sense of time. Sound on Sound looked like the exact average of every such studio of the mideighties. The floors in the live rooms were a bright shade of oak. Its décor was like that of the new offices of a moderately successful insurance company: all beiges and grays, and absolutely unremarkable. As at every studio, a tattered pile of magazines—*Rolling Stone* and trade publications aimed at engineers and studio owners, the latter being effective sleeping aids—sat on a coffee table near the couch: band distractors. The coffee was horrifying, thick and sour from the eight or twelve hours it spent warming in the carafe, but you drank it anyway. The one female intern sat behind the reception desk, where the take-out menus were kept in a folder in the top drawer. God forbid, in the eighties, she should actually be allowed in the control room.

When no music is playing, the hush of any studio's control room is womblike and deeply comforting. (Though we four dudes kamikazeing through a sleep-deprived weekend gradually made that room smell as sharp as kimchee.) Sound on Sound's was tiny, but it neatly accommodated a truckload of outboard gear, the tape machines, and the pooltable-sized mixing desk, behind which the engineer or producer sat in a rolling chair. (An engineer recorded your band. A producer rewrote your songs and told you what to play. We learned the distinction after pissing off Albini by giving him a producer credit on the first pressing of *Star Booty*.) The band sat behind the engineer, the three of us snugly wedged onto the cokey-styled, blandly modern black leather sofa against the back wall.

After something like a day straight of being awake in the studio, following a full week's work with the construction crew and a mad dash to Manhattan, and after another round of guitar overdubs on "Big Pining," I'd had enough and told everyone I needed to sleep. I flicked the light switches near the reception desk and collapsed onto a (beige) couch. A few hours later Orestes woke me to say he was leaving, that he had to get back to Boston. As he walked away I propped myself up on one elbow and blurted, "We're the best band in the world."

He repeated it back at me, because we could still say something like that and believe it. Maybe I should have quit right then. No one knew who we were yet, but it could never get better than the certainty of that moment.

* * *

AS IT OFTEN HAPPENED, OUR BOSTON SHOW WAS ACTUALLY in Cambridge, at the Middle East, a tiny room just off Central Square with surprisingly good sound. Billy Ruane, a local legend who booked shows there, had tracked us down and set it up. "Local legend" is, of course, a terrible and overused term, but anyone from Boston—even anyone in a band that came through Boston—will testify that he deserved it. Billy combed his hair up, wore loafers with no socks, and looked exactly like a drunk preppie, which is what he was. He had the pinkish skin you see on Irish guys who don't really need to shave. I always picture him in a partially buttoned white shirt, shirttail out, long before that was a common look, under a blazer or a brownish knee-length overcoat. One term was so frequently, and accurately, applied to his appearance that, were you to type his name into Google, I half expect autofill would offer up "billy ruane disheveled." Billy was notorious for jumping around at shows in an exuberant, flailing way, and I highly recommend that you go to YouTube and watch him dance. I was told there was family money, and a lot of it. Much later I learned that his dad had done well enough to warrant being described as an investor-slash-philanthropist. Billy's day job was guarding rare books at Harvard's Widener Library—really—but he lived to drink and go to shows and movies every night.

Sooyoung and I drove straight to Orestes's apartment, laughed and hugged him at the door, lugged our gear up a few flights of stairs to the sweltering attic where he kept his drums, stripped off our shirts—that again, but it was just too damn hot—set up as quickly as we could, and started ripping through our songs. We hadn't played together for several weeks, so having these guys behind me again felt like holding a jackhammer between my legs. After we'd slammed through a few songs, Sooyoung had to stop. He was laughing too hard to play, because it was so much fun, maybe more fun than ever, and it sounded even better than it ever had before. Afterward Orestes, who could drink like a camel, got us started on a mostly full bottle of tequila in his currently favored rugby-guy fashion: pour the booze and ginger ale into a rocks glass, cover the glass with a towel, place your hand on top, slam the glass on a countertop, then slurp down the foam just after the BOOM of impact. I weighed maybe 130 pounds, and I doubt that Sooyoung weighed more, but the three of us drank until the bottle was empty. Then we went to visit some friends, but neither Sooyoung nor I were much good for conversation that night.

Everything about Boston was new to Sooyoung and me: its neighborhoods of shingled Queen Annes and corner spas, its myriad insularities and strangenesses (like calling convenience stores *spas*), the omnipresence of college radio. In 1988 it was almost without question the American city that had built the best infrastructure for underground rock bands. There were a shocking number of great record stores for a town its size, like Newbury Comics and Mystery Train and In Your Ear, all of them encyclopedic about the latest stuff. Giveaway magazines like *The Noise* and *Boston Rock* focused on local bands, and college radio stations at Harvard and MIT and Emerson and pretty much every other school obsessively followed this music. Boston was the only city where bands made "radio tapes," cassette-only demos you passed off to local stations. They got airplay—in some cases, lots of airplay—and because people actually listened to these stations, every local band made them. The stores and stations and clubs and media that supported Boston bands, most of which were unknown anywhere else, fed off one another and created an ecosystem sufficiently self-reinforcing to make Billy Ruane and other superfans, like the wannabe impresario known as the Count, into something approaching local celebrities.

You needed the right kind of eyes to find bands like us in virtually every other American city, but the line between underground and mainstream was much more permeable in Boston. (The city was unusually European in that respect.) Though it may have been a bit too comfortable being a band in an affluent, welcoming college town. Once you separated out the city's hardcore scene, Boston circa 1988 was breeding lots of unthrilling guitar pop—Salem 66, Big Dipper, Scruffy the Cat, Blake Babies, Dumptruck—and many Boston bands lacked the sense of opposition, the chip on the shoulder, that fueled the psyches and ambitions and music of bands everywhere else. A different strain of Boston Disease took root in Austin, Texas, where it was so easy for weirdo musicians to scrape by on local gigs, local kudos, and part-time jobs that, in the late eighties, many of its more ambitious musicians fled to New York and Chicago. If you asked why, many said the same thing: they feared they'd just coast in Austin forever.

At the Middle East we played with a band fronted by Kenny Chambers, the guitarist in Moving Targets, one of the few bands everyone in Bitch Magnet really liked. That night, though, Kenny sang for a band that did Stooges covers, billed as "The (Fucking) Stooges." Evan Dando, long before he was a heartthrob and longer before he did too many drugs, was on the bill, too, performing a solo set of Eagles covers, which he sang while drumming, Don Henley–style. Apparently jokey cover bands were a thing in Boston. Kenny came over and chatted with us while we devoured a spread of Middle Eastern grub from the restaurant next door, and acted like he'd heard of us, thrilling the fanboy in me. We met the Harvard radio DJ before the show, too, and when she realized it was us, her eyes widened and her hand fluttered up to cover her open mouth, and I thought, *Shit—someone's actually excited to meet us.*

My hangover from the tequila had practically paralyzed me, and I was barely back to being human by showtime. There were a few technical fuckups that night, and I probably broke a string or two, because that's what always happened, but the crowd was excited—there *was* a crowd, for once—and it rubbed off on us, and it became a great night.

I soon started a brief dalliance with the Harvard radio DJ. When I stayed with her when we played her hometown of Youngstown in early September, or when she came to visit me at Oberlin one weekend thereafter, I stole her Grim Reaper T-shirt—the laughably awful metal band, not the guy who kills everyone—which I would wear onstage into the twenty-first century. I had to steal it. I still have it today. It's an absolutely perfect artifact. Not just because it brilliantly encapsulates the idiocy of most eighties metal, but because it's a reminder of how easily dreams of big-time commercial success could curdle. Black-light poster colors of purple and bright yellow, silk-screened onto the deep black of a half-polyester fabric. The front depicts a skeleton in a hooded cloak in a jail cell, bony hands curling around a prison bar and smoke seeping from ol' Grim's open mouth, over the legend LUST FOR FREEDOM. The back displays a soul-crushing litany of fifth- and sixth-tier markets through which the band death-marched for over six weeks in 1987, towns known only to their residents, places no band ever wants to see on its itinerary: Cookstown, New Jersey. Pasadena, Maryland. Salina, Kansas. Papillion, Nebraska. Lawton, Oklahoma. Some years later our friends in Codeine crossed paths on tour with an obscure Seattle band called Sweet Water as Sweet Water flogged an instantly forgotten major-label album and slogged through their version of this tour. In the lyrics for Codeine's "Loss Leader," you hear that band's story: alone on the road, utterly abandoned by their record label and everyone else, all but left to die alongside some obscure highway, as the song sadly repeats, far from home, far from home.

In 1988 you couldn't imagine the sorry fate of a band like Sweet Water, which lived in the right zip code to get scooped up in the post-Nirvana major-label feeding frenzy. Nor could the fate be foretold of an oddball band we met in Chicago that summer, with whom we'd soon play shows in Ohio. They had few fans, performed their strange, tough, and beautiful songs while wearing elaborate velvet and lamé suits, and in general acted as if they alone were in on a colossal joke. Urge Overkill's guitarist, Nate Kaatrud, and its bassist, Ed Roeser, both came from small towns in Minnesota, though both seemed far too weird and knowing for it: rightly or wrongly, I always sensed some savvy lurking beneath their generally dazed and stoney mien. Nate was a rare ladykiller in our midst, tall, rail-thin and angular, with sharply turned cheekbones and giant blue eyes. Rock-star looks, in the sense that rock stars often have odd and exaggerated features. He was a talented graphic artist, though he was too lazy to do much with said skill. He improvised absurd asides in any situation. Once, in Pittsburgh, we watched a confused drunk wallow on the sidewalk outside the Bloomfield Bridge Tavern—the sort of old dive bar that got colonized by punk kids putting on shows, to the bafflement of the native clientele. When the guy unzipped his fly and started reaching within, Nate immediately urged, "No, no, no, no. Let's keep Li'l Elvis in Graceland." If he liked your set, he wouldn't come up and say "great show" or any such standard nonsense, but he'd fix you with a bug-eyed stare and enthuse, "You smoked my butt!" People often thought Nate led the band, since he played guitar and was the most charismatic. But Ed sang most of their songs, while playing rock-solid and tuneful bass, and I secretly liked him better. He looked nothing like a rock star: short, chunky, with long hair that went stringy, not lank like Nate's. He often seemed bewildered, but if you knew how to listen, something ultraperceptive lurked in his observations. Like this: "You've got to waste a lot of fucking time to come up with something like Urge Overkill."

* * *

IT FEELS APPROPRIATE TO END THIS CHAPTER THIS WAY.

On October 26, 2010, a friend found Billy Ruane slumped in front of his computer, dead of a heart attack. He was fifty-two. All his zaniness and alcoholism were eventually recognized as symptoms of bipolar disorder. He'd been in and out of treatment, was by all accounts very casual about taking his meds, and in general never took proper care of himself. I last saw him at a Wipers show at New York's Irving Plaza in the late nineties. He was dancing his spastic Snoopy dance in front of the stage, as he always did, and though it had been years since we'd spoken, and though in fact we barely knew each other, when I tapped his shoulder, he recognized me, grabbed my cheeks, and kissed me on the lips. I miss him.

Mike McMackin recorded Bitch Magnet's second album, *Umber*, and a few songs on our last album, *Ben Hur*, as well as all of Codeine's records and a bunch of others, including Poster Children's major-label debut, *Tool of the Man*. He wisely established himself in another line of work long before the nuclear winter descended upon the music biz.

Poster Children signed to Warner Brothers. After five years and three albums they left the label, intact and with a recording studio they'd bought with money saved from their advances. Their time on a major label left them more independent, an outcome that basically never happened to anyone else. They remained an active touring band until Rose and her husband, Poster Children's singer and guitarist, Rick Valentin, had their first child, in late 2003.

A reunited Sweet Water toured with Stone Temple Pilots in 2008, so I guess their endless suffering continued into another millennium.

And, lest anyone from a mildly obscure indie rock band feel special about being asked to reunite years after they broke up—well, Grim Reaper got back together in the twenty-first century, too.

On second thought, it feels appropriate to end this chapter *this* way.

The Best Part and
the Worst Part

School years have a particular rhythm, but the rhythm I moved to during my senior year had remarkably little to do with college. I lived from show to show. I went to my classes, more or less. But mostly less, and when I did, I often stopped paying attention, hid behind my long hair, bent over my desk and started scrawling song titles and lyric fragments in the margins of my notebooks. I got a B+ on one final exam, and under my grade the professor wrote, "You seem to have done very well for someone who barely came to class. Congratulations," and suggested that it might have been nice if I'd actually spoken up on those times I did show up. There were maybe ten students in that class. It wasn't easy to hide and stay mute in such a setting, though somehow I managed.

But how could you bother with school or classes if crate after crate of new records arrived at the radio station each day, and if you played in a band? I kept devouring fanzines. Now they contained reviews of *Star Booty*. The British music weeklies, back then surprisingly and annoyingly influential in Europe and even in America, loved the record and wrote, in their typically overheated prose, comments like "A great

and necessary thing, every angst-ridden adolescent's crystal ball."
(Uh-huh.) "Bitch Magnet *worry*. Theirs is a seared, skinless sensibility,
pricked by anger, fear and self-reproach. Bitch Magnet *want back in*." (I
laughed then, but now think: pretty dead-on. For me, at least.) You
learned fast that people heard much different things in your music than
what you knew, or thought, was there. One guy in Germany compared
Star Booty's horrifyingly bad guitar sound to Hendrix. More than one
writer from Europe saw Ohio in our mailing address and imagined us
as hulking, crazed, glue-sniffing rural American freaks. They clearly
had no clue what kind of kids went to Oberlin.

We printed a thousand copies of *Star Booty,* which sold out almost
immediately, and labels in America and Europe started calling and
writing. Sooyoung and I paged through record contracts while sitting
outside the basement smoking lounge in the campus library. I ran up
WOBC's phone bill, talking to one label in the Netherlands and another
in London called Shigaku. We eventually signed with Shigaku, the
European home of Moving Targets, the Replacements, and Live Skull,
because they offered us a $2,500 advance for the European rights to our
next album. Though in true indie rock fashion, Shigaku went bankrupt
about a year later, without ever paying us a dime in royalties.

Orestes still lived in Boston with his girlfriend, but he was also seeing a woman at Oberlin, and it was nothing to get him to hop in his
truck and drive twelve or fourteen hours to practice and play a party or
a show. The good part about living seven hundred miles from him, as
anyone who's gone through the honeymoon phase of a long-distance
relationship knows, was that every meeting was a reunion and every
occasion a genuine *occasion*, joyous and hilarious. The bad part was that
we spent little time together, and the miles separating us nagged at me.

Sooyoung, meanwhile, was cranking out a new song every week or
two, it seemed, each sounding huger than the last. (Many of them
ended up on our second album, *Umber.*) One fading, college-boy-angsty
afternoon, on one of the last days of September, he turned up at my

converted-attic rental—one that shouldn't have been an apartment at all, with too-low slanting ceilings and a kitchen jammed into a space far too small—with the makings of "Americruiser," a slow and understated song with terse, spoken vocals that somehow captured all that I felt at that moment. It wasn't the vocals or the lyrics. It was everything taken together: the slow procession of the song, its loud, wordless chorus, as much what it hinted but held back as what it described. You spend so much time searching for music that names your unnameables— the hard stuff, the millions of shadings beyond "I love you" or "I hate you" or "I'm angry" or "I've been mistreated" or "I will give up everything I know for this moment of abandon" or "I'm scared but I don't know why"—and here was this guy at my school, *in my band*, nonchalantly reaching into some inaccessible recess of my brain. I remember thanking him—thanking him!—for capturing what I couldn't quite put into words.

That fall we also started playing "Motor," which eventually became the first song on *Umber*. Shortly after Sooyoung gave me a rough version of the song on cassette, a brand-new guitar slide materialized, taped to my mailbox at school. *An honorarium for you*, the note explained, in Sooyoung's neat, tight handwriting. He wanted me to use it during the intro. A brilliant idea, and I started smearing abstract slide guitar over Sooyoung's crashing, distorted bass chords and Orestes's bastardized Dixieland snare rolls. Sometimes you know right away a song is a great leap forward, and "Motor" so exploded me with joy that for a while, whenever we played it live, excitement ran so far ahead of me that I often couldn't play it correctly. Sometimes I'd end up on the floor at its ending, pelvic-thrusting with each chord flourish, wondering afterward, *Where did that come from?* It made me want to jump high enough to bang my head through the ceiling. It made me want to run with it through a brick wall. It made me want to set my guitar on fire, and maybe myself, too.

We played weekend shows as often as possible—at clubs, not campus parties—and put together a mini-tour of the Northeast during fall break. None of us owned a vehicle big enough to haul all of us and our gear, so Sooyoung and I would throw our amps and my guitar and his bass into the backseat and trunk of my car, and Orestes would jam his drums into his Isuzu Trooper, and we'd meet at wherever we were playing. I craved all the rituals of being in a band, but so many were lost to us: no late-night drives together, no shared drama of arrival, no drowsy late-afternoon stretches of highway under a waning sun. Our distance meant that much of our communication took place during nighttime phone calls, or asides in the school library, never with the three of us together. I realized that any two of us could fashion a noose for the other, quietly and out of sight, without anyone needing to fake his body language and smile and be all *No, what are you talking about? Everything's fine.* Trios often devolve into two against one. I wondered if Orestes worried about that.

More often, though, I thrilled to the social set now opening up to us, a web of associations and friends formed around this music, the bands you met and with whom you played shows. Names on the backs of records moved into your address book. Phone pals became real pals. In the summer I'd adored the "Craig Olive" single by Honor Role, another brainy and aggressive band from an unexpected place—Richmond, Virginia—that broke apart rock music and reassembled it in an interesting way. A few weeks later I was on the phone with their brilliant guitarist, Pen Rollings, setting up a show in Pittsburgh, barely able to believe my luck. I don't know if you could call it a *movement*, but all over America outcasts were finding one another with delight and relief even while many of us—myself included—still sometimes nursed a very high school fear of rejection. Justin Chearno, a guitarist and bassist who's passed through a record store's worth of bands (including Unrest, Pitchblende, Turing Machine, and Panthers), neatly encapsulated that social anxiety: "I was like, 'God, I hope this crowd accepts me. Because if these people don't, then I'm fucked.'" I knew exactly what he meant.

Anyone within fifty yards could see that the music and the excitement were leading me around by the glands, because I was not at all shy about showing how hopped-up it made me. Nor could I have hidden it if I tried. (To steal a line from Hunter S. Thompson, my nerves were pretty close to the surface and everything registered.) But Sooyoung and Orestes were as reserved as I was hyper. Sooyoung, an unusually expressionless front man, preferred recording to performing. While Orestes loved playing in any context, he despised clubs and wasn't much charmed by those who congregated within them. The one of us who worked hardest onstage, he especially hated the fog of secondhand smoke in which bands invariably performed. Before shows I bounced around the club, chatting up musicians and fans and new friends, while Orestes sat dead-eyed and bored backstage, if there even was a backstage, clutching his sticks, clearly uncomfortable, refusing any booze until after the show, eventually stirring to warm up with some fundamentals, the basic movements drummers drill as calisthenics. Neither he nor Sooyoung had much patience with the schmoozers who worked for labels, and since it appeared I knew how to talk to them, I generally drew the short straw and dealt with them. But I didn't mind. I wanted to know everyone.

We played a bunch of shows with Bastro, the band formed by Squirrel Bait's guitarist David Grubbs and—ill advisedly—a drum machine, but then Grubbs and bassist Clark Johnson recruited a friend of ours at Oberlin named John McEntire to play drums, and they got really great. Complicated, super smart, oddly chorded and in odd meters, played at blinding speed—what Grubbs did with his bizarrely tuned metallic-pink Tele was unlike anything else I'd heard before, or, for that matter, have heard since. We played together just after we both released our first records, and our shows routinely drew twenty-five people, but each time I saw them I thought, *Christ, this is one of the best bands in the world, and no one knows it.* The way they—forgive the tired term—rocked, without having the slightest thing to do with "rock." How they provided a purely visceral rush while still being so musically advanced and so thoroughly bent.

Another Squirrel Bait offshoot was far more mysterious, right down to the name: Slint. A quartet led by two extremely taciturn guys, Britt Walford and Brian McMahan, whose inside references were so intricate they seemed almost like a form of idioglossia. In 1988 we got a tape of a nine-song record, *Tweez*, before it became an LP the following year. Its songs were named after each band member's parents (and one of their dogs), and they all sounded tweaked and slightly metallic and often swung—in the jazz sense—in a way very few others in our underground could. The vocals were occasional, incidental, and sometimes started to tell stories without ever really finishing them. When the album came out, the cover was a simple black-and-white shot of a Saab Turbo—with SLINT going where the SAAB was and TWEEZ replacing TURBO, and very little information appeared on the back or the insert. I cannot overemphasize how thrilling and absolutely unique it sounded or—and this is the part that gets lost today when people talk about that band—the oddball humor underneath it all. Bitch Magnet went crazy for *Tweez*. I listened to it every day. A cassette of it turned up in a photo we used for the insert to *Umber*. In 1988 almost no one in the world had heard of them, but that just fed the intoxicating feeling that you and your friends knew secrets no one else did.

The thing I most treasured about this time was that you kept stumbling over set after set of smart misfits playing amazing, fully realized music that sounded like nothing else. All the town weirdos were suddenly in bands. Some, like Slint, were making records *while they were still teenagers* that would age as well as those made by distant rock gods like Led Zeppelin and AC/DC. In the rest of the world hair metal was king, and its bands—Warrant, Winger, Poison—ruled the radio and

MTV, selling upbeat party-time bullshit in which the guy always got the girl and all underdogs triumphed over their adversaries by the third verse, if not sooner. The bands in our underground, like those that inspired them, told stories that didn't fit into such narrow schematics. No other music so accurately evoked the black hole of self-loathing, and the power you could find within it, as "Nothing" by Negative Approach or "Black Coffee" by Black Flag. No mainstream artist drew such precise lines between us and them as Saint Vitus did in the embittered, extended middle finger of "Born Too Late," or as ferociously as Minor Threat's "Filler," or with the naked anguish of Hüsker Dü's "Whatever." If our bands didn't invent writing about the absolute abasement of romantic despair and loneliness—Leonard Cohen, Nick Drake, and Crazy Horse's "I Don't Want to Talk About It" came first, after all—nothing on the radio or MTV or any major label expressed it as clearly and starkly as American Music Club's "Blue and Grey Shirt" or "Laughingstock." Our bands even nailed standard rock topics better than anyone else around: the aimlessness of American youth, like Meat Puppets' "Lost," or the joy of libido and an open road, like Urge Overkill's "Faroutski."

And the lyrics weren't even the important part. Not when Sonic Youth and Slint and Slovenly reached heights of gorgeousness and mystery that almost never had anything to do with what they *said*. Rather, it was how they *sounded*, even on records made as cheaply and quickly as possible in studios held together with duct tape. Songs were finally liberated from verse-chorus-verse-chorus-bridge-chorus. Bands everywhere made incredibly evocative albums, like *Tweez* or *EVOL* or Die Kreuzen's *October File*, that sounded like nothing that ever came before them. Other musicians realized you could strip the exciting parts off metal's carcass—loud distorted riffs, relentless rhythm sections—and make them into something else. Something better. Very few bands playing metal in 1987 ever set their instruments and amps to "crush/ kill/destroy" as effectively as the instrumental Dutch band Gore did on

Mean Man's Dream—an album recorded live in the studio, with no overdubs, which no straight-up metal band in the eighties would ever have the balls to do.

* * *

THE MUSIC AND THE SMIDGENS OF ATTENTION WE WERE getting began to go to my head. I kept my mouth shut in high school, convinced I'd be misunderstood. Now, full of late-adolescent spunk, electrified by guitars, I was damn well going to be heard. Finally confident enough, for the first time in my life, to be absolutely straight-forward. Though the people around me might have preferred to call it "being an asshole." "You lived your life," Orestes told me much later, "like you played your instrument." I still couldn't bully anyone physically, but I could bully *everyone* aesthetically. Oberlin, a colony of art nerds and mousy nose-to-the-textbook types, was a very safe place to do this. Despite its deserved reputation for excruciating political correctness, and even though the campus newspaper's letters page endlessly hashed out the minutest aspects of sexism and racism and taking back the night, few people there knew how to put up a real fight. Passive aggression was more common: a large percentage of Bitch Magnet flyers were routinely torn down. We gleefully replaced them, and then some.

Sometime during junior or senior year I was pulling together a few bands for another dorm or house party when, with some reluctance, I approached a musician I knew. He was really annoying, and I didn't care for his band, either. When I mentioned the party and asked if they could do it, he barked out a superior prep-school "Ha ha!"—and it really sounded exactly like "Ha ha!"—and added, "Everyone wants us to play that show!" Without hesitating, I banged out, "Well, I think you guys pretty much suck. But other people asked."

He may have deserved that, but back then I sprayed that shit everywhere. I said stupid things. I *did* stupid things. On one of the first weekends of the school year, I slept with the woman at school who was involved with Orestes. I apologized to him, first on the phone and then in a self-lacerating letter, but a fissure opened that couldn't be easily closed. And I had other problems with Orestes, because he bought a dog.

I'm serious.

Specifically, a baby English mastiff he named Victor. I'm told they are delightful, but an English mastiff is a dog in the way that an aircraft carrier is a boat. Adult mastiffs can weigh more than 130 pounds, and they get big before they *realize* they're big. As a puppy Victor might see you lying on the floor and step on your face, unaware that this could break your jaw. When he leapt up to greet you, he would practically knock you down. You prayed he wouldn't cuff you in the nuts, because his paws were as big as baseballs. Each day the overflow from his panting mug could fill a few pint glasses. Luckily he didn't bark much, which was good, because when he barked, it scared the absolute crap out of you.

Orestes was too broke to kennel Victor—and god knows the band wasn't making any money—so oftentimes he brought him to shows, where Victor would wait, long-faced and lugubrious and panting and drooling, in the back of Orestes's truck while we played. Today, I understand the balm to loneliness Victor was for Orestes, but to me, back then, he only looked like an enormous pain in the ass. And Orestes was as bad as a new parent about him. One day he went on and on about how much he liked mastiffs and then he told me he wanted to get another one, and I lost it and started screaming. How the fuck would he be able to handle two mastiffs? He could barely manage one. You had to be a weight lifter—or Orestes—to take Victor for a walk. Once, when Orestes wanted to visit his girlfriend on the side, he tried, desperately, to talk me into boarding him at my parents' house for a few days. I turned him down. Possibly after a lot more yelling.

What causes most band conflicts? Disagreements and competitions over girls and boys. Money. People getting fucked up on drugs and booze, especially if different members prefer different substances. "Creative differences," which means someone's ideas are so bad you start to hate him. Orestes and I fought most avidly *over a dog*. Sometimes one tiny thing your bandmate does drives you insane.

A mastiff is not a tiny thing.

* * *

EACH JANUARY, BETWEEN SEMESTERS, OBERLIN HAD A monthlong winter term during which students completed mandatory independent projects, however half-assed those projects might be. In 1989—my last January at Oberlin—my project was playing in a rock band, which made it the second January term for which I got school credit for Bitch Magnet–related activities. We had a mini-tour booked across the East and Midwest, and had studio time reserved in Chicago to record our second album with Albini. At the last minute the recording had to be canceled, because Orestes's beloved paternal grandmother, who helped raise him, died. (Albini gave the recording time to Slint, and those recordings came out in 1994 on a two-song self-titled EP.) We still planned to play all the shows, but—

But let me start somewhere else.

A windy Saturday evening in mid-January, around dinnertime at a gas station in the middle of Pennsylvania. The temperature's dropping. There's so little light by the pumps that you have to squint to jam the nozzle into the tank. Sooyoung and I are driving my grandfather's old car, a mid-seventies Oldsmobile, primer gray, shockingly huge by the standards of the eighties and possibly by those of the seventies as well. The front seat is one big bench, with nothing splitting the driver's and shotgun seats. You can seat three people up here, if necessary, and maybe four more in the back. That backseat and the enormous trunk—the kind that protrudes several feet past the rear wheels, a duck's bill sticking out its ass—are crammed with Sooyoung's and my equipment, plus some assorted student detritus, like my milk crate full of LPs. We just played two shows in New York and are heading back to Oberlin for one night before setting off for our next dates in Columbus, Ohio, and Champaign, Illinois. I just finished putting our ten or twelve dollars' worth in the tank while the wind picked up, promising another kind of weather—no, that weather is here, and the first raindrops start slashing sideways while Sooyoung maneuvers the beast back onto Route 80, heading west.

Somewhere between Milton and Williamsport, on a lengthy elevated stretch that connects bits of land as you cross the west branch of the Susquehanna River, the car's enormous ass starts sliding. Sooyoung struggles it back into place, but then it's whipping back and forth and momentum mercilessly takes over. The brakes lock, a big, slow spin begins, goodbye to the linear, that sickening and alarmed realization instantly familiar to all who've been through it: *We're gonna . . .*

And we do. Head-on into the guardrail.

The good news is that it's not a simple thin steel guardrail but one plopped atop solid concrete, and we were going maybe twenty miles an hour when we crashed. The impact on our monstrosity, the front bumper of which seems a Chevette's length from the front seat, registers only as a sharp bump. We look at each other, wide-eyed, and quickly understand we're both okay.

But this is a narrow roadway with only a few feet of shoulder between the lane and the railing, and since the car now completely blocks much of the road, I push open my door to begin waving people around us—and put my sneaker down on a roadway so slick that I fall before I can even stand. Though of course: *Bridge freezes before highway surface.* What was light rain had become—what's the term?—a perfect "sheet of ice." As I struggle back upright I see headlights a few hundred yards behind us swerve as cars start to-ing and fro-ing and scraping and crashing.

The next part is fuzzy, because it all happens very quickly, but we calculate that we can't stay in the car. We can't stand up on the road, either, or cower by the side of the road, because there *is* no side of the road. The cars skidding toward us can't stop or steer. So we vault over the guardrail and suspend ourselves from a handhold on the railing. I've wondered for years if our feet found a purchase on something— they must have, but I can't remember. Meanwhile cars serenely glide by, moving no faster than a brisk jog, wheels locked and motionless, plowing unstoppably into each other and into our Olds, each collision ending with popping and bursting sheet metal and the cymbal crash of breaking safety glass.

Then silence.

Tiny cubes of shattered glass are strewn all over the highway, refracting and distorting the streetlights. It's lit like a disco out here.

A few other cars are clustered around ours. A woman with puffy frosted eighties-mom hair, and who looks pregnant, heaves herself out of a passenger seat, looks me in the eye, and then looks away, cradling her stomach and repeating, "Oh, my baby," in a central Pennsylvania drawl. She's fine, just frightened, and apparently a little drunk.

The Oldsmobile has a car-sized impression caved into its passenger side, right where I'd been sitting. The back window is shattered and lets in freezing rain. One guitar neck protrudes through the side of its cheap case. I touch it, then strum it. Miraculously it's still in tune.

Sooyoung snaps a picture of me on the highway, standing amid the lights and shattered glass.

I'm together enough to ask whether everyone in our wreck is all right, though if they're not, I wouldn't know what to do. (Luckily, everyone is.) Cop cars and an ambulance arrive. I have never understood how they make their way through such scenes, and I don't remember how they did here. Elsewhere on this very long bridge, I hear someone say, a tractor-trailer jackknifed. The cops tell us to sit in the ambulance. I guess they want us off the road. One guy inside with us seems confused. He was in a different wreck. He keeps saying he doesn't know where his wife is. One cop tells him she's at the hospital and they'll talk to him there, then looks away, and in the silence that follows a terrible feeling blooms.

Sooyoung snaps another picture of me inside the ambulance while I'm making a strange face. Local volunteers in their twenties, wearing thick sweatshirts, sit among us, chatty with each other and with the emergency workers. I'd say they're friendly, but they don't talk to us or anyone else from the wreck. Aren't they supposed to be handing out hot chocolate or something? They seem very casual about what has just happened. But it's comforting. I'm grateful that these multiple crashes aren't being acknowledged. The guy whose wife is at the hospital is quiet now, and I'm grateful for that, too.

Sooyoung and I don't go to the hospital, because we're fine. The Oldsmobile gets towed to a junkyard, and somehow all our gear and baggage end up with us in a motel room. I call my parents and tell my mom that there was a crash and the car is destroyed but we're unharmed. She does not take this news especially well. I find out later that people died in some of the other wrecks. I never learned what happened to the other man's wife.

The next morning we dig through the local Yellow Pages, find the closest cheap rental car, load it up, and drive, under a diamond-bright winter sun, to Stache's in Columbus, where we play with Hypnolove-wheel and cancel the show in Champaign, and afterward drive the hundred miles back to Oberlin. To get into my tragic converted-attic apartment, you have to walk up a creaky back staircase. That night, when I arrive after three a.m., I find my housemate, Susannah, wild-eyed, waiting in her bathrobe.

"I heard you guys were in a really bad car crash and you were in the hospital."

She's half-right, at least. I throw my head back and give her my best maniac cackle, saying it would take more than that to stop me. She's looking at me like I just came back from the dead. Everyone should see that on a friend's face at least once.

The rest of January was small-bore and soap-opera-y. I stayed up late, slept in, saw little daylight. We bored college kids, left alone in a frigid and snowy rural isolation, drank as much as you'd expect. There were irritations and small fights and intense bonding with others also stuck at school. Orestes and I and some other friends spent one night giggling and tripping on mushrooms, without Sooyoung. I think we wrote one new song. Whenever Orestes made spaghetti sauce for dinner, he added at least a half stick of butter, and for a while I thought this was the best way to make it, too.

When Sooyoung showed me the photos he took that night, they didn't look as amazing and otherworldly as I hoped. But I still wish I had them today. Because the crash was the highlight of that winter. Before we knew what really happened, nothing else was nearly as strange and as interesting—as magical—as vehicles turned into bumper cars, and the pure percussive crunch of each slow-motion collision on a highway suddenly as slick as an ice rink. Not a girl taking off her shirt in your room. Not another night at one of Oberlin's two bars. Certainly not the campus buildings looming over the flat, frozen landscape under gray and indifferent Midwestern skies. Bands died in wrecks. College students died in wrecks. Our classmates died in wrecks. People died in our wreck. But nothing happened to us. This is a fucked-up thing to admit, I know, about something really awful, but those still moments on the bridge, amid the safety glass glittering in the streetlights, are among the most beautiful I've known.

* * *

SCHOOL STARTED AGAIN, AND THE BY-NOW-FAMILIAR counter-rhythm returned. I'd been pursuing a preposterously hot freshwoman, and suddenly she acted interested. Full lips, blue eyes, pale skin, a hint of a British accent, a tangle of long, loose, curly hair. She moved through campus with a dancer's upright posture, wearing an expression broadcasting that no one could tell her anything she hadn't already known forever, all of which I found incredibly inflaming. She didn't seem to realize she was way out of my league. Over the years I've gotten very little play as a direct consequence of being a musician— after a show, I mean—but I know I never would have approached her were it not for the band.

Shigaku was planning a European tour for us the following fall: six weeks, something like seven countries, around thirty-five shows. Sooyoung and I scanned itineraries outside the library's smoking lounge. Orestes's grandmother had left him a brownstone in Brooklyn, and it was agreed—I *thought* it was agreed—we'd all live there after Sooyoung and I graduated. When I blabbed about it to our American record label, that factoid showed up in a press release, which didn't thrill the other guys. As always, I had a hard time keeping my mouth shut about anything that excited me, whether in interviews or in private conversations. I didn't realize that my bandmates' silence did not equal consent. Nor that they were starting to feel that I was hogging the spotlight, inasmuch as there was any spotlight shining upon us.

I sensed that things were starting to feel a bit strained with Sooyoung, and things with Orestes weren't any less complicated. He was the first male friend to whom I routinely said "I love you," but then I slept with his girl on the side and courted her afterward, which at Oberlin meant we sexlessly shared the same bed and sometimes mashed mouths while drunk. Then—and I don't know why—Orestes became a target for my rants about music. In April we played Club Dreamerz in Chicago with Slint. Afterward—all the band riding through Indiana together in Orestes's truck, for once, along with one of his old friends— I unloaded, at high volume, for something like fifteen minutes straight on a silent Orestes. Neither of us remembers what prompted it, but there's a good chance (I can barely write the rest of this sentence without laughing) I was outraged that he liked the Bad Brains come-back record *I Against I*. Orestes explained to me much later that he'd been raised in places where people didn't go off on someone like that without getting beat up, and in fact it took serious impulse control for him to keep driving and not pull over to kick the shit out of me. I kept dinging Orestes's fierce loner pride—whether accidentally or on purpose or accidentally-on-purpose. As for Sooyoung, years later he told me he was growing increasingly pissed off about day-to-day control of the band and people's perceptions of us. (My comments and story lines tended to dominate interviews and articles.) But there were girls and classes and new records at the radio station and letters from fans and fanzine interviews and plenty of other reasons to avoid confronting a growing chill.

Spring finally came, and the fields and trees sighed in relief, and the air smelled of wet earth and mowed grass and cornfields. I was six weeks from graduation, lucky to be living a luxury rare among my classmates: I didn't have to worry about what came next.

Then one evening, while I was eating dinner with the preposter-ously hot freshwoman, Sooyoung stopped by our table and asked me to meet him after dinner on the steps of the student union. "Band busi-ness," he explained, totally deadpan.

We finished our separate dinners—we no longer ate together, as we once did—and ran into each other en route to our meeting, made small talk, joked about musicians and students we knew. There was a table on the union's terrace, overlooking the expanse of grass between the library and the academic buildings, and as we sat down I cried out—a single strangulated cry, the kind a kitten makes when someone sits on it by mistake, and the kind of sound a boy in a punk rock band never wants to hear coming out of his mouth. I quickly insisted it was noth-ing, but maybe I had sensed something coming, even though there had been no hint beforehand.

Then:

"This is something we should have talked about a while ago, but Orestes and I want you to leave Bitch Magnet."

Jesus, here it is. A gasping, airless feeling I'd prefer never to feel again. I did manage to shudder out "Why?"

"I'll get to that." Though I don't remember what "that" was, because I don't remember anything else. When I interviewed Sooyoung for this book, he said one night he and Orestes had a short back-channel conversation and made a decision pretty quickly. Sometimes power struggles in a very loud band end quietly. The idea of trying to talk any of our issues through had occurred to exactly none of us.

The full extent of my life plan was: *I am playing in Bitch Magnet.* I had no long-term vision beyond recording an album in June and touring Europe in the fall. So now what?

I went looking for Martha, even though our on-and-off thing had been off for a while.

The next morning before breakfast the freshwoman saw me walking in a different direction from where I lived, wearing the same clothes she had seen me in at dinner. This led to a very unpleasant phone call later that day and a subsequent meeting to "talk," one I had to leave faster than I should have, because I was expected at *another* meeting to "talk" with Sooyoung. I left her in a bathroom with the lights out, crouched on a sink, crying. I liked her. I did. Just not enough. But even if I'd loved her madly and forever, that night I would have left her unconscious and bleeding in a ditch during a thunderstorm, because talking my way back into the band was the only thing that mattered. I didn't, but what I did do was point out to Sooyoung that it made no sense to break in an entirely new guitarist or two in the few weeks before recording an album of material we'd already honed for months, and that argument got me back in the band temporarily—just enough to play on *Umber.*

Oberlin was a small campus, where people tended to know by breakfast on Sunday who'd hooked up with whom on Saturday night, so the news spread quickly. My circle of friends was very kind to me, despite how obnoxious I'd often been to them, but the final weeks of school were awkward. How can I describe the feeling? A soft blow to the heart? The kind of mild heart attack after which everyone whispers, *He's just not the same*? Maybe that. Without the band I wasn't sure who I was anymore. What had happened felt like a rejection from every band I knew and everyone else I'd met on each strand of our spiderweb, and I experienced it with all the drama and high tragedy you'd expect from someone who in many ways was still a teenager. And the thought of losing the music—those songs—was much worse. Lou Barlow, famously and abruptly booted from Dinosaur Jr. in 1989, described that situation like this: "I was kicked out of the band because they didn't like me." But his reaction was "Who gives a shit whether you like me or not? The music we play—that's the most important thing."

Getting kicked out also confirmed the hidden, horrid, nagging feeling that I never quite belonged. And maybe I didn't. Near the end Orestes often suggested that I start playing guitar solos. I refused, partly on aesthetic grounds—this is punk rock; we do *not* play solos—but partly because I didn't think I could. Unfortunately I lacked the wit to reply: we are a trio, therefore *everything* I play is a guitar solo. Though I doubt that would have worked.

* * *

SOOYOUNG AND I GRADUATED IN MAY OF '89, AND IMMEDI-ately afterward we recorded *Umber* in Hoboken, with one of Orestes's best friends, Dave Galt, on second guitar. That fall Orestes and Sooyoung toured Europe with two guitarists: Galt and Bastro's David Grubbs. I moved to an apartment hard by the Brooklyn-Queens Expressway and took an idiot temp job. On lunch break I read rave reviews of Bitch Magnet's shows in the British music weeklies. At least Linc was still my roommate. He owned a copy of *I Against I*, but I was getting slightly better at overlooking it.

* * *

IN EARLY 1990 SOOYOUNG SENT ME A LETTER ASKING ME back into the band. We had another album to make, he explained. It would be his last record before retiring from rock forever.

We chatted briefly during a quick phone call. I was thrilled but wary. He promised to FedEx a cassette. That tape contained the makings of "Dragoon"—the ten-minute-long song that opens our last album, *Ben Hur*—and after listening to it once, I called Sooyoung and said, "I got the tape. Let's make a record."

He sent me a check for past royalties, wrapped in a letter of apology. His head got too big, he said. All he could see was his own vision of the band, and he needed to make it happen really bad. He'd made the mistake of thinking a modicum of attention was all he needed.

So we had a lot in common after all, I thought, reading it.

In time-honored indie rock tradition we rehearsed and finished writing *Ben Hur* in the basement of my parents' house in New Jersey in the spring of 1990. I hadn't seen Orestes since we'd recorded *Umber* in June, and when he showed up, I strode over and hugged him, a bit desperately, a bit overeagerly, and his body language made it clear a gulf still lay between us. Rehearsals and recording went better than ever. But Orestes got very squirrelly whenever the topic of touring came up, and shortly after we finished making the record, he visited Sooyoung and quit the band.

Sooyoung and I found a replacement and carried on. (More on that later.) I was a little sad to see Orestes go—though not much more than "a little"—and never forgave myself for fooling around with his other girlfriend. But the machine was grinding into life again, and that, I thought, could salve almost any wound. There was a record, there were fans, there were gigs, there was a van. I didn't need or want for anything else.

BOOK 2

BANDOGRAPHY

Ribbons of Flesh

DURATION: August–November 1986, more or less

LOCATION: Oberlin, Ohio

PERSONNEL: Jon Fine (guitar, vocals), Doug MacLehose (bass), Lincoln Wheeler (drums), Roger White (guitar)

RECORDS: None

Bitch Magnet

DURATION: November 1986–December 1990, April 2011–October 2012

LOCATION: Oberlin, Ohio; Chapel Hill, North Carolina; Calgary/New York City/Singapore

PERSONNEL: Jon Fine (guitar), Orestes Morfín (drums), Sooyoung Park (bass, vocals)

OTHER PERSONNEL: Tim Carper (drums, 1987), Dave Galt (guitar, 1989), Dave Grubbs (guitar, 1989), Jay Oelbaum (drums, 1986–87), Doctor Rock (drums, 1990)

RECORDS: *Star Booty* (1988), *Umber* (1989), *Ben Hur* (1990), *Bitch Magnet* (triple LP/double CD retrospective, 2011), *Valmead/Pea* 7" (US only, 1990), *Valmead* 12" (Europe only, 1990), *Mesentery* 7" (Australia only, 1990), *Sadie* 7" (US only, included with first 1,000 copies of *Ben Hur*, 1990), *Sadie* 7" (UK only, 1990), "White Piece of Bread" included on *Endangered Species* compilation (Europe only, 1990). There were some self-released cassettes early on, but I'm too embarrassed to discuss them.

Vineland

DURATION: Fall 1991–May 1996

LOCATION: Brooklyn

PERSONNEL: Countless lineups, but the final one was Jon Fine (guitar, vocals), Jerry Fuchs (drums, 1995–96), Fred Weaver (guitar, 1994–96), Kylie Wright (bass, 1996)

OTHER PERSONNEL: Bob Bannister (guitar, 1991–94), Lyle Hysen (drums, 1991–93), Jenna Johnson (bass, 1994), Eamon Martin (bass, 1994–95), Dave McGurgan (drums, 1993–94), Gerald Menke (bass, 1991–93), Mike Mihaljo (bass, 1995), Doug Scharin (drums, 1994), Dave Tritt (drums, 1994). Other people filled in for a show here and there. It's a good bet I've left someone out.

RECORDS: *Archetype* 7" (1993), *Obsidian* 7" (1995), "Beholden" included on the *This Is Art* compilation (Europe only, 1993), "Archetype" included on the *American Pie* compilation (Australia only, 1994)

Down and Away

DURATION: 1989–?

LOCATION: New York City

PERSONNEL: Jon Coats (drums), Jon Fine (guitar, 1989–90), Billy Pilgrim (guitar, 1990–), Jerry Smith (bass)

RECORDS: *Change Order* (1992)

Jon and Jerry had been in Phantom Tollbooth and were another excellent rhythm section I played with before I really knew how to play guitar. I quit to rejoin Bitch Magnet after Down and Away played one show in Boston, which I still have on tape somewhere.

Don Caballero

DURATION: 1991–95, 1997–2000, 2003–present

LOCATION: Pittsburgh, Chicago

PERSONNEL: Mike Banfield (guitar, 1991–98), Damon Che (drums, 1991–present), Jon Fine (guitar, 1999), Pat Morris (bass, 1991–94, 997–98), Eric Topolsky (bass, 1998–2000), Ian Williams (guitar, 1992–2000). Damon re-formed the band with no other original members in 2003.

RECORDS: *For Respect* (1993), *Don Caballero 2* (1995), *What Burns Never Returns* (1998), *Singles Breaking Up* (1999), *American Don* (2000), *World Class Listening Problem* (2006), *Punkgasm* 2008), *Gang Banged with a Headache, and Live* (2012), *Five Pairs of Crazy Pants. Wear 'Em: Early Don Caballero* (2014), *Look at Them Ellie Mae Wrists Go!: Live Early Caballero* (2014)

I played around twenty shows with them in 1999, after Mike Banfield left the band. Never recorded with them. Damon Che was one of the two drummers we auditioned to replace Orestes in Bitch Magnet in 1990.

Alger Hiss

DURATION: 1994–98, 2000–present

LOCATION: New York City

PERSONNEL: Jon Fine (bass, 1996–98), Haji Majer (drums, 1994–98), Jordan Mamone (guitar and vocals, 1994–98, 2000–present), Dalius Naujokaitis (drums, 2003–present), Chris O'Rourke (bass and vocals, 1994–96), Frederick Schneider (drums, 2000–2002), J Yung (bass, 2000–present)

RECORDS: *Settings for Nudes* (1995), *Graft vs. Host* (1997)

I played bass for them, when I was broadly bummed out about music but couldn't entirely quit.

Coptic Light

DURATION: 2000–2006

LOCATION: Brooklyn

PERSONNEL: Jon Fine (guitar), Kevin Shea (drums), Jeff Winterberg (bass)

RECORDS: *Yentl* 7″ (2003), *Coptic Light* (US and Japan, 2005), *Coptic Light* EP (US and Japan, 2006)

The weirdest band I ever played in.

What I Liked

After the first record came out, we got a proper booking agent and we did eight-week tours and weekend shows almost every other weekend. If something was within six hours, we'd drive there Friday night, play it, play somewhere Saturday, and then drive back on Sunday. We'd drive to Chicago for a weekend and play two shows. We'd play Louisville. We would play North Carolina. We would play Boston quite a bit. We'd play a lot of Ohio shows.

That's how you discovered the whole network. You'd meet these people who booked shows—these people running unprofitable businesses, basically. Every weekend night: setting up an out-of-town band with a show, paying them, getting a sound guy. This was happening in all these towns all over the country. Fifty, sixty, maybe a hundred people would show up.

We decided, let's see what happens with this. Everybody quit his real job. We would do temp work when we weren't touring. We did three big tours. Big, as in you have to bring two seasons' worth of clothing

*because it's going to be snowing, and then you're in L.A. and it's
75 degrees.*

*On the road you get used to having bruised hip bones from sleeping on
the floor and you get used to using your pants as a pillow, and, no
matter where you play, this is the quintessential story. You'd play
Columbia, South Carolina. No one ever shows up, but you always book
a show in Columbia, just because. You play the show, and no one shows
up, and that's fine, and at the end of the night, after you say from the
stage, "Hey, thanks for coming. By the way, if anyone has a place to
stay, we'd totally appreciate it, we're clean, we're not picky, thanks a
lot," there was always a guy in a place like Columbia, South Carolina,
who will take you back to his house, feed you not-so-great food but very
well-intentioned food, and then make you stay up watching the Sun
Ra movie.*

*In almost every town where no one will come to your show, that guy
will show up, and that guy will take care of you. He will put you up—
he's probably paying two hundred bucks a month for his entire house—
and you will have a decent night's sleep. In the morning, because you'll
ask, "Is there a cool diner here? We're going to need to get breakfast,"
he'll take you to a Waffle House, or someplace like that, where you'll
get four thousand calories' worth of food for six bucks, and then off you
go. Then you'll be in Bozeman, Montana, and you'll find that guy
again. And you'll watch the Sun Ra movie, or something like it, and
he'll play you a record you never heard of, and you'll think, this is a
crazy record, I need to find this record, and you'll write it down, and
then a year later you'll find it and realize it's the greatest record of
all time.*

*There's always that guy. Not in big cities. Not even in places like Cha-
pel Hill. But in the places where that guy is so psyched that your band
has come through, because nothing happens there.*

And it's always the Sun Ra movie. I've seen the Sun Ra movie at least eight times.

—Scott DeSimon, bassist, Pitchblende and Turing Machine

Timing is everything, even in punk rock, and starting in the latter half of the eighties, it became much easier for weird bands to do band things: play shows, make records, go on tour. The hows and whys that had been so elusive just a few years earlier were now shared through surprisingly effective samizdat and word-of-mouth networks. The bands that had done the most in a previous generation to start wiring those networks together were Black Flag and Dead Kennedys. (I am compelled to note that I still love the former; the latter, not so much.) They were the first underground bands to not just play shows on the other side of America—both were from California, and Dead Kennedys made it to New York first, in late 1979—but to tour nationally, and do so steadily, because they made a crucial conceptual leap: they decided that playing in a band was their job and started doing it all the time. What they faced and overcame in the process—Black Flag, in particular, a story probably best told by Henry Rollins in his memoir, *Get in the Van*—is rather mind-boggling. But these bands, and others, made it clear you could do it yourselves, and put particular clubs and cities on the map, and helped audiences grow accustomed to different kinds of music—first hardcore, then everything else.

Though touring early on often meant a diet of disappointment. "I remember playing in Cleveland" in the early eighties, recalled Mission of Burma's Roger Miller, whose band broke up just before key connections in the independent network were soldered into place. "These two girls came up and said, 'Wow! You guys did "That's When I Reach for My Revolver." That's such a cool song! We'll be at the show tonight.' We thought, *We're golden*. After the first song, the audience is against the

far wall. By the third song, there's zero response. Then we start taunt-
ing the audience, and there's still no response. We play 'Revolver,' and
there's no response. Then the next band comes on, and people dance.
Then we play our second set, and there's no response." And, as Miller
explains, even when it started to get better for bands, it didn't *really* get
better: "The second time we were in San Francisco, after [Burma's landmark 1982 album] *Vs.* had come out, I think there were like two hundred people there. A day later we played Los Angeles, and there were
like twelve people in the club. You'd go from thinking, *Wow! We are
finally cool!* to *Oh, right. We aren't cool.*"

Even in the late eighties we all still played music far different from
what most people expected, and club owners and soundmen would
occasionally freak out over, say, how loud you were. Or you might run
into a sound guy like the one at Cedars in Youngstown, Ohio, apparently badly in thrall to U2, who put a bizarre delay effect on my guitar
until I demanded he stop. Nor were low-level rock clubs back then
particularly concerned about Better Business Bureau–esque ethics. A
pal in a fairly well-known band played a show in a decent-sized city, met
the owner in the office afterward, and asked for the band's guarantee.
Then the owner opened a desk drawer and casually gestured toward the
gun he kept there, and my pal decided to forgo that night's wages.

But every touring band had stories like that. In a different and
smaller city the dead-calm club owner wore a sharp silver suit and was
said to be mobbed-up and to carry a gun, and when it looked as if his
promoter might stiff us, I told him that he ran a really nice club and it
would be a shame if word got around that he didn't pay bands. (Crazily
enough, this tactic worked.) Because after a couple of passes through
America and Europe, states and countries stopped being flat maps in
the dogeared road atlas we kept stashed between the front seats of the van
and became three-dimensional, with memory and incident and images
and the people we met: Newport, Kentucky, where the amazing hillbilly
speed-metal drummer in the opening band looked twelve but was

twenty-four; Cincinnati, where everyone played a bar called Sudsy Malone's that contained a Laundromat and where, in 1993, a guy tried to pick me up; London, Ontario, where the sole hot girl at the afterparty kept squealing that hearing the Stooges made her come, but her boyfriend was way too drunk to take advantage of this information; Brixton, where we stayed in London, where someone broke into the van and made off with most of our gear and merch; Athens, Ohio, where we played a dirt-floored and underheated venue in January until the cops shut us down for being too loud; the small town in Austria where we cut the set short because the PA malfunctioned and the crowd seemed menacing and I'm still not sure if I really heard anti-Semitic mutterings or was just paranoid; Osijek, Yugoslavia, where the primitively Xeroxed gig flyer advertised GUITAR FLAME NOISE, and where we didn't spend enough time with the lovely guy who'd set up our shows there: a budding minister of culture, who understood everything about music and art, was endlessly curious about both, and managed to find us a bottle of Jim Beam in a broken, barely post-Soviet state that used a currency that lost all value as soon as you left the country. Before we left he gave us his address, painstakingly writing YUGOSLAVIA in capital letters at the bottom, before observing with a shrug, *Of course there won't be a Yugoslavia in a year*, and he was right.

You learned fast that doing it yourself applied to many more things than calling clubs to book your band and pressing your own records. "We played the Khyber Pass in Philadelphia in 1994 and stayed with [longtime local promoter] Brian Dilworth," remembered Andrew Beaujon, the front man for Eggs. Dilworth lived in an industrial, isolated, possibly unsafe part of town, where, luckily, there was a fenced-off lot in which Eggs could park their van. When the band arrived, though, cars were arranged in a way that left no space big enough for them. So Brian turned and told everyone, *All right, guys. There's like thirty people here. We're gonna pick up one of these cars and move it.* And they did. Or you might arrive at an Elks Lodge in Louisville for your first punk rock show, as Jeremy DeVine did long before he became the founder and owner of the Temporary Residence Ltd. label, and find people hammering together scavenged two-by-fours and wood planks to build a stage because the Elks Lodge didn't have one. (And, as soon as that show was over, they broke down and discarded what they'd built.)

Still, as the eighties became the nineties, the bigger battles had been won. A network of clubs spread across America, and a far nicer one traversed Europe. Many important American underground bands could barely scrape together a hundred fans for hometown shows, but the British music weeklies *Melody Maker, NME,* and *Sounds* wrote about them extensively—as did major press outlets on the Continent— and much bigger crowds greeted them when they toured overseas, at clubs that treated them far better, with ample food and beer backstage, and real meals after soundcheck. There promoters put bands up in *actual hotel rooms.* (Not in England, though. Because promoters knew you were going to play London no matter what? Because there were different touring economics? Because the Continent has always valued artists and culture more? I still don't know why.) Eventually endless tours by third- and fourth-rate American bands exhausted European audiences, and their appetite for this music collapsed in the midnineties. Until then, though, Europe was our yellow brick road. Orestes would have been happy only touring Europe and never playing the States again, and his was not a unique opinion.

But it wasn't mine. I liked touring America as much as I liked touring overseas. Because I liked everything about this thing of ours.

To pinch something that Elizabeth Elmore—who led the bands Sarge and the Reputation—once told me, I loved the surprise of each day on the road. I loved waking up in the morning not knowing what the night would bring. Or that, five or ten or twenty years later, I might still be in touch with someone I met at that show.

I liked plotting weekends just as Scott DeSimon described: scanning mileage charts in the back of a road atlas to see how far you could drive and still make it home in time for work on Monday morning. I liked it when, driving southeast on a Sunday after playing Boston with Vineland the night before, stuck in traffic but not unhappily, our bassist asked where we'd play next, and I rolled the idea around for a moment and declared, "Richmond and Pittsburgh," and a few weekends later, we did.

I liked the long, empty highway spaces: the zen boredom of the generic American interstate, the lulling rhythm of the ride, the continuous forward motion. I liked being anywhere in a vehicle groaning from a full load of gear, on stretches of highway in West Virginia or Michigan or even Iowa, where the major roads almost always intersect at ninety-degree angles, on which you made long, straight drives through endless flat landscapes. I liked the giant standing irrigation rigs alongside the road in the fields of Indiana, those metal spiders the size of football fields. I liked how being stopped in traffic at a forgettable bridge in Delaware could be transformed into an event by a startling sunset.

I liked the voices you heard on college radio stations while driving on the interstate, for the ten or fifteen minutes before static buried them. They sounded like people you could know. No. They sounded like people you *did* know, and since some invisible connective tissue joined us, in a sense you did. I liked hearing my friends' bands on the radio in unexpected places. I liked hearing my own band on the radio in unexpected places, even though it didn't happen much.

I liked arriving at a club in the late afternoon, the few people in the hushed beer-and-cigarette-smelling room only starting to yawn and stretch into another day. (Even if the first thing that always happened was that everyone in the van employed subtle machinations so as not to get stuck with finding parking for an oversized vehicle with inadequate rearview mirrors in a city during rush hour. Unless it was a club that had parking spaces set aside. But it almost never was.) I liked the ritual of pulling up to the curb, inert bodies groaning into motion again, unthunking the van's back door, disassembling the gear puzzle one more time: the procession of speaker cabinets, drum cases, amp heads, drum stands wrapped in blankets, guitar cases, boxes of merch, everyone's duffel bags, toolboxes or milk crates stuffed with cords and distortion pedals, everyone's backpacks or briefcases. Walking past the manager adding up figures from the night before or hauling cases of beer and the sound guy wearily uncoiling speaker cables and setting out mike stands as you hefted everything onstage: the drummer rebuilding his kit, everyone else reassembling their rigs, staring off into space while the sound guy miked the amps and drums and trudged back to the soundboard to start the soundcheck—kick drum, snare drum, toms, hi-hat, then the entire drum kit. (I stood in the middle of the club for this part, because a good drum sound was crucial, but I also loved watching good drummers rip.) Then the bass, then the guitars, then the vocal mikes, then a song or two. I liked chatting with club owners I saw more than once—Dan Dougan at Stache's in Columbus, Bruce Finkelman at the Empty Bottle in Chicago, Peter Weening at the Vera in the Netherlands. I liked Louise Parnassa, who managed CBGB, even though whenever you called the club, she always seemed to be in a very foul mood, because a couple of times I think I made her laugh. Her phone manner and growl made me picture a stooped, chain-smoking sixty-year-old, so it was a shock to meet her and discover she was not only around my age but also pretty cute—long hair, smoky eyes, a knowing smirk—even after spending all those hours in that lightless cave.

I liked how our rehearsal room smelled of old amp tubes heating up. I liked the staticky way the PA crackled into life after you flipped its switch. I liked the ancient and unbelievably crude graffiti in the hallways where we practiced, especially the extraordinarily specific screed that instructed "you, the faggot," to suck diarrhea from a fat black man's asshole, with a straw, so that "he doesn't even have to push." (The detail that shot it into the stratosphere, I thought, was using the word *fat*.) I liked having a nodding acquaintance with Ronald Shannon

Jackson, the ultra-badass drummer who'd played with Albert Ayler and who practiced down the hall. I liked how, whenever we loaded in our gear at three in the morning after a show, we'd hear him drumming to what sounded like a CD playing backward while a thick scent of pot drifted toward us. I liked knowing I could go to the practice space late at night if I needed to, because sometimes I needed to, when it was my only friend. I liked how Sundays were practice day, so starting with whatever show I attended Friday night, it was basically all rock until Monday morning.

I liked—no, I *loved*—my guitar rig, once I figured it out: a Gibson Les Paul Custom, or a Yamaha SG-2000, each with a Seymour Duncan JB pickup in the bridge position, into a Rat distortion pedal and a four-input Hiwatt Custom 100 amp going into a jet-black custom-made speaker cabinet that weighed more than I did, which we nicknamed the Beast. I liked reading about weird seventies guitars and amps and effects and trying to track them down, long before the Internet indexed everything and bargains disappeared. (I don't like remembering the crazy deals I missed out on while broke, like the gorgeous sixties Fender Jazzmaster on sale in Cleveland for four hundred bucks in 1991. Today it would cost four grand, at least.) I liked discovering a once-grand music store that lasted for decades in Newark, even as the surrounding neighborhood grew deserted and scary, and rooting through its boxes of old effects pedals, panning for gold, for something old and obscure that still worked or could be fixed. I liked finding an original and unused Orange head from the seventies there and buying it for slightly more than $300 in 1989, because with it I achieved my favorite guitar sound on record—the power chords on Bitch Magnet's "Ducks and Drakes"—and because that amp still sounds great today. I liked the tiny adjustments I learned to make to my guitars, like tweaking intonation and replacing pickups, because this work was profoundly calming.

I liked handwriting the set list each night, and I liked identifying songs by shorthand or in-jokes so no one in the front rows could know what was coming. I liked being onstage, even if, for many years, I wasn't quite sure what to do once I was up there and remembered so little of it afterward. Not because I went into a trance, or because I walked onstage into a dream that made no sense once I woke up, or because the excitement created a blur in which only a few moments registered, like images glimpsed while riding a roller coaster, though every show was its own roller coaster. But because everything that happened up there vanished once the music stopped, lost in the stage lights and the adrenaline and the confusion from surfing so many currents at the same time: the songs, the sound, the volume, the crowd, the tiny changes bandmates made onstage, the parts I improvised every night. I liked having long, curly hair to hide behind when a show was going bad, and to fling around when it was going well.

I liked how some people in the crowd watched with real intent while you were just setting up. I liked how diehard fans planted themselves by the lip of the stage for all the opening bands and grimly held that position all night, never leaving to pee or grab a beer. I liked finding that guy—or was it having that guy find us?—in Columbia, South Carolina; or Worcester, Massachusetts; or Savannah, Georgia; or Eugene, Oregon. The smaller towns could surprise you. The first time Bitch Magnet arrived in Morgantown, West Virginia, we had no idea what to expect—and we found a packed room, and when we played, more people stage-dove than at any show I ever played, anywhere. I booked Morgantown on every possible tour thereafter. The shows were always good, though the local economy was always depressed, so the crowd was too broke to buy much merch. But pretty much everyone there had weed, if that was your thing. (Though by then, alas, it wasn't my thing.)

I liked staring into the eyes of random people in the audience until they looked away. I liked alternating coffee and beer before the show on the nights I was tired. I liked drinking two beers, no more, before the set, but I also liked the nights when I drank one or two too many and was a little looser and sloppier onstage. I liked how playing in a band was license to talk to anyone at the club. I liked working the merch table just after the show—wired, sweating, hollering—because how could you not like meeting people there and hearing them say, in sometimes stammery syntax, how much your band meant to them. I liked meeting the biggest music nerds in each town and hearing about the good local bands, even if those bands weren't always as good as you wanted. I liked having a backstage to escape to, even if backstage itself was often a shithole. (People *fucked* on those sagging, cigarette-pocked couches that stank of armpits and stale grief? Yes. They did.) I liked the club at the end of the night, after everyone had left, because I liked knowing the arc of a full day there and not just the brief interval its customers saw.

I liked how being on tour moved you in a perfect counter-rhythm to the nine-to-five world: your adrenaline rose when it ebbed for those at work and peaked after they went to bed. I liked how unmoored, how far out from shore, you were after a few weeks on tour. The minor insanities of your day-to-day: the fast food and cheap beer, the cumulative fatigue and hangover, the rising preshow tension and its ecstatic onstage release, the ringing ears, the squalor in the van and the houses where you crashed. I liked the drug-dealer feeling you got on tour from carrying a bag containing thousands and thousands of dollars in cash, sometimes in a jumbled rainbow of many different currencies. I liked learning that the smell of American money is like sour wood and sweat, gamy and slightly sick-making, which you didn't know until you kept a lot in a very tight space. I liked hearing other bands' disgusting, tragic, and hilarious road stories, the strange things each band did, like how members of A Minor Forest would shove dozens of slices of steam-table pizza from all-you-can-eat joints into a shoulder bag, dump them on the dashboard of their van, and survive off them for the next several days, or how they'd buy twenty or more breakfast tacos from Tamale House every time they played Austin and do the same thing. ("They would stay pretty well," their drummer, Andee Connors, assured me.)

I wanted to stay on the road forever: *Sell the house sell the car sell the kids find someone else forget it I'm never coming back*, not that I had any of those things to sell or anyone to not come back to. I hated how each tour eventually deposited you, without mercy, at work on Monday morning after you barely made it back home a few hours earlier, blinking bloodshot eyes at the bright fluorescent lights, feeling abandoned and far from love.

I liked the eight or ten or fifteen fanzines I read religiously, and the excitement I felt when they irregularly appeared. I liked See Hear, the all-zine store in a basement on New York's East Seventh Street. I liked that I could make it there and back during lunch hour from the small architecture firm where I worked my first job after college, from late '89 until the following fall, when I quit to tour America and Europe with Bitch Magnet. It was the only thing I liked about that job.

I liked cassettes—demo tapes, mix tapes—their covers made from colored markers and collages on photocopy machines. These were perhaps the defining relics of this culture's handmade ethos, and today they exist almost entirely as pure objects, since only diehards like me kept their tape decks. I liked the tapes and letters that would arrive at the band's post office box from fans with whom we'd traded addresses while on the road. I liked opening that PO box with a sense of anticipation that I never felt when opening the mailbox at my apartment, and I didn't even mind waiting in the achingly slow line to pick up packages sent there.

I liked dubbing cassettes of my band and sending them to labels, along with a self-addressed postcard, on which they sometimes responded. I liked staying late at work to make flyers for upcoming shows on the office copy machine, and I liked carefully carrying home thick stacks of them, still warm and smelling of ink and chemicals. I even sort of liked mixing wheat paste and water in a bucket until it reached a disturbingly semenlike consistency, and hanging flyers all over the East Village at night back when you could do that without getting arrested. I liked how a few Vineland flyers stayed up for years in some nooks along First Avenue.

I liked walking around on weekend days, searching for sights or an association or a scrap of an overheard conversation from which I could squeeze a line or two, a seed for a song, like the homeless guy shaving the other homeless guy in a doorway, who turned up in the Vineland song "Archetype." I liked staying up all night with people I just met. I liked—and was always awed and moved—when people in each new city adopted you for a few hours or a day, took care of you, showed you around, showed you cool stuff you didn't know. I liked the intensity that attached itself to those relationships, and your condensed togethernesses whenever you met on the road or in each other's hometown. I liked hosting other members of our tribe in my city and taking them to my circuit of dive bars, record stores, and cheap restaurants. I liked meeting people whose records I knew. I liked the way people reflected where they grew up and where they lived—Seattle, Cleveland, Richmond, Charlotte, Austin—as well as our commonalities that transcended origins and accents. I liked learning local slang in one region and introducing it to another—"dookie" for "shit," years before Green Day stole it; "dodgy" for "unreliable"; "wheef" for "pot." (*Wheef* came about when we almost certainly misheard something said by Urge Overkill's Ed Roeser, but we liked saying *bad wheef* way too much to drop it.) I liked coming back from Europe with a few affectations that let those who could hear the dog whistle know where you'd been: a phrase in German, some new British slang, a taste for a cigarette hard to find in the States, like the red-pack Gauloises Blondes one friend bought by the carton from the duty-free after every tour. I liked leaving graffiti for friends in other bands backstage at clubs in Europe: LYLE HYSEN: CALL YOUR MOTHER. BRITT AND BRIAN: MAKE SURE YOUR VAN HAS SEATBELTS.

I liked the way all this effectively organized and structured my life. I liked that we all found this way to stay young, well into our twenties at first, and then well beyond. I liked believing that we knew something most everyone else didn't. I liked believing that this culture was going to change music. I liked believing that it would last forever. Because, for a while, that was easy to believe.

Why We Never Smiled Onstage

Late one weeknight in the late nineties I sat in a bar in Chicago with Damon Che, the drummer for Don Caballero, the instrumental quartet for which I briefly played guitar. Broke full-time musicians hold a few trump cards, and we were playing one: nights were our days, we had nowhere to go in the morning, so tonight we'd stay out forever. We nursed our drinks, savoring the practically empty room and the quiet settling over the city.

Damon is an enormously talented drummer and guitarist, but often it seems his primary skill is burning bridges. To cite just one example, while on tour with Bellini in 2002, he quit the band onstage in Georgia, loaded his gear into the van, and drove home alone, leaving all the other members stranded. This was especially bad form since two of the three remaining Bellini members live in Sicily. So, yes, Damon has a bad temper. When I first practiced with Don Cab, witnessing his rages was unsettling, since he's around six foot three and his head is roughly the size of my torso. (The other members of the band were so inured to such displays they looked bored whenever he erupted, an affect I soon imitated.)

Still, Damon had spent practically every sentient moment since grade school thinking about music or playing it or both. However enormous a pain in the ass he could be, he came up with stuff, on drums and guitar, that no one else in the world could. He also had an autodidact's unique perceptions of music, and of any other culture that interested him. This last part made him a very good person to get slowly drunk with after midnight on a Tuesday, and as we did we got to talking about a musician we knew. We both liked him and all, but Damon, like me, was pretty *whatever* about his band. They were really great guys, but "really great guys" is the absolute kiss of death if it's the first thing you say about a band.

Damon's beef was that the band was unrelentingly modest, in the manner of many at that time: understated, too shy for grand gestures, and whatever color they applied stayed very much within the lines. But this was the interesting thing. He didn't say the band *sucked*. He said that he didn't *understand* it. He wanted to know: why would anyone aim for something so plainly unambitious?

Exactly, I thought. Both of us wanted something more from music than mere entertainment. Something much more than merely cerebral, "cerebral" being a very easy fallback for a subgenre that practically required a college diploma from its participants. Too much music, we knew, only tickled the surface and never explored the vast untapped areas that were just sitting there. I liked playing music that came from the head, guts, and crotch. Anything else was pointless. If you weren't going for power—or just to be really weird, or to do something that hadn't already been done a thousand times, or *something* big—I didn't understand why, either. We had such powerful weapons in hand—guitars, distortion, drums, amps, volume—so why charge toward such a small hill? Cormac McCarthy voiced the literary version of this idea back when he gave his first interview in 1992: "A lot of writers who are considered good I consider strange," he said. They weren't dealing with life-and-death issues, and McCarthy didn't see the point in writing about anything else.

I wanted to play, and hear, music that was physically involving. I wanted sound to physically affect the audience. I wanted it loud enough to *feel* it. Some people want a song to speak to them. I wanted to disappear into the sound. I know, I know, I'm supposed to say that you can't crescendo at 125 decibels all the time, and there's supposed to be that blend of light and shade, as Jimmy Page famously wanted for Led Zeppelin. But screw that. Because some of my favorite records, like Minor Threat's first 7″s or Slayer's *Reign in Blood* or Prong's *Primitive Origins*, do nothing but amp up every moment to the absolute max.

Bland bands had always popped up in American indie rock, but as the eighties turned into the nineties, such bands—watered-down, polite, *average*—were getting harder and harder to ignore. In the fall of 1992 I walked out of CBGB, utterly bored by a hotly hyped band from Chicago. I didn't see the point of the Smashing Pumpkins, and nothing I heard later by them changed my mind. They struck me as middling arena rock crafted with some slightly different ingredients: better guitar sounds and heavier distortion, basically. I didn't mind the arena-sized ambitions, which you could sense even then. I minded how dull it all was. Even before then, I remember my heart sinking when the Pixies started getting big: there was so much else going on that was so much more interesting. *This* was what people were going for?

But I still don't think I'm explaining this properly.

If I could reach through these words, grab your throat, and squeeze until you struggled to breathe—would you understand me then?

If I played you a song and the final chord in each verse crashed upon you like a piano falling from a skyscraper, as it does in Fucked Up's "Crooked Head"—would you understand me then?

If the drummer drags the beat with his kick drum, sending the sensation to your reptile brain that rolls your eyeballs toward the back of your head, if the guitarist's overtones are so intense you start seeing angels, if the singer screams not like every other singer has screamed since the dawn of time but instead surfaces the terror and dread that you spend *your entire waking life* trying to tamp down—

Would you understand me then?

Then maybe you can understand everything that a well-crafted, essentially polite rock song can never express.

✱ ✱ ✱

SOME PERFORMERS ARE DESPERATE TO BE LOVED. THEY want to ingratiate. They're part of a long tradition that encompasses vaudeville—though I'm sure it was around before then—and most performers in musicals. In her prime Liza Minnelli was likely its apotheosis. A slightly more recent example is Ozzy Osbourne, who performs as if his life depends on an audience clapping along—save Tinkerbell! but more metal!—and who's been screaming onstage, since the earliest Black Sabbath shows, "We love you ALL!" over and over again, a boyfriend saying he loves you so you have to say you love him back. Aside from the Clash's sanctimony and overall Springsteen tendencies, another reason I never liked them was that Joe Strummer struck me as an overly needy front guy. He wanted agreement. He wanted approval. (And Joe was no Liza when it came to working it.) Bands playing the softer styles of indie rock were generally ingratiators. Salem 66, the jangly Boston band, showed up on one album cover dressed up and hanging out around a dining room table, in what appears to be the aftermath of a dinner party. But "Hey! come join! civilized fun!" is always a questionable idea to telegraph with your cover art, unless you want people to associate your record with *brunch*.

Other performers want to dominate, like Beyoncé and Madonna and James Brown and Black Flag and Miles Davis and Swans. They don't want to be loved, though they may be happy being worshipped. They aren't solicitous of an audience. They're there to overwhelm. Another kind of performer, like Sonic Youth in their prime, plays as if the audience isn't even present. Performing, for them, is like breathing, or drinking coffee: natural and very cool, in the sense of "removed." But you have to be really good at that sort of detachment to make it work.

I liked the natural approach. But onstage I wanted to dominate. I didn't want to see smiles in the audience. I wanted to see people looking slightly stunned, as if something very large had just struck them and they were trying to calculate whether that collision was very bad or very good. I wanted awe, not affection. I didn't even need applause. Sparse and tentative clapping was enough, if the crowd seemed sufficiently concussed and they were still slowly processing what had happened. (Though hearing screams was always pretty great.) Bitch Magnet played the Kaikoo festival in Tokyo in 2012, and we ended our set with "Sea of Pearls," a fairly poppy song by our standards. Halfway through it I saw a woman in the front row smiling and wagging her head to the beat from side to side, back and forth, back and forth. I immediately thought, *Shit, ugh, failure.* Pop songs—songs that ingratiate—elicit this blandly pleasant side-to-side bop. Songs that hit harder make an audience snap heads up and down: the headbanger's response. That's what I wanted to see.

When friends and family who hadn't spent years obsessing over punk rock saw my bands play, they almost always mentioned one thing: we didn't smile onstage. They found that puzzling. But not smiling made perfect sense to us. For one thing, we were playing fairly complicated and athletic music, which required concentration. But there was more to it than that. You smile when you're nervous. You smile while on a bad date. You smile during excruciating job interviews. You smile greeting the relatives you hate. But you don't smile when you come, when you cross the finish line after running a marathon, when a good Samaritan pulls you from the surf onto wet sand, rescued, when the firemen save your house from burning down, or when the surgeon, in his scrubs, trudges to the waiting room to tell you that everything turned out fine.

In February 1986 I saw Hüsker Dü headline the Phantasy in Cleveland. They were touring behind *Flip Your Wig*, a fairly toned-down record, but the night was strictly old-school Hüskers: all the songs sped up, running into each other without pause, at an ungodly volume. The show was basically one giant, continuous grinding sound, like a truck dumping a load of large rocks. Sometimes I thought I recognized a lyric. Down front, where I stood, was too chaotic and unformed to warrant being called a pit. As the show went on, row after row of the old-school bolted-in theater seats—the classic red velour ones that snap upright when you stand—got destroyed. The entire night swung wildly between ecstasy and absolute terror, and at any moment it was impossible to tell which pole you'd be flung to next. Sometimes I think I'd have to survive another car wreck to feel that way again. I don't know what to call that sensation, though I desperately hope I have it a few more times before I die. Whatever it was, it didn't make me smile. But I didn't go to punk rock shows for fun. I needed something that, for just a moment, got its hands around everything too complicated and intense for language. I didn't want anything *happy*, and I hadn't for a very long time.

One night when I was sixteen, stoned and sitting in a friend's borrowed beige Chrysler outside a convenience store, a pal bolted from the front seat to chat up a girl he knew. I watched the entire conversation, and she seemed really happy. She smiled the entire time, big enough to crinkle the corners of her eyes. Her eyes shone in the parking lot lights, and inasmuch as eyes can *laugh*, hers did. It was winter and the windows were closed, so I couldn't hear anything, but she cocked her head back and forth whenever she spoke and looked like she punctuated everything with a little giggle. She was really cute, too. And I hated her. I hated her because she was happy and I wasn't, and back then I thought if you were happy, you had to be an idiot. I thought, *She doesn't know how important it is to hate something. She doesn't know the joy of being hated and hating back. She doesn't know the power of being hated and having nothing to lose. She doesn't know what it's like when it's February and you don't have a Valentine, because you never have a Valentine, and the sky's been a giant bruise for weeks, and the streets run with slush, and everyone is shuffling through their midwinter light-deprived catatonia, but you know you have a secret, shining like a newly formed sun—this determination to get back at everyone—and it not only keeps you moving but you catch yourself thinking,* I don't care if it's never summer again, I have all the wattage I need.

No. She didn't know any of that. Nor the buried-deep, hot nuggets of self-hatred that feeling fed on. Nor the moments of sudden violence common to male adolescence.

A few months later I went on a first date with the freshman girl with new-wave hair in my French class. Sarah. She lived in Millington, a town more rural than mine, in a big old house atop a hill, which you reached by following a series of short dirt roads. I picked her up one night after spring rains had made them muddy. I pulled out of one intersection a little too fast and sprayed some mud on the car behind me. Or at least that's what the guys in that car were screaming when they pulled up beside us at the next stop sign.

Mistake number one: I poked my head out my window to see why they were yelling. One of them snatched the eyeglasses right off my face. Mistake number two: I got out of the car.

As with sex or performance, the particulars of physical confrontations are blurry afterward, and in this case they were particularly blurry because I couldn't *see* anything. But very soon after I got out of the car, I was mopping mud off their car with my denim jacket. Then these guys—swarming and jabbering, stinking like hyenas—started throwing me onto the filthy hood, hard enough to send me scudding up and onto the windshield. After a few rounds of this, they tore off my T-shirt, shoved my glasses into my hand, and drove off, laughing and hollering. Happy first date, punker!

I ended up wearing Sarah's sweatshirt that night, and later she taught me how to French kiss, or, rather, I guessed correctly enough, and we became a thing, and for the next few months we rubbed against each other and stuck our hands inside each other's pants at every possible opportunity, thrilling to the headspins of teenage desire. But what I remember most isn't that, lovely as it was, and it was very lovely. What I remember is how I just accepted what happened that night. How I didn't really fight back.

You carry that knowledge with you every day, and then you're supposed to go home, turn on MTV, and watch the fucking *Romantics*?

That's why I didn't smile onstage.

On these stages, in these crowds—here, at last, was the arena in which anger and sadism and revenge and submission finally all made sense. When I was onstage, I wanted to destroy. But when I was in the audience, I wanted to be shoved around by how bands sounded and what they played.

One chilly, gray day at Oberlin—sorry, redundant—I walked around with Sooyoung seriously discussing which was better: being in a band or having a girlfriend. Even though we teenage punk rockers pined, often quite sappily, for a girlfriend, we both picked the band, and it wasn't that hard a choice. Contrary to traditional rock mythologies, we didn't form a band to meet girls. (As you may have guessed from the name.) And, yes, I loved the music. But everyone says they love music. What I really loved, once I got my hands on a guitar, was the power. The electricity it shot straight into your heart. That's why we— well, I guess I just mean me—were doing it. For the voltage you generated by fitting a few distorted chords together with a scratchy vocal line on top. Once you added drums, it got so much bigger. And onstage it got bigger still. It didn't matter if that stage was a corner of a living room in a rented house slowly being destroyed by a different crew of college kids each year, or in an old man's bar on a weeknight, with only five people there. It didn't even matter that it took years for me to understand that being onstage—and finding a way to be onstage that had nothing to do with the arena rock theatrics we hated—required as much practice as playing an instrument. In time, the best of us learned how to fill bigger stages, and those with the right kind of imagination starting having much more fun with the power of such settings.

The Jesus Lizard once played a sold-out show to about a thousand people at the Masquerade. Atlanta's version of the biggest place in town for a touring punk rock band, and a club with a giant dance floor, not a sea of seats. At one point, between songs, David Yow told the crowd that the band had planned something really amazing, but it required the entire audience sitting on the floor. The audience wasn't having it and hooted down the idea. But Yow kept at it, telling them that this thing would be *really* cool, and unforgettable, but if they were gonna to do it right, everybody had to sit down.

Amazingly enough, a thousand people shrugged and scrunched themselves onto the floor. Yow took in the sight for a long moment.

Then he burst out laughing, and the band launched into the next song.

The Glory,
the Madness,
and the Van

The earliest stages of any band were lousy with longing for the moment you could finally stop saying "*a* van" and start saying "*the* van." Because nothing was more central to this culture's tiny mythology than our beat-up, barely running vans—they signaled independence, they signaled seriousness, they signaled that we didn't need a tour bus and a driver—no matter how squalid most of them became, no matter that civilians would peer inside, their eyes would go wide, and they'd slowly back away. Everything happened in the van, and much of it stayed there. The wadded McDonald's wrappers covering the floor, mud prints on the top layer from the last time it rained, alongside convenience-store coffee and soda cups, empty plastic bottles, gum and candy wrappers, half-eaten and long-forgotten snacks. Most of which inevitably migrated to the door wells, so every time a door was opened, the van puked out debris. But on the road the van was our home, our castle, our magic carpet, sometimes the setting for a hurried tryst in the parking lot in the back of the club, or even while parked on the street. Half our legends revolved around vans. Like:

Just before another all-night drive the guitarist and bassist ate a bunch of trucker's speed and became so hysterically motormouthed for the entire trip that the other guys demanded that they never, ever do that again. Or: They drove through Nebraska so often that the drummer made a game of trying to make it all the way across the entire state without stopping to pee. Or: They had to drive straight from Oregon to make it to their next show in Chicago, and they each took six-hour shifts and stopped only for gas and bathroom breaks and they made it. Or: They had to drive straight home after the last show of the tour because the bassist had to be at work at 8:30 the following morning, and they drove all night and dropped him off at 8:25.

After one crappy Boston show we wanted to leave town so badly that we started driving back to my parents' house at 2 a.m., until the wind and the rain pushed us around on the road and my eyes kept closing, and I managed to pilot us off the highway to a quiet country road, where we slept a few hours. I drove home from CBGB after the show, even though it was very late. We drove home from Providence after the show, even though it was very late. We drove home from Philadelphia after the show, even though it was very late, because it was St. Patrick's Day, and I expected all the loud guys and women in high heels and too-short dresses to start puking in the gutters and worse. We drove home from Charlotte after the show, even though it was very late, but home was then New Jersey, and once Orestes and I got to Maryland and it was well into the next day, I understood that this was a very stupid idea. We drove home from Boston after the show, even though it was very late, got back to our practice space in Hoboken, unloaded the van, took the subway to our apartments, showered and changed, got back on the subway, and went straight to work.

The van was a blue Dodge we bought for six hundred bucks, and the following day we found two unused tickets to an Ace Frehley show in Minneapolis wedged into the backseat (which I flash for a second in the video Bitch Magnet made for "Mesentery"). Or it was a Mercedes rental in Japan, and I climbed into the back to sleep alongside the gear, wearing earplugs to block out sound and an eye mask to block out light, and the bassist leaned over the backseat to snap a picture that looked as if it should accompany a ransom note. Or it was a maroon Plymouth minivan that didn't have enough seating for all of us, so for the duration of the tour we stood a cinderblock between the sliding side door and the back bench, and each morning one band member would grab a pillow, fold it onto the cinderblock, and perch on both for the entire day of traveling. Or it was the generic white Ford Econoline, with only ten thousand miles on the odometer, the floor lining still slick from whatever the car dealer used to wax it, and a power strip that we ran from the front cigarette lighter to charge our laptops and phones, all of which felt luxurious after years of creaking, half-dead vehicles. Or it was the yellow-and-green Dodge from the eighties, previously owned by a lawn-care company, in which, even after years of touring, you could still smell the raw chemical undertone of old fertilizer.

The best place in the van was the loft: the shelf atop all the gear in the back, which you wriggled up onto from the backseat. A simple sheet of plywood nailed onto a very simple frame of four two-by-six posts screwed into the van's floor to keep it stable. You hid the gear underneath, and it also provided a place to store small or squishable items, like sleeping bags and pillows and merch boxes and winter coats. The shelf was rarely more than sixteen inches from the roof of the van, but privacy is hard to come by on tour, and it was an excellent place to nap or escape during the long drives. Shelf life was deeply meditative, because there wasn't much you could do while nestled within such a shallow space, hemmed in on all sides by boxes of records and CDs and sleeping bags and whatever else got stuffed up there, apart from lying on your back and looking straight up at the sheet-metal roof of the van, vibrating along with the ride. Amazing how thin, how unadorned, that membrane was. The steady white noise of the road was louder up near the roof, and lulling. Once you comfortably understood that you'd be pizza should the van roll over in a wreck, the setting was remarkably restful.

The shelf was also a very good place to whack off into a dirty sock, one of which I mistakenly left up there while on tour with Vineland in 1994. (Sorry, guys.) To steal a pal's observation, the only chance you had for sex in a touring indie rock band was if you played a town where an ex-girlfriend lived, and the privation of such sexless surroundings led some bands to hold tour-long whack-off contests: who could rack up the biggest number? Story goes that one band took this seriously enough to keep track of each member's tally on a patch of sheet metal behind the driver's seat. Said band is driving late one night after a show. Everyone's too tired to talk, and all seems hushed and still. Then one of the guys in the backseat shifts his weight, reaches over, and adds a fresh hash mark beneath his name. Every band had some version of that story—something stomach-turning to the rest of the world that, from inside the van, didn't seem so bad.

Anyway, the disgustingness of any band's van generally hinged on three factors:

1. whether its member were slobs
2. whether they ended each show drenched in sweat
3. whether they used piss bottles

Bitch Magnet was a no for numbers one and three, but every band I ever played in sweated onstage like it was summertime in New Orleans. I didn't discover that some musicians *didn't* sweat onstage until I interviewed one member of a much gentler band. (Not judging. No, I'm totally judging. Make an effort, for Christ's sake.) Not us. One Vineland drummer sometimes hung his sweat-drenched show shirt in the van after the show so by morning it was dry, albeit crispy from all that salt. Vineland was also not particularly good about item one, which is a nice way of saying we were total slobs, but we were a no for item three. Don Caballero, unfortunately, ticked the yes box for all three items.

So I guess we gotta talk about piss bottles, the portable emergency commodes often used by bands, especially those that day-drank the previous night's leftover beer. They were especially popular in bands with more than three members, in which, practically speaking, not every call to nature can be answered with a bathroom visit, because any rest-area stop inevitably meant thirty to forty-five minutes off the road: someone has to use the pay phone, someone else gets on line for a burger, two people mysteriously wander off, and the next thing you know the sun is setting. (Rule of thumb: time spent at rest stops increases exponentially with each additional passenger leaving the van.) Each stop also meant significantly longer drives to the next show, because the longer you dithered on the highway, the more likely it was that you'd get mired in the swamp of any city's rush-hour traffic, which meant you'd probably miss soundcheck, and maybe the show, and I've got to get out of this paragraph right now, because just thinking about this is totally giving me an anxiety attack.

Therefore: any large empty Gatorade or soda bottle starts looking like a solution. Ideally widemouthed bottles, not because everyone had giant dicks but because such vessels forgave bumps and jiggles and imprecise aim. (Physiology meant that women musicians were more apt to use a piss *cup*. Big Gulp or larger, please.) In time, you and your van mates developed quite a casual relationship with piss bottles. On one tour I left my camera in the van while I drove to a couple of shows in my car, and when I later developed the film, I found photos of the other guitarist pissing into a one-liter Gatorade bottle in the backseat while the woman who sold our merch rested her head on his shoulder, watching, nonchalant. Even a liter bottle can be, occasionally, technically insufficient but in a pinch would keep you traveling until the next real bathroom stop. This interval could last a long time, so it was important to save bottle caps—crude though our sanitation instincts were, we knew that much. But then sometimes you'd find orphaned piss bottles that had been fermenting peacefully for five or eight or ten days under the backseat.

I knew that everything happened in the van, but what I *didn't* know until very recently was this: people shit their pants in the van much more often than you'd think. On tour with Scratch Acid in the eighties, David Yow was smoking hash oil in the back, took too deep a hit, and got into a coughing fit so ferocious that he crapped his pants. Unfortunately he was wearing his favorite silk suit. Doubly unfortunate: he wasn't wearing underwear. The driver pulled over so he could clean up on the side of the road. But Yow didn't want to just *throw away* the pants, though the rest of the band—quite understandably!—didn't want them back inside. Which is why, for several hundred miles, a pair of sharp but badly stained gray silk suit pants flapped in the breeze, tied to the roof rack atop Scratch Acid's van.

All this amid the day-to-day of life in the van:

They fought constantly as they drove from show to show. They never said anything as they drove from show to show. They laughed and drank beer as they drove from show to show, and realized that they liked each other and that this band could work, and twenty years later they still make records and tour. They decided, as they drove from show to show, to start an urban legend on one end of the country and see if it ever made its way back to them on the opposite coast, and the rumor they tried to start was that Dave Thomas—the comically mild-mannered Wendy's founder—was convicted of manslaughter in the sixties. (My embellishment: he'd killed a man with his bare hands.) Two bands toured America together, and the practical jokes they inflicted on each other's vans culminated in hundreds of crickets being dumped into one, and I'M DRUNK AND I LOVE COP CUM scrawled in the dust on the back of the other, with an accompanying illustration. No one in that van noticed until a highway patrolman pulled them over, demanded that the driver step outside, and showed him the graffiti. "I don't care," said the cop, "but lots of people have been calling and complaining." Then, "Wait. You guys are in a band? What kind of music do you play?" When someone mumbled, "Rock music," the cop said, "Oh, like Aerosmith?" and, sensing an exit, the guy said, "Yes, *exactly* like Aerosmith," which was much easier than telling the truth, and they got away without a ticket after gifting the cop a CD. We were driving through Pennsylvania and, as a car full of girls passed, we thought, *Hey, why not?* but the only note we could come up with to hold out the window while we passed them read, WE'RE IN A BAND, and then they passed *us*, holding up a sign that said, WE'RE NOT, and that was pretty much the end of that. Once when we were overseas, a young roadie who didn't speak English very well confided that he had bought a vibrator for his girlfriend and was excited to try it out. A few days later he told me he had, and when I asked how it went, he frowned and said, "She pee," and I kind of did a spit take and repeated, "She *pee*?" and he nodded sadly and said, "She pee, and she cry."

✳ ✳ ✳

I ASKED EVERYONE I INTERVIEWED FOR THIS BOOK FOR THE grossest van and tour story they knew, and the winner came from Rjyan Kidwell, who performed in a solo electronic project called Cex (say "sex"), and Jeremy DeVine, the label head of Temporary Residence, who tour-managed Cex on an ill-fated 2003 tour of the UK and Europe, a tour for which DJ Beyonda opened.

> **JEREMY:** We played in Nottingham, and instantly after the show Rjyan and I both hooked up with beautiful women. They lived together, so everything is super cool, and we go back to their house.

> **RJYAN:** We parked in front of their apartment building. I was really wasted, and there were stairs, and we were like, "Do we have to bring

everything up?" And the girls were like, "No. There's a security camera right there." They pointed to the end of the block, and there was a security camera pointed right down to where the car was parked. So we were like, "Perfect." I brought almost nothing inside.

JEREMY: Rjyan goes up, hooks up with this woman. I hook up with this other woman. Everything's great. The next day . . .

RJYAN: It was pretty early, and I needed to go down and get my clothes and toothbrush and stuff. Sander, the driver, went ahead of me. I went to the back of the car, and the door was swinging open, and I asked, "Sander, you opened this door, right?" He said, "What? No."

JEREMY: The van has been broken into. All the merch is gone. Rjyan's suitcase, his passport, all gone. This is something like day two of a twenty-one-day tour.

RJYAN: I had just made this awkward "Okay, we live in other countries, so no number exchanging" goodbye. Then I had to turn around and go back up the stairs and say, "All our shit was taken. What do you think we should do?"

Then we looked up at the security camera that had been staring at our van the night before. It had pivoted ninety degrees during the night and was now looking down another street.

JEREMY: The only way to get a passport is to go back to the American consulate in London. So we do the drive. And Rjyan snaps, but not in an aggressive way. He snaps like, "You know what? I'm going to take ownership over this thing that happened to me, because these people do not own me. They can't make me miserable. I'm going to own my own freedom." I said, "Okay. And how is that manifesting itself?"

He said, "I am not going to bathe for the rest of the tour."

RJYAN: I had one set of clothes. I bought a skirt at Camden Market and just wore that for the rest of the tour. I thought, *You're going to take all my stuff? I don't need stuff.* I also didn't shower at all. Like, *You can't bring me down. I'm going to wear the accumulated stress. And everyone is gonna have to deal with it.*

I don't totally remember what the thinking behind that position was.

JEREMY: Me and the other people in the van said, "But that doesn't resolve anything. And eventually it very slowly tortures everyone around you." And he just said, "It's going to be the smell of freedom."

RJYAN: That does ring a bell.

JEREMY: We didn't take it seriously. Day three, day four rolls around. He still has not bathed, and he's played a show every night. Day six, day eight. Wow. He is really going for it. He's wearing the exact same clothes.

For the rest of the tour he never bathed. Eventually it got so rancid in the van that we couldn't drive without all the windows open. Even if it was cold. Sander, the hired driver, was getting visibly more upset as the days went on.

RJYAN: Very early on I feel like we figured out that Sander was not psyched about us at all.

JEREMY: We play a show in Paris. We play in a club that looks like a pirate ship. The ceilings are only eight feet high. It's really close quarters. And you can smell him. A stench is permeating the room. I don't know if the crowd knew it or not, but it's him.

RJYAN: Maybe to other people it's not like this, but I feel like I can tell when I have B.O. It's not as bad as anyone else's smell. It doesn't have that weird garbage, rank, sour smell. Mine has this nice, sweet smell. It smells like chalk or something.

JEREMY: That night he goes home with some woman he met at the show. I was thinking, *He smells homeless and dead. There's no way that is attractive.*

RJYAN: What I thought was, that's pheromones. That's how you find out who really likes you, when you're really kicking out those pheromones. It smells gross to people who are not suited to be your mate, and it smells awesome to people who are.

JEREMY: They hook up. Which really disgusts me. It really bums me out. And I'm a total hobo. I don't shower every day. But I shower every *other* day. And I change my clothes.

It ended up in a fistfight with the driver in the van. Because eventually Sander just snapped: "You have to fucking bathe! This is ridiculous!" And they get into this strange and existential argument, because Rjyan kept saying, "This is the smell of freedom!"

Sander is kind of meek. He's not someone we ever felt threatened by at all. And he punches Rjyan in the face as hard as he can. Then keeps driving and never says another word.

RJYAN: I actually don't remember that. But it probably happened. I feel like I just took it, and honestly, I feel like it wasn't a hard enough punch to have a memory of it. There was a period when I actively tried to forget a lot of things from this tour.

JEREMY: I said, "I don't know, dude. I'm going to be honest with you: that might have been deserved."

He smelled very swampy. Like a Cajun corpse. Louisiana *Walking Dead*–type shit. I think at the end of the tour I literally threw what little money I had left at Rjyan and walked away.

RJYAN: It was at some café or diner. No one was there but us. I can't remember what I said, but I feel like I provoked him, with some kind of matter-of-fact thing like, "This has been the worst tour I've ever been on. Thanks." Something shitty like that. Then he threw the money at me, and then I felt bad.

I gave everything that was left over to Beyonda. I feel like she was invited along on the pretense of my being a successful electronic musician, so this is going to be really easy and fun. She endured a lot of hardship for no reason.

Jeremy and I did two records after that.

Doctor Rock

realized I was very different from the guy we called Doctor Rock one morning around 2 a.m. while I was entwined with a very recent acquaintance on a living room floor in Madison, Wisconsin. This was during the last round of Bitch Magnet tours in 1990, the ones right after Orestes quit. Doctor Rock was his replacement. He and I both had girlfriends back home, but that night we had made fast friends with two young women who'd driven eighty miles from Milwaukee to see the show. One of them told me they'd gotten stoned and listened to *Umber* every day that summer.

I was pretty anti-pot by then, and the stupidity of weed was a running inside joke. Sometimes onstage, as we paused mid-set, I'd step up to the mike and declare: "This is a song about smoking pot." But since we rarely smiled onstage, people often missed the point. In Columbus a soft-bellied, sad-eyed guy sought me out after the show, begging for weed, claiming it was impossible to find any. Of course you can't, I told him, deadpan: we have *all* the pot. Still, the image of two cute girls getting stoned to our record during long, flat, hot Midwestern summer days was quite picturesque, and I ended up with Mary. She was blond—Catholic, I guessed—and when I introduced myself, she gestured in the space between us and said, "John and Mary!" I could tell she was spelling my name wrong even as she said it, but beyond assuming it was some New Testament reference, I had no idea what she meant. But I just Googled "John and Mary" and discovered that it's the title of a movie, released in 1969, wherein *goyishe* Mia Farrow and Jewy Dustin Hoffman meet in a bar and end up in bed. Was that what you meant, Mary? Did I miss *the whole point until now?*

After the show we maneuvered our new friends out of the club. That night a fight had broken out on the sidewalk and ended up on the hood of our van, leaving blood trails smeared across the windshield. After windshield-wiping the bloodstains away, we drove to the house where our hostess, a kind and shy friend from college I'll call Sarah, turned the living room over to us and tactfully disappeared.

There it was: the fluttery feeling of new lips, new mouth, new body, my hands under her shirt tracing patterns on her smooth and wondrous skin. But distractions quickly started pinwheeling: *I have a girlfriend. What am I doing? Do I, like, fuck Mary right here, in front of everyone? And—oh, shit—Sarah is friends with my girlfriend. How will she not find out?*

The foreknowledge of regret. The dickless indie rock anhedonia kicking in. Before getting too entranced by the cool of Mary's skin, I contrived some excuse—*too tired, long drive tomorrow,* something like that—kissed her good night, rolled over, and closed my eyes. Approximately eight feet from my head Doctor Rock and Mary's friend were going at it like they were playing tackle football, she sounding simultaneously like the opposing team and the cheerleading squad. Sooyoung was sleeping, or pretending to sleep, or—I dearly hope—calmly writing his recollections of the day in his notebook, eyes fixed to its pages, in the farthest corner of the room.

Sooyoung and I had very active governors on our ids. Doctor Rock's was innocent of any such mechanism. (Not for nothing did he earn that nickname.) Maybe nothing pushes a hedonist to comical extremes more than the company of ascetics. Now, I'm not judging Doctor Rock, though I certainly did then. But we had no business playing together, for reasons that were becoming brutally clear.

*　*　*

DOCTOR ROCK WAS SEVERAL YEARS OLDER THAN SOOYOUNG and me. He was compact and lean with a round face and big, white Midwestern teeth—the sort of face you could tell freckles had once spread across, and there still remained something very boyish about his enthusiasms and petulance. His shoulder-length red-brown hair had thinned and often went Albert Einstein on him, which was not a good look. Even before his audition, it was clear he did not speak our language of punk rock cred and correctness and hadn't spent years going to hardcore shows, reading zines, and hanging out at a college radio station. (Though neither had Orestes, and that worked out great.) When I called and left a detailed message for Doctor Rock with his live-in girlfriend—*We're in this band he knows, album's coming out, we need a drummer more or less immediately for upcoming tours of America and Europe*—she immediately asked if "management" would pay for relocation. My response: "You're talking to management, and we can't."

Just after we met, he enthused about how cool it would be to have an electronic kit that triggered various industrial sound effects. 1990 was a long time ago, but not so long that this notion was in any way novel. There he is, locking eyes with me, miming hitting a cymbal and vocalizing a robotic *Rrhhhooonnngggkk*. There I am, trying to look noncommittal about a totally horrifying idea for this band. Still: he was a *really* good drummer. Powerful, precise, and at ease playing both the complex and the simple. He was a metalhead, but that could be kind of cool and might help in a conflict I knew could arise between my desire to get heavier and weirder and Sooyoung's pop sensibility. Then again, he'd also played the glammy fake-metal crap we hated during a stretch of the eighties he spent in Manhattan, where he briefly lived in an illegal basement apartment in Alphabet City. (The toilet was a simple drain cut into the cement floor.) Anyone reasonably familiar with that time and place will not be surprised to learn that his most promising band collapsed when key personnel, himself included, got too familiar with narcotics. The coup de grâce came when a bandmate stole most of Doctor Rock's possessions, including a pretty nice stereo.

So, yes, he had a few miles on the odometer. But he'd cleaned up, and, unlike the only other drummer we tried out, he auditioned well. Welcome aboard, Doctor Rock. He threw his drum kit and some clothes into his Honda station wagon and drove down from the upper Midwest, moving in with a couch-tenderized South African Spicoli type I'll call Strom, whose accent rendered his favorite phrase as "ab-so-lewwt-lee NAHSSING!" To hear it, you just had to ask what he'd done that day. Strom's dedication to lassitude was so heroic that he affected a limp and wore a knee brace while working as a paralegal, to avoid having to do any physical work *at a law firm*.

* * *

YOU NEVER FORGET THE NEW SENSATIONS OF YOUR TEENS and early twenties. Or maybe it's that certain transitional moments in your life stick with you, and something about the way you find yourself waiting within them, in a pleasant sort of limbo between two destinations, etches them into memory. I loved those few weeks before we went on tour. I'd uprooted myself to North Carolina—Chapel Hill, where Sooyoung had moved after college. Once there, jobless, I aimlessed my way down the main drag a few times each day, chatting with people I'd met in clubs or at bars or through the whole brotherhood-of-bands thing. Sometimes I scammed free food from a Bitch Magnet fan who worked at the pizzeria. I was dead broke, but Taco Bell served unlimited iced tea and 39-cent tacos, and one day I was able to feed myself with the spare change I found on the floor in my room. The Char-Grill in Raleigh served tea so sweet it made your teeth hurt, and shakes so thick that, as I believe Thurston Moore once observed, sipping them through a straw was like trying to suck a wrench out of mud. Sometimes I loitered outside Cat's Cradle when interesting bands came through, to charm my way onto a guest list. (When Sonic Youth played there, they arrived in a tour bus with FRAMPTON emblazoned in the skinny front window where buses once announced their destination.) I pulled long late-night sessions in the twenty-four-hour Kinko's—where Laura Ballance, the bassist for a new band called Superchunk, sometimes worked nights—constructing and Xeroxing show flyers and press kits, then skulked the deserted downtown, stapling flyers to telephone poles and bulletin boards while crickets sawed at the moist night air. My girlfriend lived hundreds of miles away, and contacting her required careful budgeting or a stolen credit card number. But this was a very contented time, and even today I can remember the tickly feeling spreading: *So much was going to happen.*

The only problem was that Sooyoung worked, and lived with his girlfriend, so Doctor Rock was my primary activity pal, and he seemed a bit bewildered by the setting and by us. Sooyoung and I didn't drink much, weren't into big hormonal displays, and our ambitions and demeanor, onstage and off, didn't exactly match Doctor Rock's. He adored the juicy, dirty pleasures of rock and the showmanship of an earlier era. We'd never play footsie with major labels or be in nakedly commercial gutter-metal bands in New York—and if we had, we *definitely* wouldn't have worn eyeliner and scarves, as he did. He had never heard of the bands we held closest to our hearts, though his mind was properly blown once I played him Voivod and Honor Role and Slint and Gore. (Not for the first time, I thought, *See? This stuff is so great it can convert anyone!*) Though he was full of great and horrifying stories. In one he went on a hiking trip with his ineffably gentle Midwestern parents while secretly coming off heroin. I made him retell these tales, howled in appreciation, then filed them in the mental ledger that tallied his faults.

* * *

A TRIO ON TOUR IN AMERICA SANS DRIVER OR SOUNDMAN OR other helping hands, as we were, is forced to get workmanlike pretty quickly. The days tick by: drive to gig, unload gear, soundcheck, set up merch table, grab quick dinner nearby, sit at merch table, play, have someone dash to sell merch right after the set (prime time for sales), get paid, load van, drive to sleeping quarters, unload van if necessary, sleep, repeat. The profit margin depends on finding strangers' floor space. Three of us sharing one motel room? A rare luxury. In other words, ours was not a party van. Before the tour began, our booking agent showed me the standard contract rider his bands used. In the part outlining what food and drink we required backstage, I crossed out *one case of beer* and wrote in its place *one twelve-pack of beer.* At one point Doctor Rock confided to a mutual friend that the tour felt like being among scientists. He hadn't been in a band like ours: sober, somber, serious, somewhat distant. Somewhere in Ohio the bassist in an opening band—a ferrety, older Johnny Thunders type whom I immediately distrusted—said he had Seconals, which astonished me. *Seconals? Who in the '90s was still eating reds?* I don't think Doctor Rock indulged. But that night he had more to talk about with that guy than he had with us.

Anyway, it wasn't that Doctor Rock was so much older. It was that he seemed so much younger. At an afterparty following the last show of the American tour—in case this sounds in any way exciting or louche, it took place in a college dorm lounge, lined with grayish institutional couches and ablaze in fluorescent light—he exulted, as hopped-up as a twelve-year-old, over our upcoming tour of Europe. Throwing his hands in the air, pumping fists, all that: "Yes! I'm going to Europe! Yes! I get to go to Europe! Yes! Yes! Yes!" The veteran of a zillion bands, he was butting up against the realities that being thirty brings into sudden sharp focus—and here he was, high-fiving strangers about a trip overseas.

Having been kicked out of my band for being a loudmouth, I'd internalized one lesson from that experience: If I was ecstatic about something, I assumed I was always best off *keeping it to myself.* I'd grown very conscious that how I acted affected everyone's emotional weather. I hadn't considered how much Doctor Rock's behavior would affect mine, to say nothing of Sooyoung's. Not for the first time, I stared at our new bandmate in disbelief. Where had this guy come from?

* * *

AT THE END OF THE AMERICAN TOUR, SOOYOUNG AND I DID some basic accounting and discovered that, on a series of dates that seemed well organized and reasonably well attended and that paid us decently, we'd lost something like fifty bucks. A few days later Sooyoung called a band meeting, where he announced that he'd enrolled in grad school and would start shortly after we returned from Europe.

Doctor Rock took this all in. Then he announced that, given this development, well, with great reluctance and with many thanks for this amazing opportunity and a great time all around, after this last round of dates he was going back home. He said all this with great Midwesternness. Great modesty and affability, accompanied by many smiles and self-deprecating head bobs. There was a touch of insincerity around the edges if you fixed him with a penetrating gaze. But I couldn't blame him if he'd had enough of our nerdy, solemn ways. And of course he had reason to smile: a decision had been made for him. (I should probably say here that both Doctor Rock and Sooyoung later told me that this meeting was not the first time Sooyoung made these plans known, but I assure you, the news was a giant surprise to me.) Anyway, it didn't seem like there was much reason to stick around, so I, too, said I'd go back home. There was just this entire European tour to get through first.

* * *

THE GREAT CULTURAL DIVIDE WITHIN BANDS LIES BETWEEN the drummer and everyone else. If your band is at all serious about impact and power, your drummer's job is the most physical and violent, and by far the hardest. Other musicians can half-ass it—distortion is a remarkably forgiving tool—but the drummer must be both caveman and mathematician, and has a far smaller margin of error than anyone else. While the task is to bang the staff on one rock, loudly, the drummer also has to know, to the millisecond, when to start whacking the next one. You don't want someone just good enough: you want someone *great*, someone obsessed with drums and rhythm and beats and cymbals, who plays for hours every day and subsists on raw meat and steroids and pornography and power lifting. You want sheer fucking power tempered with just enough finesse, and if you don't, I'm basically not interested in your band. Such a regimen won't civilize your average young adult, which is where the cultural divide starts. Those who write lyrics are thinking about *poetry*. The drummers are thinking about murdering animals with their bare hands. (Or should be.)

Orestes likes to talk about how everyone needs to let the demon out, so long as you know when to usher the demon back into its cage. Hearing him say that always made perfect sense to me, because pursuing drumming with the singlemindedness that excellence requires can make anyone go completely insane. Even someone like Doctor Rock, who, despite all those thousands of hours spent practicing, was far more lover than thug. But upon landing in Europe, he let the demon run amok and never tried to drag it back to its cage. Maybe it was that the end was now in sight. Maybe he held back on the American leg of the tour, worried that he'd freak out us geeks. Maybe the right combination of environment and availability flicked an invisible internal switch. In Europe he became caricature. In Europe we started calling him Doctor Rock.

* * *

DECEMBER IN NORTHERN EUROPE. I WON'T BE THE FIRST PER-
son to say it, but much of that continent doesn't really understand heating. Our van was tiny and lacked seatbelts, which I hated, because
without them your ass slid around the slippery backseat, making it
impossible to sleep, while the chilly weather gradually leached out all
your body heat. A few scenes of snowy alpine glory, but much was just
lightless and gray. We pulled into each city at twilight—no, it was *always*
twilight—while passersby hunched their way home through streets
and sidewalks coated in soot-covered snow. Parts of England still stank
from coal smoke. After we played our first show of the tour, opening
for the Wedding Present in London, our van was broken into, and we
lost both of my guitars, my amp, Sooyoung's bass, and a bunch of
merch and cash, which didn't do much for morale.

We argued in the van, in hotels, backstage and onstage. Sometimes
moments before the show began. Sometimes during the set.

I went days without speaking to Doctor Rock. (Sooyoung went longer.) But it didn't seem to bother him, once he discovered the greater
volumes of free booze, the occasional availability of speed, and that
larger crowds meant lots more women at each show. Early in the tour
we played Hamburg, a town that, as every touring band knows, has an
actual red-light district. Another American band opened for us, and we
all checked out the Reeperbahn afterward. Available women sat in lin-
gerie in storefront windows, lit by low ambient light. They had mastered
an almost-subliminal signaling system: you never saw any of them
knocking on their windows, you just heard ghostly taps echoing down
the alleys.

We tried to find the cheapest place with topless dancers. Not the best
strategy if one wants a good show. To his enduring credit, a googly-eyed
Doctor Rock posed the same question to all the barkers who stood by
the entrances: "Is it decadent?" (A question we all found profoundly

amusing. Also kind of the right one to ask!) We finally found a suitable one—by which I mean the cheapest one—and paid the minimal fee. Each of us entered his own booth, a wall opened, and we found ourselves looking into a giant round room, staring directly into one another's open booths, while a tall blonde gyrated and shimmied without any enthusiasm. She asked where we were from, and the guitarist from the other band said, in the flattest American-news-anchor accent possible, that we were all English. The absolute highlight was when she straightened up, pointed at her chest, and, apparently seriously, pronounced, "Tits." The show ended after that, and Doctor Rock trotted off to explore the sights.

The rest of us went to another club, which had a sloped and polished painted-concrete floor, like a roller rink or skate park, and was about as big. Immediately two or three blond German girls, nude but for high heels, descended upon me, and one tried to strike up a conversation.

Attractive Naked Blond Girl: Hello! Where are you from?

Me: Um. New York.

ANBG: Would you like to come with me to a private room?

Me: No. [*Exit.*]

Doctor Rock, meanwhile, was enormously complicating his evening by forgetting the name and address of our hotel, then spending all night trying to find it. At one point he went to a police station with this sad story. I was interested in hearing how Hamburg's constabularies responded, once they stopped laughing. But after seeing an exhausted and angry-eyed Doctor Rock glaring at the rest of us over breakfast—he managed to find his way back just as we started eating—I thought it better not to ask.

I could say that Doctor Rock drank a lot, but it would be more accurate to say that if he was awake, he was drinking. We played a shitty show in Innsbruck—literally shitty, in an absolutely freezing room in a squat that was home to a pack of dogs that left scattered frozen clusters of droppings everywhere. As disheartening as that sight was, it was nowhere near as disheartening as what happened when the heat finally went on and the room filled: the poop unfroze, mingled with the snow on everyone's shoes, and was tracked everywhere until the entire floor was sloppy with a thin, foul-smelling muck. Before the show Doctor Rock drank a beer while flying around on someone's skateboard. He hit a patch of frozen dog shit, or something, and took a pretty serious tumble. But he didn't let go of his beer bottle—interestingly—and he landed on it, opening a nasty gash. I saw him howl and flail a bloody hand and immediately thought, *Tour over*. But Tanco, our unflappable Dutch driver/tour manager/Doctor Rock minder, wrapped it neatly in gauze and tape, and within minutes Doctor Rock was relating and reenacting his accident to a crowd of new friends.

He did not appear to require sleep. He was awake when we went to bed and awake when we woke up. Sometimes he would doze in the van during the day, then suddenly sit up, reach for a beer, and down it.

He seemed to find a woman at every show. In Austria (or Germany, or Switzerland, I really don't remember), one stuck around in the van for a few days. She must have hoped for a better time than what we showed her, because, if I understood correctly, she had put her job in danger by coming along. Had I spoken to her at all, I might be able to tell her story now.

Long van rides lead young men to hash out theories, and on this tour we started wondering whether Germany was so uptight because its men scorned cunnilingus. One morning in Karlsruhe or Kassel or Bremen or Dortmund, outside our hotel, following an impressive make-out/mauling session with the previous night's conquest outside our idling van, Doctor Rock described how he had gone down on her the night before, making her softly exclaim in wonderment, "What are you doing?" We all developed the theory, but Doctor Rock did the actual lab work. Credit him for that, I guess.

Some of this was kind of funny and made for great stories, even if the day-to-day sucked, as it inevitably does when you live with someone who's always in character. The complications came from realizing that the joke-doll version of Doctor Rock was easier to deal with than the talented and disgruntled drummer who was ill-suited for our band. Encouraging him by chuckling at the cartoon had queasy moral aspects, even if, to paraphrase Orwell's brilliant quote, he was quite happy to let his face grow to fit the mask. I kept him at arm's length and laughed at his excesses because it was the easiest thing to do. Not my most shining moment. It never occurred to me to say, *Hey, what's up? Maybe it's time to slow down.* Anyway, the general codes of the road dictate that someone has to be found unconscious with a needle in his arm to warrant an intervention, or to be so fucked up he or she starts ruining shows. Doctor Rock never did that. Which is not to say that his metally flourishes were working or welcome.

The last show of the tour was in the Netherlands on the next-to-last day of 1990, and the following night there was a huge New Year's Eve party in the well-appointed squat where we stayed. (On this tour I learned that no country did squats as well as the Dutch.) I stayed in my room, reading fanzines, watching TV. I was worn out, feeling shy, also sad that this was the end. Doctor Rock, of course, was roaming the halls but had divined that our host had a small cache of speed, and every half hour or so he asked sweetly for another hit.

You don't want to see someone you know acting like this, but the tour was over, as was the band, and we were finally going home. Well, *most* of us were. Doctor Rock had received a vague offer to drum with an expat American guitarist of minor renown. Perhaps some caution light should have flashed, since he found said guitarist hanging out with a clearly junked-out opening band one night, but, whatever, he was no longer our problem. He planned to stay at the squat for a few days and then . . . well, we didn't know and we didn't ask, because Doctor Rock was finally off our hands.

An article in a British fanzine, written just after Sooyoung and I limped home, closed with the image of Doctor Rock riding toward the horizon, heading deeper and deeper into some rock fantasy, until he disappeared from sight.

The reality was different. A few days after I got back to the States, while licking wounds at my parents' comfortable and massively un-punk-rock house—unemployed, band over, no clue what to do next, sitting with them each night at the dinner table, joining them uneasily in front of the TV afterward—the phone rang. It was Doctor Rock's dad, an extremely gentle white-haired academic, who had some questions.

Among them: "Now, Jon. I have to ask you something. And I understand if you feel you can't betray a friend. But was my son having problems with drugs when he was in Europe?"

No, I said. But he was drinking heavily. (I didn't bother mentioning the speed.)

"Well, if it was just drinking . . ." his dad started to say, but I didn't want to give him any false sense of relief. It wasn't that I gave a shit about Doctor Rock. I was basically hoping I'd never see him again. But his parents were so kind when we stayed with them on tour. I also sensed that his dad had made this call before, and that thought made me squeeze my eyes shut.

No, I said. He was drinking *heavily*. Really, really heavily.

Meanwhile, Doctor Rock's girlfriend, understandably upset that he was, you know, *not coming home*, called my girlfriend, whom I'd made the mistake of telling many things I assumed she'd keep in confidence. (Getting through that tour required a lot of venting.) But when Doctor

Rock's girlfriend called her, she shared what I'd recounted of his mul-
tivarious dalliances, and afterward told me about this discussion. Like
me, my girlfriend also went to Oberlin. Unlike me, she was still influenced by the most excruciating aspects of the school's exhausting lef-
tydom. She argued that sisterhood prevented her from lying or shading
the truth when asked about Doctor Rock's faithfulness. I pointed out
that she had betrayed my confidences, and by doing so screwed me and
some other people as well. But by then scorekeeping was moot.

Doctor Rock's parents contrived a way to bring him back home,
though I don't recall how. They didn't inform him that, upon arrival, he
was going straight to rehab. Though they did tell me.

Before we flew to Europe, he had left his car in my parents' driveway,
and it fell to me to pick him up at the airport. He'd already gotten an
earful from his girlfriend, so: awkward. But he was nowhere near the
asshole that he had every right to be. In fact, he was almost cheerful.
Or at least he, like me, desperately did not want any kind of scene, and
he, like me, just wanted to get on with what was left of his life. I did not
bring up any touchy topics. (I was happy being pretty Midwestern-
indirect about everything myself.) He stayed at my parents' house just
long enough to shower, while I reflected upon the shitstorm awaiting
him, and then he hopped in his car and disappeared in the direction of
the interstate. He left as cheerfully as he came in, even though he also
talked about what he thought was coming—that he would have some
serious explaining to do when got back home.

But he had no idea what was coming. A few weeks later I got a letter
from rehab.

"I'm sorry to be writing this, but anger must be vented," it began in
seething and tiny handwriting. It went on from there to denounce my
betrayal, my disingenuousness, and my eternal complaining while on
that last tour. (Right on all counts, by the way.) I stewed for a couple weeks,
feeling guilty, again, that I'd tacitly encouraged his worst instincts.

Finally I sent a few perfunctory sentences conceding certain points while asserting that he had no one to blame but himself.

I couldn't help it. You couldn't have helped it, either. Something about rehab forces clichés out of everyone.

This note crossed in the mail with a sunnier, blame-accepting letter from a clean, sober, and steadier Doctor Rock. What a shitty time we had all along trying to communicate. We couldn't even time apologies and accusations correctly. Our correspondence dwindled to nothing after that. I got a postcard from him about a year later, gently, cheerfully—Midwesternly—chiding me for not sending him live tapes of the European tour. He ended up in a band we knew, but left after one album. I ran into him on the road in the mid-nineties, while I was on tour with Vineland, and we had an awkward conversation. Like many dreamers and seekers, he ended up out West, where he spent years drumming for a show in Las Vegas. He's married now, with kids.

I DIDN'T SPEAK WITH HIM AGAIN UNTIL LATE 2013. FUNNILY enough, after completing a PhD in music, he taught university classes in pop music: he really *was* Doctor Rock. I'd told him I was writing this book and wanted to talk about our time playing together. I wanted him to take some shots at me, fair being fair and all, but no matter how much I prompted, he demurred. I didn't expect the conversation to be easy, but it was clear that I was ripping off many old scabs, and the way he wallowed in apology was hard to hear.

I asked: What happened in Europe?

"I fucked everything up. Isn't that what this is about? I was the guy who fucked it all up."

No, I said. That's not what this is about. What happened?

"I was having the time of my life. I'd never experienced anything so amazing." I'd forgotten that, despite all those years of playing in bands, he'd never really gone on tour before. "I imploded. I didn't know how to handle how cool it was. At the end I just didn't want to go home. I didn't want to leave. I didn't want it to end."

Clay Tarver, the guitarist from Bullet LaVolta and Chavez, once told me that going on tour is so much fun it makes you crazy. I love this line, because as soon as he said it, I knew what he meant. It sort of happened to me, early on. It definitely happened to Doctor Rock.

In retrospect, I said, there was no way to replace Orestes. No one else would have worked. (I've successfully replaced drummers in other bands, but it's really hard to swap out a musician in a trio. Though neither Sooyoung nor I knew that.)

Doctor Rock said that he loved the band and thought we sounded great together. He asked over and over again if I would make him the villain when I told this part of the story. I told him I wouldn't.

Did I?

Or is the villain the guy who encouraged his worst instincts, talked shit about him behind his back, dropped the dime on his on-tour indiscretions—and then wrote about almost all of it in a fucking book?

* * *

DOCTOR ROCK, DOCTOR ROCK, YOU ASS PAIN, YOU OF THE dubious aesthetics and wince-inducing ideas, you who helped sink one of my most cherished bands, you who in so many ways needlessly complicated my life—well, you were completely right about a few things. Many of us indie rockers knew nothing about pleasure back then. The band you joined certainly didn't. We didn't drink much. Smoking pot made my heart race from nameless dread, and anything harder than pot was unthinkable. We didn't fuck nearly as much as we should have. We didn't even dance.

And you know what else? I wish that I, too, cut loose, went mad, drank beyond the point of knowing anything, accepted any pill or powder that floated my way. I mean: I was twenty-two and touring in a rock band. It wasn't like I had to wake up and go to work in the morning. I wish that I, too, ripped the tights off young, giggling German women and tongued them until they experienced the ultimate pleasure. But something held me back. Something that, for good or ill, I had and you didn't. The fix and rush of the music was enough for me. The hormonal thrill of being inside it, instead of watching from the crowd. You and I both chased a buzz we were powerless to resist. It just wasn't the same one.

Jonathan Richman Has Ruined Rock for Another Generation

In 1994 or 1995 a band from Providence called Small Factory played in Manhattan at Brownies, and for some reason I went to the show. The drummer, Phoebe, was inept, and wrinkled her nose and made a funny face every time the band went slightly out of time, and they went out of time a lot. The guitarist, Dave, looked thirty-five, at least, but the entire band dressed like they were eight—bowl haircuts, stripey T-shirts—and acted like they were six. Their songs sucked, and they couldn't do a single interesting thing with their instruments. But—and this was the worst part—*it didn't matter*. The crowd was there to love the band, no matter what, and have the band love them back. A cuddle party, not a rock show.

Cities change. Even cities that, like Indie Rock USA, are just a state of mind. A very naïve form of twee pop had started going around, like a flu, and was afflicting many along the Eastern Seaboard. (Ultimately, the best-known bands that had a foot or two in this scene were Belle and Sebastian and the Magnetic Fields.) This all started in Olympia, Washington, with Beat Happening, with whom, strangely enough, Bitch Magnet once played at the CBGB Record Canteen. Beat Happening basically purveyed a more sexualized and arch version of Jonathan Richman—he's been doing nasal and childlike since the seventies—largely because their front guy, Calvin Johnson, had tons of charisma and wit. (I still wasn't a fan, though I always liked the oral-sex reference near the end of "Indian Summer.") Still, in the early nineties the consummate observer/superfan of our underground Nils Bernstein—who later ran publicity for Matador and Sub Pop—was prescient enough to make a few batches of T-shirts that declared in bold type: CALVIN JOHNSON HAS RUINED ROCK FOR AN ENTIRE GENERATION. As many bands influenced by Joy Division oversimplified a brilliant band into much bad minor-key goth, the post–Beat Happening stuff was much like Small Factory: bowl haircuts, stripey shirts, smiley faces, utterly bereft of sexuality. Summer camp after grade school, minus the aggression. D.C.'s Tsunami, which started the Simple Machines label and, like Beat Happening, established themselves as a maypole band for this kind of stuff, actually sang the line "You say punk rock means asshole. I say punk rock means cuddle." (Actually: no, not at all. Punk rock means—pick one—*self-determined* or *self-sufficient* or *individual* or *steadfast in the face of opposition*, not *asshole*, and definitely not *cuddle*. But you already knew that, right?)

Blandness became an aesthetic. Tempos strolled, never grinding, never speeding. Little was heavy, and even less was interesting, amid this bunch of shaggy-dog bands wanting to nuzzle you and a crowd seemingly eager to regress to childhood. Had eBay existed, prices for Archies and 1910 Fruitgum Company records would have skyrocketed. I was desperate not to grow up, too, but I thought the point was to be forever twenty-one, not a kindergartner. I liked adulthood, and most trappings of adulthood, like drinking and sex and living on my own. I hated all these bands, and I especially hated that they were starting to shove aside the music I liked most. In his book *Our Band Could Be Your Life*, Michael Azerrad identified a fear of sexuality—an unwillingness to embrace the complications that come with any of it, straight or gay—at the heart of the indie pop childishness. I just saw the childishness. What was the point?

***

THINK OF THE KICK DRUM/SNARE DRUM INTRO TO JUDAS Priest's "Living after Midnight":

Boom-CHA boom-boom CHA, boom-CHA boom-boom CHA
Boom-CHA boom-boom CHA, boom-CHA boom-boom CHA

Now count the beats by finding the *pulse*—the steady heartbeat beneath it all: 1-2-3-4, 1-2-3-4, 1-2-3-4, 1-2-3-4. A textbook example of rock in standard 4/4 time—four beats per measure, with the snare drum emphasizing the second and fourth beat.

Now think of the main piano riff for Dave Brubeck's "Take Five":

Bum-BAH, bum-BAH, bum-BAH
Bum-BAH, bum-BAH, bum-BAH

and count this one out, too: 1-2-3-4-5, 1-2-3-4-5. Five beats per measure, with accents in different places, most notably on the last two beats of the measure. Now count out the main instrumental riff in Peter Gabriel's "Solsbury Hill." You'll find it's in seven.

When I mention odd time signatures or odd meters, I mean fives, sevens, and elevens. In rock they were generally the domain of prog-rock eggheads like Rush and King Crimson—I mean this in the best possible sense of "prog-rock eggheads," since I actually like both—though Led Zeppelin was confident enough to play around with them, too: much of "Four Sticks" is in five, and "The Ocean" gets into fifteen. Occasionally they turned up in bona fide pop hits. Like "Solsbury Hill," Pink Floyd's "Money" is in seven, and with "Hey Ya!" Outkast somehow created an infectious and danceable song with verses in eleven. (For purposes of keeping this bit short, I'm using few examples, but aspiring time-signature geeks are directed to Crimson, Meshuggah, and Voivod for more advanced study.)

What I liked about odd time signatures, once Bitch Magnet and bands we liked started messing around with them, was how they made songs swing and groove in different ways—it was still rock and all that, but the feel was deeper, darker, more complex. Switching time signatures when you go from the verse to the chorus or from the verse to the bridge—Rush does this lots; to cite just one example, much of "Red Barchetta" is in 4/4, but the guitar solo and the subsequent refrain of one main riff slip into seven—was a gentle way of throwing in a subtle emphasis, or throwing *off* a listener's equilibrium in a way that always interested me. It can, of course become a contrivance. In the mid-nineties a bunch of bands had all these lurching, awkward songs because they were trying so damn hard to turn riffs that wanted to be in 4/4 into seven or five. And I got to the point in Vineland where a song didn't feel quite right unless it had two different time signatures, if not more.

When you're cocooned within a cultural bubble, you might start mistaking your circle of friends for a broader reality. You might start believing that whatever obscure thing you treasure most—like, say, rock played in odd time signatures—is about to take over the world, and you might believe that that thing will therefore thrive forever. Beatniks did. Hippies did. I couldn't stand either, but I, too, believed that the revolution was here and my side would win. Because you have to, right? You have to *believe*, even when the world throws so little love your way, because you have to find some way to get out of bed in the morning. Losing candidates do it every election. The star pitcher on the last-place team does it. And you—you work your crap job every day for nine hours, where someone shoots you a nasty look during each personal phone call, so tonight you can fill a dirty plastic bucket with that disgusting comelike cornstarch solution and dodge cops while plastering flyers all over the East Village until 2 a.m. Are you gonna do that if you think you're doomed to fail?

In the mid-nineties I could rattle off names of many bands that worked the specific angles I most cherished: those odd time signatures, odd guitar tunings, heavy, largely instrumental. Caspar Brötzmann Massaker. Slovenly. Wider. Gore. Slint. Bastro. Breadwinner. Voivod. Don Caballero. Pitchblende. There were likeminded people everywhere, or so I thought, because we all found one another at the same shows. In real life there weren't that many fans of this music—only those really deeply into it will recognize most of those names—because few normal people care enough to spend time parsing which measure is in five and which is in seven. The guys interested in details like that—and they were almost all guys, most of whom wore glasses and reveled in finally finding nerd athletics at which they could excel—were frequently musicians, or they quickly became musicians, since the membrane between fan and performer was so porous. This was one of the greatest things about this culture, but it's a problem when your only fans are the other musicians on the bill each night. Though you might not *notice* that it's a problem if you're spending too much time inside your bubble, where it's too easy to disappear up your own asshole, and be fully convinced that the rest of the world will soon join you up there. One friend at college who lived on Manhattan's Upper West Side was shocked when Reagan won in a landslide in 1984. Everyone she knew voted for Mondale, so how could Reagan have won? Precisely the trap into which we were falling. "You're in the studio," explained Turing Machine's Justin Chearno. "You've only listened to your five songs for two weeks, and when you're done, you really think, *We've created this new thing called music, and the world is going to hear this thing, and it's going to change their lives, and* Saturday Night Live *is next*. You just get so caught up. Then when nothing happens, you're like, 'Oh. Right.'"

Life in Indie Rock, USA, wasn't what I'd cracked it up to be. What had started out as free and welcoming ended up becoming as rigid and rule-bound as everything I'd hoped it would replace. (I was totally part of the problem, having been completely doctrinaire about music since forever.) "There was a lot of 'you're doing it wrong,'" recalled James Murphy, who drummed in Pony and Speedking long before he started LCD Soundsystem. Entering this world, he said, was like "your parents saying, 'You're gonna leave the farm. We're going to send you to this really good school.' And you're like, 'I am so excited!' Then you get there, and everyone's like, 'What kind of shoes are *those*? Oh. The *country kid* thinks they're *cool*.'" And since everyone in indie rock thought of themselves as a precious little snowflake, many claimed a uniqueness that was hard to square with the facts. "I used to get into all these fights with bands," Murphy recalled. "They'd all be like, 'I don't listen to anything. I listen to Edith Piaf,' and I'd be like, 'But you sound like Slint! You don't sing cabaret music! You're playing a guitar that's tuned funny in seven!'"

We weren't the only ones growing disillusioned. "There's this notion that indie rock has this intelligence. I think it was the opposite. More like know-nothingism," Andy Cohen, the guitarist from Silkworm, remembered. "Most of these bands were terrible, and they couldn't even play their instruments, in a bad way—not like how the Sex Pistols couldn't play their instruments, in a *good* way. Most bands were unambitious, and couldn't even execute their shitty little ambition." What bothered Cohen most was exactly what bothered me at that Small Factory show: laziness and low expectations. "You don't go to that famous opera house in Milan and suck and not hear about it. You go to the Apollo and you suck, you get knifed. But if you were in an indie rock band in the nineties and you sucked, you'd do well if you had the right friends."

The mainstream still sucked, but you always knew it would. Now our thing was starting to suck, too. Suddenly the weirdos—all right, *my* weirdos—were no longer winning, even in our little underground. "Indie rock became a genre of music, and it was very jangly and poppy," said Juan MacLean, a founder of Six Finger Satellite, who's now a renowned dance music artist and DJ. "That's why I quit. I grew up with hardcore, and then the Butthole Surfers. It seemed like their goal was to fuck with as many people as possible. I loved that. And I was so angry that indie rock became like what I actively rebelled against in the first place."

Lots of bands playing our circuit were only half a step from the mainstream—remember that the Smashing Pumpkins, Hole, the Pixies, and Beck all started on indie labels—and in the wake of platinum and gold records from Nirvana, Soundgarden, and Helmet, major-label reps drew targets on most every middling band with a soupçon of indie cred. Things got so strange that those reps also signed some bands that were actually oddball enough for me, among them San Diegan eccentrics Three Mile Pilot and the all-instrumental Pell Mell. (Those bands' major-label records died a very quick death, of course.) College radio veterans and guys from punk rock bands ended up on staff at Atlantic or Sony or Geffen, the token young people told to go out to their favorite hangouts and find the next big thing. The bands they courted received some version of The Spiel, often at fancy restaurant dinners attended by label execs and their flunkies. Ted Leo fronted Chisel and then Ted Leo and the Pharmacists, so his career has spanned multiple commercial booms for indie bands, and he's heard The Spiel in a few different decades. He recalled it like this: *You guys are doing something great. We want you to have a home where you can make the records you want to make and have the funding to do it.*

Further conversation, of course, revealed that reality in the big leagues wouldn't necessarily fit that frame. You might be told that the drummer or bassist or even the entire rest of the band had to go. When Sebadoh went to record *Harmacy* in 1995, Lou Barlow was pulled aside by someone on the project, who told him, "If you want this to be a big hit, you gotta get rid of your drummer. And you gotta do it now." (It's important to underscore here that its technical wobbliness was part of

Sebadoh's package, much like the Pogues' drunkenness or Motorhead's facial warts.) "I knew he was right," Lou recalled. "And I knew I couldn't fire my friend in order to make a more dynamic, post-Nirvana-sounding record." To his credit, he didn't. And *Harmacy* didn't sell like *Nevermind*. But hardly anything did.

The tally of indie bands broken on the shoals of major-label indifference is, frankly, far too long to get into here, but in time everyone had friends in bands like Die Kreuzen or Walt Mink or Tad who had very detailed and unhappy stories. Among the recurring themes: the guy who signed us got fired and suddenly no one returned our phone calls; the guy at the label strung us along with teases and promises for over a year and then didn't sign us and we finally broke up from frustration and inertia; the release date of our record kept getting pushed back until we finally broke up; we got dropped right after they released our record.

Even some bands that seemed primed to succeed crapped out. Urge Overkill had their look and concept extraordinarily well thought out. Their cover of Neil Diamond's "Girl, You'll Be a Woman Soon" gave them a star turn on the soundtrack of *Pulp Fiction*. For their 1993 major-label debut, *Saturation*, they had the full promotional power of Geffen's machinery behind them: significant commercial radio airplay, a tour with Nirvana and Pearl Jam, and a video for "Sister Havana" that ended up in MTV's *Buzz Bin*, back when that all but guaranteed you'd soon hang a gold or platinum record on your wall. To date *Saturation* has sold about 270,000 copies. A total that would have any indie label freaking out with joy. But for a band in the nineties that received a full-on major-label push, that figure is flat-out disappointing. "The people spoke," Urge's Ed Roeser told me. "It didn't work out." To employ the gentlest form of understatement, drink and drugs became a problem, and the band's dark and underbaked follow-up, 1995's *Exit the Dragon*, tanked. Urge had played a glamourpuss-rock-star shtick for laughs pretty much since they started, but now it looked like they could no longer tell which parts were a joke and which weren't, which even Ed admits now. He quit, and the band fell apart—or vice versa—and fell apart in the worst way. Many fans never forgave them for leaving for more-monied pastures. Smarter ones just questioned the wisdom of their tactics. "They probably would have been a much more successful huge rock band if they hadn't been *trying so hard* to be a successful huge rock band," said Tortoise's Doug McCombs.

As for me, after indie pop triumphed and virtually all indie-to-major signings failed, I ended up getting into the continuum of sludgy hard rock bands that ran from Blue Cheer to Saint Vitus and Melvins to Kyuss and Sleep, the most recent examples of which were being described with the unfortunate term "stoner rock." In these bands I found the physicality and visceralness I no longer found among my indie brethren. Unfortunately I also found a decided Doctor Rock-ness to many of the musicians. Dave Sherman, then the bassist in Spirit Caravan, once told me he was calling his new band Earthride, "because we're all just"—here he paused, looking off into space, before concluding—"riding the earth." Then he described the art he wanted on the cover of Earthride's first album, a blond woman straddling the earth, at which point he started demonstrating that image. (I'd love to be able to say that album—whose cover features no such blonde—is pretty great. But it isn't.) By then I'd abandoned many of my indie rock prejudices, but I just couldn't hang with how these guys defaulted to standard party-time rock modes. Nor how, once you got past the best of this breed, quality declined so precipitously. Nor how, for many of them, punk rock never happened. Also, theirs was a different tribe. Outsiders, yes, but bikers, not nerds. No way I'd ever pass for one of them, even with my long hair.

* * *

AROUND 2003 TED LEO MET WITH ANOTHER MAJOR-LABEL A&R guy, who had a slightly different spiel: "We want to think of you as another Bruce Springsteen. You've got a life here with us." Afterward

Ted went directly to an interview with a twentysomething magazine writer and mentioned what he'd just been told.

Ted said that writer told him, "'I gotta tell you, from the perspective of a lot of your fans, we'd be really bummed if you signed to a major label.' And initially I was like, 'Fuck you. That's not for you to decide.' But my other reaction was practical." He now understood that the A&R guy feeding him those lines could well be gone in a few months, and Ted knew no one else at that label. And he realized something else: "They're not going to make me into a star. I was thirty-three or thirty-four, writing political pop songs. That's not the equation for hits. *And* I'm going to lose half my existing audience? That sounds like a loser of a move." Ted's very smart on the challenges that middle-aged indie rockers face—Google any recent interview he's given for proof—but even he had to watch a generation of indie bands fail on major labels before reaching that conclusion.

VINELAND ITINERARY 1996

Thurs., April 4: depart NYC.
Fri., April 5: arrive in Chicago, evening.
Sat. April 6-Wed. April 10: record.

Thursday 4/11: Minneapolis, Uptown Lounge (w/Pervis from Austin)
Fri: 4/12: Chicago, Empty Bottle. (w/Storm and Stress)
Sat. 4/13: Detroit, Zoot's (w/ Storm and Stress ($75-$100)
Sun 4/14: Cleveland, Grog Shop ($100)
Monday, 4/15 Chicago-Lounge Ax, with Silkworm, -dis, and Panel Donor Tuesday,
4.16: I. City/Oberlin/Madison.
Wed. 4/17: Champaign (w/Cibo Matto)
Thurs 4/18: Pittsburgh, BBT, with Storm and Stress
Fri 4/19: Morgantown, W.Va., Nya Bingie, with Mule. ($150 plus points)
Sat 4/20: Charlottesville, VA, Tokyo Rose (w/Sliang Laos) ($100 plus points)
Sun 4/21: Philadelphia, Nick's
Mon 4/22: Richmond, VA, Twisters, (w/Jettison Charlie and Sliang Laos)
Tues 4/23: drive/Charlotte, NC???/DC???
Weds 4/24: Atlanta, BLT's
Thurs 4/25: Savannah, GA, Velvet Elvis, with Bug Hummer
Fri 4/26: Athens, GA, The Landfill (w/Freemasonry)
Sat. 4/27: Chapel Hill, NC, Lizard and Snake, with Cole and Bug Hummer
Sun, 4/28: nyc??dc??
Mon 4/29: NYC, brownies.
Tues: 4/30 Rochester, NY, Bug Jar (w/Hilkka)
Wed 5/1: Boston, Middle East (w/Erdody's new band; Crown Heights?)
Thurs, 5/2: Ralph's, Worcester MA.
Fri 5/3 umass/Portland/vassar college
sat 5/4
Sun 5/5
Mon 5/6: ???

reasonable ending: Boston/philly/Rochester/northampton or Worcester/dc, if need
be; all easily accessed. show in NYC??

"Reasonable Ending": This itinerary is a key prop for the next chapter.

Walter Mondale, George McGovern, and Your Shitty Band That No One Likes

All bands fail.

—Joe Carducci, former co-owner of SST Records, author of *Rock and the Pop Narcotic*

Some bands fail more spectacularly than others, and some fail very quietly, with no witnesses. But that failure doesn't feel quiet if you're in such a band and you find yourself confronting something tougher than the general outcastness of playing weird music: blank stares from those who actually *like* weird music. I don't mean "no widespread recognition" or "no pots full of money." I mean *nothing*. No labels putting out your music. No fans coming to your shows. Because there are no fans.

If you've played in bands or spent any time within the social swirl surrounding music, you're familiar with the interested titter or two that typically greet a band's first few shows. That ripple of recognition is an amazing feeling when your band is new, and thrilling in its potential. At those first shows you come onstage and see the crowd moving toward

147

you through the darkness. The stage lights are shining in your eyes, so you can't make out any faces, but you still sense the curiosity and eagerness in those bodies. The problem arises when it's three or four years later and your band has silently glided past new and kind of interesting and is now familiar and unbeloved. Your friends make excuses for not coming to your shows. You play to empty rooms, and the songs feel like cardboard, and you stand onstage atop unsteady legs, avoiding the eyes of anyone still watching. (Often all we had was conviction. When that went, what else was left?) But you still have to act like you believe, even though the evidence overwhelmingly indicates that no one else does, and that evidence gradually gnaws a hole in you. Once your band lands here, there's never a late-career comeback. There's no rock band equivalent to *The Rookie*. You're dead. The only question is when you'll realize it, too.

Peter Prescott was the youngest member of Mission of Burma, and at a very tender age he saw terms like "legendary" applied to his band. Nothing else he did in music—he played in Volcano Suns, Kustomized, and the Peer Group, among others—made such an impact, though, to be fair, not much else did. But he told me a very cool thing: "I'd be kind of bummed out if I didn't experience the more modest pleasure of being in a scrappy little messed-up band that thirty people in each city care about." I'm grateful I experienced that, too. The problem is when that's your audience and most of them drift away.

I started Vineland in late 1991. Bitch Magnet had been a trio, so this would be a quartet: two guitars, very loud, songs built around alternate tunings and odd time signatures, very aggressive and, for lack of a better term, very rock. Riffs but no big major-key singalong choruses. By then the tyranny of vocals exhausted me—it still does sometimes—so in this band the singing would be understated, primarily spoken, fighting to be heard above the band. Having learned a lesson from getting booted out of Bitch Magnet, I made myself the key man: songwriter and singer. Since I was going to be so annoying about vocals, it made sense to just take the bullet. Also, the last thing you ever want to do is audition frontmen. David Lee Roth is great in Van Halen, but you do not want to live with that every day. (Evidently neither did they.)

Vineland lasted four and a half years. We released two singles and appeared on one Australian compilation and one Spanish compilation. If you, too, perceive something uniquely heartbreaking about the phrase "appeared on one Australian compilation and one Spanish compilation," well, imagine *applying it to your own band*. We also recorded two unreleased albums—or, to be more precise, we recorded one album and then rerecorded much of it with a new rhythm section a year and a half later. We toured America three times, going as far west as Kansas City, as far east as Boston, as far north as Minneapolis, and as far south as Savannah. We played lots of weekend shows clustered in cities within a day's drive from New York. The bubble of mild enthusiasm—I mean this in highly relative terms—that greeted us when we formed quickly dissipated. We didn't hear a whisper from anyone in Europe, that dream fulfiller of every loud indie band, no matter whom we barraged with tapes. At no point was any serious record label seriously interested, unless you count the nice postcard Jonathan Poneman of Sub Pop sent us. (I don't.) We went through four drummers and five bassists, even more if you count people who filled in for one or two shows. For the last few years I was the only original member. Our longest—and final—tour, in 1996, lasted for a month. By then maybe fifteen or twenty people turned out for our hometown shows. In other cities, even less. Beyond the numbers, a dead feeling hung over those rooms. Twenty-five people in Cedar Rapids on a Tuesday night is fine, if you can feel their excitement, and you always can when it's there. On our best nights we'd draw forty or fifty souls, mostly friends and friends of friends, who'd shake my hand afterward and say something *tactful*, obligation weighing them down like a heavy coat. All the people who were there wished they weren't.

In the spring of 2013 Zack Lipez wrote an excellent piece for *The*

Talkhouse newsletter, "I Threw a Show in My Heart and Nobody Came," describing how he broke up his band, Freshkills, because, as he put it, "we had more ex-bassists than audience members." Shortly afterward I met him in an apartment in lower Manhattan on a humid afternoon. Zack, who's now the singer of Publicist UK, is tall, with chunky round black glasses and pale skin and dyed black hair. A young thirty-seven when we met. (I might have guessed thirty-one.) Skinny but slightly potbellied, prickling with a nervous energy, like the frontman he is.

"The only time I almost broke down and cried was when I got the record sales back from our last album," he told me. The tally: 336 physical copies and 27 digital tracks sold. (*Twenty-seven!* Jesus.) "Our drummer just said, 'There's no positive way of spinning this.'" There isn't, and here's how I know: Vineland self-released—by which I mean *I* self-released—a thousand copies of our second single in 1995. About four hundred of them remain entombed in a bedroom closet at my parents' house. Maybe there are more. I could count them, I guess, but to what degree must I quantify how many fans we didn't have? Meanwhile, those in search of sibling rivalries will likely find the following facts interesting: in the mid-nineties Sooyoung's band Seam toured America and Europe constantly and released well-received records on Touch and Go, while Orestes was making a living as the drummer for Walt Mink.

* * *

THE GUITARIST IN THAT FINAL VERSION OF VINELAND WAS Fred Weaver, who first got in touch with me by sending a postcard to the band's post office box to offer us a show in State College, Pennsylvania. When I wrote back to say, hey, thanks, but the guitarist quit and we need to find another one before we can play any shows, he responded by saying that he wanted to try out, and he drove to New York from a small coal-country town in central Pennsylvania called Clearfield. He was twenty and shy, tall and thin, and barely needed to shave. But he could play, understood what I was trying to do, was insanely motivated, and, though I didn't need any more convincing, owned a van. He joined up and took on too much—like more or less singlehandedly sound-proofing the practice space in our loft—without ever complaining. He also harbored his own ambitions to start a band. All of which meant tensions arose in difficult situations and in small quarters, and since we played in a struggling band and lived in a loft in which anywhere from four to six guys shared one bathroom, we spent plenty of time in both.

Our drummer was Jerry Fuchs, long before he became a legend and drummed for everyone from !!! and Maserati to MGMT and Turing Machine and, briefly, LCD Soundsystem, and longer before he became my closest friend to die young, in a stupid accident in a busted elevator at a party in Brooklyn in 2009. He dropped out of the University of Georgia and moved to Brooklyn to join the band in 1995, when he was a very young twenty, still sporting a bit of baby fat and a great deal of social awkwardness. He was also built like a pit bull: shorter than me but twice as wide, and god knows how much stronger. I'm susceptible to drummer-crushes—you've probably noticed—and I totally developed one on him. I couldn't believe my luck: Vineland was already going nowhere, but we'd grabbed one of the best drummers I'd ever heard. Kylie Wright, a dark-haired, pale-skinned photographer, played bass, joining not long before that last tour. I was twenty-eight, and she was around my age, so we were the grown-ups. Kylie was Australian, but her accent emerged only if you got enough drinks into her. She had tiny, delicate hands, but she was a really strong bassist.

I had a generalized guilt about having hired Jerry—he dropped out of college for *this*?—and I still feel as if I should apologize to Kylie, too. Because on that last Vineland tour I often thought we were touring like burglars, if burglars felt remorse. We played many cities with local bands we knew, all of whose hometown draws were much bigger than ours, since they lived there and nobody much liked us anywhere. But we'd get more than our share of the door, because we'd driven a long way and because our culture always took care of touring bands. Jerry was aghast at this practice, but we convinced him that it was either that or forgo food and gasoline. Or, rather, we didn't convince him and just did it anyway. Every night, when we got paid, I'd look down at the bills—a hundred and fifty bucks, a hundred bucks, often less—muttering thanks as I jammed them into a front pocket and quickly walked away, swallowing hard, feeling undeserving, and having taken advantage.

The plan that tour was that everyone would get a princely $10 per diem for food, but finances became so disastrous so quickly we couldn't manage even that. We were all broke, irregularly fed, and extremely crabby. At lousy fast-food joints I gobbled my burger and stared at anyone eating slowly, waiting for leftovers. There are people who live in a state of hunger. We weren't them, by any stretch: we had jobs back home and families—to paraphrase something the writer Cheryl Strayed once said, we were the impoverished elite, not the actual poor, and that's an enormous distinction—and this was someplace we were merely visiting. But still, on this tour, we were measuring wealth by the french fry. Something I jotted in a journal during that tour: *When you're this broke, your relationship with food changes. If it's in front of you, you eat it, and anything on the table is fair game. You stuff yourself, to stave off hunger for as long as possible, then do it again. Eating less and lightly is for rich people.*

I overweighted Chicago on the tour, because playing Chicago was more or less the entire point. Chicago was home to lots of friends and bands and studios and labels. Something could happen there. Or at least some people would show up. But I got greedy and booked us Friday at the Empty Bottle and the subsequent Monday at Lounge Ax. These were rival clubs, each suspicious and paranoid about the other, and they hated it when bands played both places. My move, once discovered, pissed everyone off and cannibalized our tiny draw. Silkworm headlined the show at Lounge Ax, so there was a decent crowd. Afterward

Sue Miller, the owner and manager and a generally beloved person, kachinged the cash register behind the bar and handed me a few bills. "Here's some money for your band, Jon."

Seventy-five dollars. In Chicago. The one city where I thought we'd do well.

I was very sensitive about money, mainly because I didn't have any, and though I told myself over and over that money didn't matter, being this broke so close to thirty was frightening. Around this time I co-wrote and performed a score for an NYU grad student production. My fee, for several weeks' rehearsals and a week's worth of shows, was five hundred bucks. No argument there: I'd agreed to that sum and was happy just getting paid. Except that I *wasn't* getting paid, and I really, really needed the money, so I visited a theater prof named Nance, the faculty adviser for the show and the closest thing to an authority to whom I could complain. An assistant milled about her office as I asked, politely, for my check. Nance told me to keep waiting for it. And, she suggested, if I *really* needed the money now, I could always borrow it from the director—she knew he and I were old friends.

Always question the judgment of anyone willing to be called *Nance*. I still regret not throwing a stapler, or saying something, or even staring for a long moment with a cocked eyebrow. Something. Anything. But I didn't, because I was ashamed, and shame can make you freeze. (And, worse, someone else witnessed that shame.) As I was ashamed when Sue handed me the few bills, and I found I couldn't refuse or complain. Charity once more. And had I heard a hint that we were being done a favor we could never call in again?

Here's some money for your band.

* * *

VINELAND'S ENDGAME HAPPENED DURING THE WANING moon of that era in the nineties in which major labels were lunging spastically toward virtually any established indie band. Even though, by then, many signings had resulted in sales that were visible only with a microscope. Vineland or Freshkills numbers, albeit for giant entertainment corporations that expected six- or seven-figure sales. (The one record on Geffen by Hardvark—its drummer was Bob Rising, who'd formerly played in Poster Children and Sooyoung's band Seam—sold 372 copies, according to Soundscan.) But there were still a few late fluke hits from bands we knew. Hum, from Champaign, was briefly all over the radio in 1995 with "Stars." Hum primarily played a pedestrian version of the this-is-the-soft-part/NOW-THIS-IS-THE-LOUD-PART thing, and their drummer had a huge thing for Bitch Magnet. Vineland played a few shows with them, and the drummer invariably cornered me to ask incredibly picayune questions about Orestes's drum gear and technique. That year, I'd drive over the Williamsburg Bridge to go drink at Max Fish on a Friday or Saturday night, listening to the big FM rock station, and "Stars" would come on. The following Wednesday Vineland would play to a dozen people in a basement in the very pre–*Sex and the City* Meatpacking District. Hum's subsequent work went nowhere, but they still squeezed through one of the occasional wormholes in the musical universe and scored a hit big enough to sell a few hundred thousand records.

I didn't want to be like Hum. I didn't want the major-label deal. I didn't want to be a rock star. I didn't want to get rich. It was a drag to know that bands I didn't like toured all the time and only returned to their hometowns, glamorously exhausted, to rest and drink and tell road stories until they all got in the van again—maybe even a fucking *bus*—for another six-week circuit around the United States or Canada or Europe. I wanted what I called just-enough. I wanted people to hear my band. I wanted to be known and respected. I didn't want the tour bus. (I did want the van.) All I wanted was just-enough people buying our records, so there was just-enough of an audience to tour ambitiously. Just-enough was probably ten thousand to fifteen thousand people worldwide. Zack Lipez wrote that he wanted Freshkills to be Murder

City Devils famous: successful enough to get by on touring seven months a year while bartending a few nights a week when he was at home. Needless to say, neither Freshkills nor Vineland had just-enough. Not even close.

* * *

EACH MORNING ON THAT LAST VINELAND TOUR, AS WE headed off to the next city, I saw a vanful of deflated faces and knew better than anyone that nothing would get better that day, or the day after that, or the following week. I started asking, "What, you expected this to be *fun?*" Often several times a day. Meanwhile, Jerry and Fred were becoming best friends, forming an impenetrably tight circle with its own inside references and van rituals inflicted on everyone else. One of them involved choosing a radio station and keeping it on until the signal faded. Fred and Jerry routinely sought out the worst classic rock stations they could find and insisted on singing along to Spacehog's "In the Meantime"—the noxious song of the moment—while playing it at top volume. I had a very low threshold for tolerating classic rock, not to mention Spacehog. Which they both knew.

No boss ever experiences the workers' camaraderie. Though the boss at a real job gets certain perks, like making more money. In indie rock the boss *loses* the most. (As I did.) And it's especially lonely to lead a band when Daddy can't feed the family. One lunchtime or dinner, before playing the Bug Jar in Rochester—a venue so idiosyncratic that any band had to split itself up between two tiny stages—I sat alone while my bandmates chose a table across the room. There I marinated in bad vibes, thinking, *They're talking about me. I know they're fucking talking about me.* Over and over again. Couldn't make it stop.

In Pittsburgh we played at a coffeehouse, opening for a ferocious and then-obscure trio from Portland called Sleater-Kinney. Someone wrote JON FINE IS A DICK on the wall in the women's bathroom. That someone, I learned much later, was probably in my band. But the other indignities of that last tour weren't colorful enough to make for funny stories, like the time Eggs' Andrew Beaujon, hung over and huddling miserably in his sleeping bag on a long van ride, puked *into* said sleeping bag. Or the time a barefoot Anne Eickelberg, the bassist in Thinking Fellers Union Local 282, stepped into a pile of fresh dog shit while looking for the bathroom late one night while bunking at an unfamiliar house. Or the time, many years later, when, bereft of any other option, Fred was forced to shit in his toolbox while stuck in traffic on a treeless highway during a solo tour. Nothing like that happened to us. And no matter how bad any tour was, you still spotted random dazzlements amid the vast strangenesses of America. In one rest-stop bathroom near Macon, Georgia, unbelievably detailed pre-Craigslist men-seeking-men graffiti instructed interested parties to show up in a specified location and "touch cock" to signal interest. While on my way to dinner before the show in Richmond, I paused to light cigarettes for two grateful quadriplegics. And at our last show, in surpassingly depressing Worcester, Massachusetts, the small crowd went batshit. The kind of night in a small town where no one knows you but you make the most unlikely new fans, like a middle-aged auto repair shop owner who for some reason showed up, still wearing his work uniform. I'm sure that show sounded good—wound up tight, pissed off and burning. Bands about to break up often do, if they channel the tensions correctly.

By then Fred had quit, after a blowup one night in Georgia, though he agreed to play the shows we'd already booked. A major complication, since he owned the van, and he and Jerry and I all still lived in the same loft. After Fred left, and one bad post-tour practice as a trio, Jerry called a band meeting, at which he very gently announced, "I don't want to do this anymore."

I was dicking around with a bass, to relieve tension. *So there it is*, I thought. I put the bass down and said, "Me, too. How about you, Kylie?" Band over. It didn't take five minutes. I probably went out for a beer afterward, alone. By then Fred and I were barely speaking, and I was ready to avoid Jerry for months. But he wouldn't let me, and I loved him for it.

* * *

WAS VINELAND GOOD? I THOUGHT SO. AND ON THAT LAST tour we reached our peak. Each night onstage Fred and I threw all our frustrations into acts of musical passive aggression that somehow worked. Besides our unspoken hostile amplifier standoff every night— *I* will turn down mine as soon as *he* turns down his—we each embellished our individual parts more and more without working said bits out with each other, without even *listening* to each other. Judging by the tape from one of our last shows, a skull-crushingly loud one at the Middle East in Boston, this worked much better than it should have, the songs constantly assuming new shapes before quickly snapping back into the correct forms. But it's no loss to humanity that the final Vineland album remains unreleased, even if it's the first full album Jerry recorded. Once I could stand to listen to it again after he died, I was horrified at how snug a box I had forced his drumming into. Also, I hated my voice. My singing sounded thin and strangulated and nasal—a whine, not a growl—even after I had learned to breathe in time with the music onstage, to have enough air for each line and keep my rhythm in sync with the band. It felt weak, and I grew to despise it.

We'd built the band to my specifications. I wrote the songs, sang them, and had veto power over most aesthetic decisions. (Here I could fault myself for adding too much sentimentality and poppy touches, out of insecurity, but let's set that aside for now.) I contacted clubs and labels. It didn't happen for us. If we weren't as good as the other bands I played in—it's still hard to think this part through, but sometimes I suspect that's really the story—and didn't go as far as they did, any blame goes on me. I know I should be stoic and expect nothing from a band except the joy of the music. I know I should be thrilled I wrote a few songs for Vineland that I'll sing to myself forever. But Vineland broke me. After we split up, it killed any desire to start a band, which had been my sole animating impulse since I was twelve. And while I still identified as a musician—what else could I be?—I lost much of my appetite for playing music, and all my confidence. I went back to an anonymous cubicle job writing and editing a newsletter with a minuscule readership, halfheartedly played bass in Alger Hiss, and tried not to think about it too much.

I also realized something important, even if I wasn't proud of it at all: there were people brave enough, and strong enough, to place all their bets on music, no matter what happened, and I was no longer one of them.

✳ ✳ ✳

BUT I'VE BEEN DOING ALL THE TALKING, AND THE SUN IS SET-ting over the Hudson, and Zack is just sitting here.

Zack? Are you heartbroken? Relieved?

"Both," he said, and then doesn't talk about relief at all. "I'm heartbroken that nobody liked my band. I did it for nine years, and nobody liked my band.

"I'm not sad to be out of Freshkills," he continued. "I'm sad that nobody ever gave a shit about any single fucking thing we ever did. It's a constant sorrow. I'm going to take it to my grave."

True story: Walter Mondale ran into George McGovern not long after Mondale lost to Reagan in 1984. They had a lot in common. Two liberal senators from prairie states. Two candidates who lost forty-nine states to an aloof Republican opponent they plainly regarded as unworthy. Mondale asked McGovern, who was crushed by Nixon in 1972, "George, how long does it take to get over a big loss like this?" McGovern replied, "I'll let you know when it happens." Ha-ha—though not really. McGovern repeated this line for the rest of his life, until he died, in 2012.

I didn't share this with Zack. It's rather overblown to equate the heartbreak of your band's failure to the heartbreak of someone convinced he'll be the next president—and who spent all his time trying to convince everyone else that he would be the next president—but then finds out, very quickly and very definitively, that he never will. But this is how I feel about Vineland, and how I imagine Zack feels about Freshkills. One day I'll get over it. I'll let you know when it happens.

I Was Wrong

ut I'm not telling the whole story. Because I missed so much of it while it happened.

I keep saying our world was ascetic, boring, so not-like-rock. So little sex. So few drugs harder than pot. Sometimes I saw this wasn't quite true.

In the mid-nineties a friend who played in a band in Los Angeles visited New York every few months and we'd hit the bars. He liked to get losing-your-language drunk. After a certain hour, if you heard him on the phone, you'd think he was drooling. *That* drunk. But just before that he'd suggest, then demand, that we find some coke. I had no idea how, and always tried to change the subject, but even in a strange city he could parse any room within five minutes: *I can't get coke here, I can only get E, let's go.* Then he'd tell me about the threesome he had with an icy blonde and a male friend, whom, he insisted on assuring me, he *did not touch at all, not even once,* during said encounter. But that was L.A. Not New York. Here we dressed badly and burrowed inward. Here we so rarely acted on what we wanted. Our fuel was unfulfilled desire, channeled elsewhere. Right?

Or maybe I wasn't understanding what was really going on around me. One night I was out late in the East Village, getting drunk with a woman who was also a musician. Pale-skinned, giant eyes, she was everyone's crush, and I felt fortunate to be there with her and a woman she knew. After the bartender announced last call, we walked toward an apartment, tightly pressed together, with me in the middle. At least that's how I remember it.

When we arrived, the musician—let's call her Maroon—sent her friend upstairs and pulled me aside to chat on the street corner. The look on her face suggested she knew secrets and felt far more confident than I did. A confusing conversation, out there at a quarter to four. Confusing to me, at least. Maroon asked me, half-smiling and looking sideways, to come upstairs for a while and then leave. *So she's hitting on me*, I thought. She recently broke up with her boyfriend—someone I knew, who was also in a band, of course—and I wanted to know if fooling around with me was some rebound or revenge move. I started in on *Are you doing this because of him?* Looking important and off into the distance, for effect. Taxis drowsed their way up First Avenue, beyond an overflowing orange garbage can. No one else was around.

Then her face rearranged into bewilderment and (I thought) a mocking grin. Maybe you saw this coming, but I didn't: Maroon was after her friend, not me.

Then *why did she want me upstairs at all?* I didn't ask, because I was humiliated that I had misunderstood her, and still felt like I misunderstood what might happen next. I followed her upstairs, gulped half a beer, ran out the door. She protested that I shouldn't go, but it didn't sound sincere. I ran past that garbage can, hailed a cab—a luxury in those days—and headed to my practice space, where I grabbed my guitar, turned my amp way up, closed my eyes, and played until long after sunrise.

Looking back now, I think: threesome. You fucked up. But I still don't know. Do you?

It wasn't that no one got laid on tour. Once in Detroit, late at night after the show, a musician disappeared to make a quick phone call, came back chuckling, and said he was leaving to visit his cousin. Everyone else rolled their eyes. Because, they knew, he had cousins across the country. All of them women, all of whom he only saw late at night, all of them unknown to his live-in girlfriend.

My friend from L.A. wasn't the only one who wanted serious drugs. Eventually I realized why the first drummer in a band that would later get famous was so often dazed and distant and falling asleep, even at shows and parties. Or why I once ran into him as he walked west from Avenue C and he laughed and said he was out of money. Sometimes at night I ran into Jim or Travis, which are not their names, when their blue eyes looked especially beautiful. For a long time I didn't know why: dope had erased their pupils. I last saw Travis one Sunday night around eleven as he packed up his drums. He'd found someone to buy them right then. It was a classic, gorgeous old kit from the sixties. Ludwig, maybe, or Gretsch. He might have gotten a hundred bucks. Far less than they were worth, but I think the buyer sensed that it was a distress sale.

One of these guys overdosed and died. Another records himself reading poetry and posts it online. Heroin is very bad for you.

In Six Finger Satellite's early days, half the band were junkies. Even on tour. Which, by the way: *crazy.* How can you feed a habit when your band makes two hundred bucks a night? For one thing, their drummer Rick Pelletier told me, someone was FedExing dope to them as they traveled the country. (Important to note: Rick was *not* one of the junkies.) "We'd go to some mom-and-pop indie record store and say, 'Is there a package here for Six Finger Satellite?'" Rick said. "The unknowing counter person would say, 'Yes, there is.' It was filled with drugs. Which would then be taken very quickly."

"Quickly you resort to stealing," admitted Juan MacLean, who *was* one of the addicts. "Even from the other guys in the band. J. [Six Finger's singer J. Ryan] caught me breaking into his apartment." J. was also one of Juan's closest friends. Previously Juan admitted to a different technique to solving a different dope-on-the-road problem: when faced with border crossings, he hid his drugs in his bandmates' suitcases. Anyway, Six Finger was on tour, had just played a show, and they all were bunking at some punk rock house. Late that night or early the next morning, a resident did dope and turned blue. Panic. "Someone wanted to call 911. I said, *You're not calling*," said Juan. "I remember unplugging the phone." Luckily that resident lived. When Six Finger Satellite got back from that tour, the other guys dropped off Juan and the other junkie, fired them both, and told them never to contact the rest of the band again. Juan went to rehab and got clean, which is why he's still making records. The other guy didn't. He died.

Not everybody was in the monastery. Many of us had a crooked-grinning, slippery side and locked ourselves in bathrooms or snuck over to Avenue D when no one was looking. And, really, it was okay, because you could convince yourself that everybody did it. Everybody needed their cousins. Everybody wanted a taste of something sweet before turning out the light in their tiny rooms, and a dollar brownie or a carrot juice from the corner deli wasn't doing it anymore.

I knew you could get by on crumbs while living this life, as long as sometimes a woman's in your room at 4 a.m., or a few bartenders or baristas or taco stand employees slide you free drinks and food, or, occasionally, an excited fan stops you on the street. These made up for the times you checked the bank account on the first of the month, rent due, and saw you had $97, made up for wearing the same shabby clothes for years, made up for buying canned tuna only when it went on sale. You'd be amazed how sustaining those little moments were. You could live off any of them for another week, easy. Until they stopped happening.

I thought music alone could feed us forever, but it turned out to be too slender a diet. I thought we were about opposition. I thought this was us and them—them being the big-time music biz and commercial radio. I thought we were supposed to keep fighting. But how long could you accept your half-assed lot of being fanzine-famous—no, just fanzine-*known*—and kind of starving? Was this why the standard indie rock emotional response was to duck your head, avert eye contact, not admit to wanting anything—because you were never going to get it? Were twee bands here because adulthood meant adult desires that the world would never satisfy?

I saw more and more bands in which no one onstage seemed to be trying. They looked like they didn't give a shit, and not in the interesting way: the way a waiter at an indifferent café at 4 p.m. doesn't give a shit. I'd see them and think, *Why are you doing this?* One night I saw Helium when Mary Timony played with her then-boyfriend Ash from Polvo. I loved Helium's early records, and Timony's track record offers plenty of evidence that she's a serious badass. But live, that night, the two of them were so sleepy and uninvolved I was like, *Christ, you two. Take a nap.* They both seemed exhausted—in the sense of having nothing left to offer—and absolutely without joy, or vitality, or sex, or much of anything, really. I went to see Bugskull—excited, because I adored their singles—and watched the singer shamble through the set, simpering, unable to meet the audience's eyes. He kept telescoping his head into his shoulders, like a turtle; he kept shrinking back from the microphone and the lip of the stage. I left disgusted. Couldn't anyone *pretend to believe a tiny bit* in what they were doing? Move beyond the rut of modesty and understatement that we stuck with so long it became its own cliché? After ten or fifteen years all our indie rock modesty and seriousness only meant: no pleasure. Not much hope. No fun at all. A sameness had descended on a culture once so sprawling and uncategorizable. So remind me again: why were we here?

I found myself thinking, *I wish I could quit.* I'd have money in the bank. Wouldn't be pissed off all the time. Life would be easier, I knew, if *I could just fucking stop.* But I couldn't. Even after Vineland fell apart. "I don't mean to be melodramatic, but there are times when it feels like an affliction. A terminal illness. You're never going to get rid of it," Tim Midyett, the bassist from Silkworm, once told me.

I couldn't let go. Not yet, anyway. I wore the same T-shirts over and over again. The same flannel shirts until they frayed off my back. And suddenly you were in your thirties. You hadn't worked at a real job in years, unlike your old pals from college. Some of them still made a fuss over your band and sometimes came out to see you play. (At least on weekends. Not many made it out during the week anymore.) To them, you were interesting. Maybe even famous-ish. But they were married. Some had kids. Jobs became careers. Meanwhile, you knew some things they didn't. Your record sales had plateaued, or were shrinking. Your crowds and guarantees weren't getting bigger. You played the same clubs in Berlin or Minneapolis or San Francisco or Dublin each tour, and each time you saw the same faces. Aging faces. Suddenly the crowd was older. (Were you, too? It dawned on you: yes.) You'd stare out at the crowd and think, *Maybe this is as big as it gets.* Or *Maybe a few years ago was as big as it gets.* You still swore up and down you'd never sign to a major label, but this wasn't exactly a choice. They stopped being interested a long time ago. If they ever were. So what the fuck do you do?

No, really. What the fuck do you do?

*** *** ***

BY THE MID-NINETIES THINKING FELLERS UNION LOCAL 282 had been around almost a decade. They'd released four impressively sprawling and idiosyncratic albums on Matador. A fervent fanbase adored them. They got reams of great press. They also played the same clubs each tour, and they toured a lot, and were all well into their thirties, surviving on a band salary that peaked at seven hundred bucks a month. Then, in 1995, they got an offer to tour with the dreadful band

Live, back when Live was one of the biggest bands in the world. According to their bassist Anne Eickelberg, this is how that went:

> We kept saying, "We want to tour with bigger bands. Let's get more exposure." People kept coming up with really insane things. Like "You want to tour with Toad the Wet Sprocket?" Where does that even come from? Then: Live. We didn't know who Live were. But then we were like, let's just do it.
>
> It was a full tour. Twenty-something shows across the country. Secondary markets, mostly. Total test of character, because the audiences fucking despised us. We got stuff thrown at us all the time. Kids just screaming, "You suck!" for a whole set. Sometimes it was like a high that you could ride, because it was just so ridiculous. In his tour diary Brian [Hageman, her bandmate] said something like "We're standing there looking like their fucking mom and dad, and we're the obstacle between them and Live, so they're really, really angry about it." But you'd be done super early, go back to catering, have really amazing food, have people move all your shit for you. Play a half-hour set and get paid a lot of money.
>
> It was great fodder for future conversations. We played an outdoor venue in Knoxville, and after our set one guy in Live nonchalantly came up to me and said, "I cracked the window on the tour bus. You guys sounded all right." Another day he breezed up to us in catering, shoved Billboard at us, and pointed, so we could see that Live's record had reached number one: "Just showing this to you because I can." We were also there to see the delivery of their matching robes, which had the album logo on them.
>
> But we knew within a couple days: there's no way we could ever do this. We're too weird. We're not right. This will not happen.

Other bands found that the world had stopped caring. Mudhoney's third album on Warner Brothers, *Tomorrow Hit Today*, came out in

1998, and sold roughly a tenth as many copies as their earlier records. Sebadoh released *The Sebadoh* in 1999 to what Lou Barlow describes as the open disdain of their label, Sub Pop. It sold a fraction of the band's previous releases, and Sebadoh toured in front of a rapidly disappearing audience. "Our last show in that cycle," Barlow recalled, "was playing to like twenty-five people at the Gypsy Tea Room in Dallas. A place we had sold out a year before." The Gypsy Tea Room's capacity? Approximately seven hundred. Barlow now shrugs, "I just thought, *Message received.*"

Meanwhile, the real estate and stock market boom during President Clinton's second term reshaped the American city. Which is a dry and academic way to say that, as happens to every generation, cheap neighborhoods became unaffordable as demand kicked in for real estate in the places we helped gentrify. Beginning in 1992, Unrest's Mark Robinson lived in a house about five miles from Washington, D.C., at 715 North Wakefield Street in Arlington, Virginia, and ran his label Teen-Beat from there, too. He and some fellow musicians rented it for virtually nothing. Andrew Beaujon of Eggs recalls paying $234 a month, a bargain good enough to overlook the rats that lived there, too. Eventually the landlord offered-slash-demanded: buy this house for $135,000. Which, for the residents, might as well have been three million bucks. (At its peak, Robinson said, Unrest was a full-time job for its members and paid them twelve grand a year. In Beaujon's highest-grossing year as a more or less full-time musician, he made about $9,000.)

The denizens of Teen-Beat House were evicted at the end of August 1998. The house sold for $160,000 the next month, sold again for $381,000 in July 1999, and in 2005 sold for $857,000. In other words, the featureless, poorly maintained, and frankly unattractive group house where underemployed indie rockers dodged rats is now probably a million-dollar home. The same happened in neighborhoods we all could afford in the nineties: Silver Lake in Los Angeles, the Mission in San Francisco, the East Village and Lower East Side of Manhattan,

Wicker Park and Ukrainian Village in Chicago. As always, artists and musicians didn't leave those cities *en masse*. They got pushed to other neighborhoods, or Philadelphia. But losing your cheap foothold in your chosen city tends to inspire reflection.

"I got kicked out of Teen-Beat House and moved to a much more expensive house," Robinson said. "A lot of record stores were closing or had already closed. It seemed like the whole thing was disappearing." He moved to Boston, took his first full-time job, got married, and essentially closed the book on being an active touring musician. Among the bands we knew, stories like his played out endlessly. In 1996 Thinking Fellers quit touring. "I just felt like I was on this accelerating train, and I better jump off pretty soon and learn how to do stuff that could help me stay alive," Eickelberg said. Sooyoung's band Seam released their final album in 1998 and broke up in 2000. "I was a math major," said an ever-succinct Sooyoung. "The numbers didn't add up." Orestes left Walt Mink in early 1997, after the band got dropped by its second major label. Disgusted, he quit music, packed up his gorgeous wine-red Yamaha drum kit we both loved, enrolled in the University of Arizona, and began working toward a masters in engineering.

* * *

THEN IT WAS 2000. I WAS THIRTY-TWO. I STARTED DETUNING my guitars to C—lower means heavier—but wasn't sure what else to do with them. I had no band. I had no job. I lived in Williamsburg in a third-floor walk-up apartment filthy from years of grime and neglect, a baked-in filthiness you couldn't scrub away. My living room was eye level with the Brooklyn-Queens Expressway. (Some people who live very near a highway will tell you the road sounds eventually become a soothing white noise, like the ocean, or a summer breeze through leafy trees. They're wrong.) At night a fast-moving stream of red brake lights zipped past, so close that, when the wind was right, you could spit from the living room onto passing cars. When trucks passed, the entire building trembled. An endless stream of soot crept past the decaying window frames, whether the windows were open or shut, and settled on the floors, blackening socks and feet. The only sink was in the kitchen, so you brushed your teeth over unwashed dishes. I watched mice hang out across from the desk where I attempted to eke out a living as a freelance writer. They huddled beneath the radiator, bobbing up and down as they breathed, staring at me. I stared back. Some afternoons that was it. That was all that went on in the apartment.

I never thought I had good game with women, but a few had sex with me *after* seeing this place, so maybe it was better than I thought.

Manhattan was unrecognizable. Cell phones sprouted out of everyone's right hand, except mine. Back in Brooklyn, my musician friends got their first decent jobs, started spending $200 on jeans, and knew all the new restaurants. What I spent on clothes each year was enough for a couple new pairs of black Levi's—505s, thirty bucks at Canal Jean—and band T-shirts I bought at shows. No one else still wore black jeans, and mine were all a little too baggy and caught in the no-man's-land between "still black" and "nicely faded." My hand-me-down dresser was packed with ill-fitting extra-large T-shirts. The size we all bought in the eighties and early nineties because *why*? I refused to cut my thinning hair. I had great hair in my twenties—those long, springy curls that went halfway down my back. I grew it out when I went—in my mind, at least—from loserdom to belongingness. I thought it made me cool. I thought it made me attractive. But the top was getting sparse, and the look was getting very Ben Franklin. In my bad clothes, in my bad hair, I thought, *Where was my tribe?* I felt homeless. And was coming close to dressing the part.

One afternoon in the spring of 2000, looking forward to celebrating a friend's birthday that night, I realized that I was out of money. I lived from check to check, but sometimes they came late. There was, basically, nothing in the bank or in my wallet. I called my girlfriend Anne Marie at work for a very unpleasant conversation. I'm glad I don't remember it. But that weekend she sat me down at the rickety, stained kitchen table wedged next to the radiator, a pad in one hand and a pen in the other, and demanded to know my debts and income. The latter was pretty bad. This was when I would labor a week on a lengthy music piece for an alternative weekly, which would pay about a hundred and fifty bucks. (If I was lucky, I resold it and earned another hundred.)

The debts were much worse. Close to twenty grand on credit cards, with interest rates approaching 20 percent. Also a four-figure sum I owed to the IRS.

Anne Marie stared at me from across the table. A tiny Filipina who worked at a sports magazine, she'd gotten a late start in journalism, but she was ambitious and worked harder and longer than anyone else I'd met. She knew a bit about music, and my being a musician once made me more interesting than the other guys pursuing her. We fell madly in bed with each other, as the saying goes, she essentially moved in before we knew each other at all, and we had lots of sex, until we didn't.

She had such a beautiful face, but there was no love left in her eyes and it was hard to meet her gaze. When I looked down, I saw the stained tabletop and the sheet of paper with her neat columns of numbers.

Sometimes you see exactly who you are. I was no better off than any embittered sad-sack rock guy working for the one record store in his small town, the guy with receding hair and a belly that hung over his jeans a little more each day. The guy who had essentially stopped trying.

It was time to give in. The cost of living like this was way too high.

The first day of my first real job in a very long time was June 6, 2000, when I started working as a reporter for a magazine called *Advertising Age*. Anne Marie was so plainly happy about this that it felt good being around her again, judging from the few photos taken of us that summer. She and I didn't last through autumn. (Sometimes it's only a few months from "you're the best thing that ever happened to me" to "I don't want to do this anymore," but that's another story.) But by then I had a steady paycheck, something to do, and somewhere to go every day. What a surprise to discover how comforting that routine could be. I had been fired six and a half weeks into my last real job, and while that memory and the nerves every new employee experiences sometimes soured my stomach and kept me up at night, soon I felt the everyday satisfactions of doing a job well enough: a small sense of mastery, an understanding of what was required, a degree of confidence that you could do it. The relief of having found a place. A few months into that job, I started another band.

I was alone again, but the early aughts were a very good time to be single in New York. It was time to try hedonism for a change.

This Is Me, I'm Dancing, and I Like It

Maybe this part starts in the small living room with a stage where the pirate radio station put on shows. An illegal and unpermitted venue in the middle of a quiet block in Brooklyn, above which a movie-set view of the Williamsburg Bridge loomed. A gargoyle hung from the building's façade. To enter, you walked up a narrow staircase that squeaked and groaned until you arrived in a compact but perfect space, maybe twenty feet by twenty feet. Getting in cost about five bucks. The lights were dim, and all the walls were white. I don't know who built the stage, but it was elevated, framed by a proscenium, and looked absolutely natural up against the front window, as if it had been there forever. There were a couple of street-sized plastic trash cans filled with ice, bearing bodega beers on sale for a buck or two. The lighting was low and, like everything else there, effortless. Shows happened here for years. Very strange bands played. Women in the audience churned their hips like washing machines to whatever crazy, noisy destruction was onstage. You had to load in your gear up that flight of stairs, but even so it was one of my favorite places to play, anywhere. I wish I had some photos, because it still feels like we dreamed it.

Or maybe it starts at Rubulad, the very long-running party that, by the time I went, had moved to the enormous Brooklyn basement of a grimy and unremarkable building across from the bridge. If "basement" sounds close and claustrophobic, then I'm not expressing the scale correctly. Imagine a gymnasium. Maybe even two. Parties at Rubulad sprawled into many rooms, and outdoors, and onto a tar-papered roof. The dance floor was as big as a basketball court. Just past it was the room where you could buy a green-gray goop with resiny black flecks said to be absinthe, which was still illegal, and gave you a drunk mingled with the whizzing feeling you got from E and hangovers that made your entire face hurt. In another room there were pot brownies.

But maybe it starts in the side hallway to Plant Bar, its de facto backstage, amid stacks of Sheetrock and plywood and piled-up refuse, where friends drank and sometimes broke laws governing the possession and use of certain substances.

If you knew where to look in the first years of this century, New York was full of places where all rules were suspended. It was a great gift to be permitted a second adolescence here, at the last possible moment, while I was in my early thirties: still young enough to have both a real job and the stamina to arrange each week around nightlife. (It was also the last era in which you could hide being in a band from everyone at work.) A real-er job meant that you had a bit more coin, and in 2000 you could live really well in Williamsburg on a thirty-year-old's creative-class salary—with your own apartment, nights out in bars and restaurants, ample street parking for your beater used car—as the neighborhood offered up its last gasps of wildness. There was no better place to stage your last years of being single. Musician pals were suddenly DJs, and dance floors filled with women grinding into you—a miracle after decades spent in sexless and body-denying indie rock. The discovery that dance music was body music, wasn't always twee and poppy, and could be as visceral and reptile brain–based as heavy metal. The realization that there was nothing wrong with pleasure. A huge relief, after over fifteen years in an underground that seemed entirely uninterested in it, where bands felt that the correct thing to do, when a song became popular or even liked, was to stop playing it live. My bands did that. My friends' bands did that. We *loved* doing it—being what a pal once called *a band that doesn't give you what you want*. Around 2000, though, a different New York. A different culture. A different audience, younger and incredibly adventurous, all of whom dressed way better than the record-store clerks who set the fashion template for my generation. (Another revelation: jeans that fit.)

A band like Black Dice—so abstract as to approximate musique concrète, whose performances reliably exceeded 120 decibels—routinely drew hundreds to gigs at one-off semi-legal spaces on the border of Williamsburg and Bushwick or Greenpoint and Queens. Music that was "difficult"—which generally means "not at all song-based"—coexisted with the joy-seeking you'd expect to find among postgraduate art kids who discovered drugs and underused warehouse spaces big enough for circuses. Parties lasted past sunrise, so deep in the boroughs' underpopulated industrial outskirts that you sometimes saw rabbits or raccoons dashing down the streets.

Like all lovely collisions between art and music in New York, that time is now over. But it lasted far longer than I ever thought possible. Some reading this will argue that these days were far removed from Williamsburg's true wild years, when the neighborhood was desolate, wholly inhospitable to outsiders, legitimately lawless, and dirt-cheap, which I believe means you could get by without having any sort of job. They're probably right. But how about we just talk about the neighborhood bar that openly sold cocaine?

Which some genius named Kokie's Place.

Where some genius *hung out an awning* that read KOKIE'S PLACE, an awning that presided, in fading glory, over an increasingly well-trafficked stretch of Berry Street. I first heard about Kokie's at a rooftop party in 1999. Three of us went the following Saturday night. (I left first, around 7:30 the next morning.) Chatter claimed it had been named for the coquí tree frog found in Puerto Rico and the Dominican Republic. Kokie's—no one used the second word—sold $2 mini-bottles of Budweiser, those tiny seven-ouncers you can disappear in a gulp without even trying. Two giant yellow Igloo coolers filled with ice water sat on either side of the bar. Call me crazy, but I felt that more profit was generated in the "DJ booth," where a "DJ"—always a very large man who did not appear to enjoy his work—would open the door, accept your twenty, and palm off a tiny clear or blue plastic bag. Crucially, Kokie's also provided a curtained-off area in the back room for snarfling up the goods, though "curtained-off" sounds fancier than what it was: a framed-out closet behind a shower curtain or a stained baby blanket. A bouncer—also very large and unhappy—controlled access. Five or six people could cram in there, if you really smushed into each other, and you did, getting all up in some stranger's space as if in a packed subway car, your face inches from theirs, both of you with a housekey halfway up a nostril and snuffling like warthogs. Interesting conversations were struck up here, and interesting connections forged. A friend still swears he once did bumps alongside a mother and her daughter. Such moments were part of Kokie's charm, though these were secondary to the charm of Kokie's openly selling cheap cocaine.

What tickles me to this day is how the large, unhappy bouncers got extremely agitated if you did coke in the bathroom, instead of in the closet in the back room, and threw you out *tout de suite* if they caught you. This made Kokie's something like the *exact obverse* of every other bar in the city. As the mornings wore on, condensation beaded on the oozy paint—a kind I seem to see only in south Williamsburg, which always looks sticky—that covered Kokie's walls, in dark reds and urinary yellows. Two small windows in the front room were always tightly shuttered, although if you got right up next to them, you saw daylight around the edges, because it was eight in the morning and you'd been there for six hours.

The consensus was that Kokie's sold horrifyingly bad coke, but whatever it was, it worked. Once you got past the lengthy catalog of implied threats that its unsmiling staffers broadcast, everyone at Kokie's was happy, social, beaming. Sweating Latinas danced endlessly to whatever music was playing. (Allegedly a live salsa band performed in the early evenings and on Sunday afternoons, but I never saw it. It's a point of pride that I never went to Kokie's for brunch or dinner.) Strangers talked to one another. Lord Jesus, did they talk. Management kept the lights low—mercifully—but not so low that, after 4 or 5 a.m., you could avoid noticing that the lips of the person chattering at you were ringed with dried spittle. But I got very quiet, very internal, when doing coke. I liked listening to my pulse pounding in my ears, and running the tip of my tongue over my front teeth to determine how numb they were. Those two data points, I believed, provided highly accurate readings of exactly How High I Was At That Moment, and whether or not it was time to queue up again for the curtained room.

My first night there I met a wiry Latino I will call Orlando, who had a thin mustache, long hair, and mournful eyes. He wore a wifebeater, a few thin gold chains, and a straight-brimmed Yankees cap. He did his coke off a black Bic-pen cap, after bending the last sixteenth of an inch of its thin plastic tongue to make a mini coke scoop. It looked like he knew what he was doing, and I was impressed. But Orlando was generally worried, and as the night wore on he got worse. I tried talking to him about it, but communication was difficult. I was coked up and very terse, and he seemed able to discuss only two things:

1. various unnamed people who were very unfriendly, and
2. that they would beat the absolute shit out of you if you displeased them.

Or that's what I *think* he was discussing. He never quite completed his sentences:

Orlando: Man, they, you know, they just . . . [*Shakes head.*]

Me: I know. Yeah. I know. I know. [*Runs tongue over front teeth. Eyes dart.*]

Orlando: And if they don't like you, man, they just . . . [*Shakes head. Looks down.*]

Me: [*Nodding quickly.*] Yeah. Yeah. [*I jerk my head toward the coke closet, because there's no line. Orlando, my friend, and I slip behind the curtain. My friend offers a bump off his key. Orlando shakes his head and goes back to his pen cap, still worried.*]

You might suspect that terrible things routinely happened at Kokie's, but people understood the parameters and obeyed, perhaps because plenty of muscle was in view. Kokie's had been around since the eighties and lasted a preposterously long time even after becoming commonly known among the hipster sets in several cities. It existed just before smartphones and social networks became ubiquitous, although, Jesus, I can't imagine that the bouncers would have countenanced customers playing with iPhones. (I don't recall seeing a cell phone in use there, ever, and sure as hell never touched mine.) Newcomers kept showing up each weekend—stifling gleeful giggles upon entering—and word spread. Soon local publications like *Time Out New York* and *New York Press* ran unmistakable veiled references to it. I think I saw Kokie's named outright in a review somewhere that concluded with a sentence along the lines of "I hope it never, ever, ever, ever, ever, ever, ever closes." Though it did, of course. A bar called the Levee now stands in its place.

Under no circumstances will I suggest that it's a good idea to do drugs, and—oh, God, I can't say that, who am I kidding? Even if I have good friends who lost years to drugs and almost died. This time was a useful way station, one that helped clear out bad feelings and old habits.

It changed the way I walked. It was very not-indie-rock in spirit, in its hedonism and in its moral indefensibility. As a friend of mine says, when you buy coke, you're never more than two people removed from the guy with the machine gun. But moral indefensibility was the point. As was realizing, sometimes, I needed my cousins, too. Though I'm glad all this happened during my early thirties, after I'd had years of therapy and developed a decent sense of myself, and not ten or fifteen years earlier, when I knew much less. I don't know if I would have come and gone so quickly had I known about Kokie's then.

* * *

EVERY STORY IN NEW YORK CITY IS A REAL ESTATE STORY, AND everything I could tell you about what we saw and did in the Brooklyn that's now considered "Brooklyn" is how much of it took place within cracks in the pavement. Illegal or forgotten spaces, like Kokie's or the pirate radio station or warehouses in areas blissfully ignored by all authorities, where something strange and free arose. If you knew how to look, great treasures still lurked in plain sight. I rented a practice space in a narrow warren of basement practice spaces. At our entrance the staircase leading up was covered with plywood and padlocked shut to prevent us lowly musicians from wandering through the building. But the skinny and cunning among us found we could slide through the stairway bars, so we did, and held secret Fourth of July gatherings up on the roof, because it was a tall building one block from the water with an absolutely clear view of the fireworks over the East River. We stood there, slightly stoned, sipping beers, underneath the brilliant display, in the glory of a quiet, private space amid a mad celebration. The last street whores of north-side Williamsburg—a brutally low rung of the trade—worked this block well into the first decade of the twenty-first century. Neighborhood rumors claimed that their clients were truckers and Hasids. Also on that block, for a few weeks or maybe even months, a cracked-out guy spent evenings shadowboxing beneath a streetlight across the street as we walked by, hefting our guitar cases, or loaded out for gigs. Some nights he chalked graffiti onto the sidewalk and pavement, bragging about himself, the great boxing champion. All stuck around even as the gentrifying forces of new construction and rising rents kept marching in, faster and faster. In the summers you saw skin and flesh and skimpy summer dresses and short shorts everywhere, nipples visible beneath tank tops, and it was wonderful, it was awful, the heat was relentless, you felt every breath in your crotch. I remember one white-trash-themed party, the dancing grindy and pelvic and plainly voracious. I thought, again, *Good god, why didn't we dance in the nineties?* Boys left the dance floor with hard-ons straining their jeans. A haze of desire hung in the air. I heard someone say he was waiting for everyone to start fucking so he could go jack off in the corner. I wasn't single, and my girlfriend was out of town, but I walked home alone, quickly, sweating, ablaze with desire, feasting on the images. Once home, I left the lights off, got into bed, pounded on myself, and went to sleep in my hot, under-air-conditioned apartment, the window fan roaring by my head.

It wasn't all happy faces, and dancing to lose yourself, and the wonderment of a new New York opening its arms and legs. A tightly coiled angry kid still remained in me. But even he could learn new tricks. A different way to be with music. The epiphany of a crowded dance floor: a mosh pit's much more fun if girls are there, too. And once again there was a great and simple happiness in playing guitar. I returned to standard tuning—E-A-D-G-B-E—and I'd been away from it for so long that it, too, had become new again. At night I rented movies—the strangest stuff I could find, or the Herzog or Kurosawa classics I hadn't seen—popped them into the VCR I could finally afford, watched them on the TV that sat directly on my linoleum floor, leaned back on my scavenged couch, and moved my hands around my guitar, playing as abstractedly as possible, responding only to the images, hoping to get to parts unknown.

* * *

IN NOVEMBER 2000, WHILE BUMPING ALONGSIDE THE BED-ford Avenue portion of the New York Marathon, I ran into my old friend Kevin Shea, an eccentric, ethereal dude and a very bent and powerful jazz drummer. He had just moved to New York with his girlfriend. He suggested we get together and play. I told him, sure, and did nothing. But Kevin kept calling.

A couple of weeks later I went to see some bands on a Friday night at another semi-legal venue and showed up wearing a Magma T-shirt. A guy named Jeff noticed and proceeded to talk my ear off about music.

Jeff Winterberg was short, scrawny, excitable, and funny. He knew his stuff, from hardcore to all manner of weird seventies prog. He, too, had played in bands—Antioch Arrow was the best known—and was an even bigger music nerd than me, which was saying something. A dim lightbulb went on as we spoke. I left with his phone number and e-mail address.

I called him that Sunday—it took him a long time to get to the phone because, he explained later, he was quite stoned—and told him I knew a drummer and we should all get together. He asked if he should bring a guitar or a bass. I hadn't thought about it, and when I told him to bring either, he paused and said he'd bring the bass. On my way out the door, almost as an afterthought, I grabbed my looping pedal. We met at the rehearsal space and plugged in. Kevin started pummeling one of his sideways, spasmlike drum solos—but it never ended. Jeff joined in with something fluid and note-y on the bass, and just like that I was playing a music I'd never played before. Looped and layered, extended solos, note-based, and not much chording. Very filigreed and very dense at the same time, without a single acknowledgment of standard rock structures. If this wasn't what the MC5 meant when they talked about "free," it should have been.

After a half hour straight of playing purely nonlinear music that somehow held together, we stopped and stared at each other with dazed joy and disbelief: the kind of look your new girlfriend gives you when she realizes how good you are in bed. We took the name Coptic Light. We did not play easy music. There were no vocals, our songs often exceeded ten minutes, few parts repeated, and our drummer basically soloed the entire time. (As did our bassist and guitarist, come to think of it.) Also, we were really, really fucking loud. I often played through two half stacks, each powered by a four-input Hiwatt Custom 100—still my favorite amps, and absolute beasts for volume. Jeff constantly had to upgrade his bass rig just to be heard, and we blew out more speakers in our first couple of years than all my other bands combined.

Coptic Light let us all forget any rules of formatted music—that tyranny of leaving space for the vocal line, and even the tyranny of verse and chorus. Ignoring every single rule felt magical, given how indie rock was now nothing if not rule-governed. I loved how it gave us license to be completely unreasonable aesthetically, so long as we all agreed. Our early years were the most fun I had playing music as a grown-up. I spent my days working at magazines, torturing blocks of text, and it was such a relief to come to the practice space, set up, turn the lights down, and blast away at something having absolutely nothing to do with words or structure. To depend entirely, for a few hours, on the other side of my brain. Some nights the music gave me a buzz so strong that I wanted to leave my loops running, unplug my guitar, and pirouette. The long solos, which at last I could finally play, the open-ended lengths to many parts of our songs—I would have fucking *hated* Coptic Light when I was a hardcore kid, and that realization filled me with glee.

It was different now, being in a band. Having a serious job made twice-weekly practices challenging, though not impossible. (That tighter schedule also lent focus.) I liked Kevin and Jeff well enough, but it was clear we wouldn't be best friends, and that was fine, too. I didn't need my band to be my family and my gang anymore. I wanted Coptic

Light to be a democracy, in part because being so busy at work kept me from taking over. For the first few years we taped every practice—literally taped, on cassettes. Songwriting involved listening to everything we improvised and then—painstakingly, piecemeal—assembling bits to make rough song structures. In theory, a novel experiment. In practice, a huge pain, because anyone could veto anything, and did. Bands don't really work when they're communal endeavors. They require leaders. Veto equality exacerbated personality mismatches and led to friction—I'm sorry, "creative differences"—that eventually chafed badly. But I was now old enough, and settled enough, that my world didn't depend solely on my band.

For a few years plenty happened to keep us interested. The American label No Quarter put out our CDs, as did Dot Line Circle in Japan. We went to Japan twice, which was a huge deal to us, as hardly anyone we knew toured there in the eighties and nineties. Those tours were pure delight—a country as sheer visual abstraction—and the crowds were more receptive to our very strange thing than they were back home. In Coptic Light's last eighteen months we played more shows in Tokyo than in New York, where we primarily performed in Williamsburg and Greenpoint, often in those semi-legal, illegal, or temporary spaces. That pirate radio station. An old garment factory, converted into an arts space. The upstairs annex to a bar on Kent Avenue, which, according to neighborhood legend, was won by its owner in a poker game. The back room of an extremely sketchy dive bar. Trashed loft living rooms, in buildings that seemed minutes from the wrecking ball. Not every venue had a stage, so bands often set up on the floor, sometimes in the middle of the floor. Being surrounded by the crowd was thrilling, as it was thrilling to be doing something new, and to be around something new, as you moved deeper into your thirties.

We lasted until 2006, amid another good era for music in New York. Bands like LCD Soundsystem and the Rapture and !!! and Interpol got the most attention, but so much more excellence lurked below: Battles,

Orthrelm, Black Dice, Gang Gang Dance, Turing Machine, Sightings, Zs, a million others. A pleasing jumble of everything mashed together in the practice-space complex where most of us rehearsed: krautrock, metal, art, dance beats, punk rock, synths. Doors opened, and spring breezes wafted in. One night a new, mostly vocal band opened for Coptic Light and Battles at North Six. All I knew was that a friend from a coffee shop sang and played guitar for them. He had a huge beard, a huge afro, and, I found out that night, a voice like an angel. Kyp Malone's band TV on the Radio wouldn't stay an opener for long.

* * *

It might have been my birthday. I don't even know. But they gave me an E, and I went fucking crazy, and I had the best time ever. I came up on "Tomorrow Never Knows," which is my favorite childhood song. I open my eyes, and some really hot girl is grinding on me, and all my friends are cheering, and I'm like, "Why did I not do this all the time?" It made me realize, "I'm dancing. I know I'm on a drug, and I know the drug is lowering my inhibitions. But this is me, I'm dancing, and I like it." When it was over, I wasn't like, "What did I do?" I was like, "This was fucking awesome." After that, I went dancing everywhere. I was comfortable for the first time ever.

—James Murphy, LCD Soundsystem, Pony, Speedking, co-founder of DFA Records

NO MATTER WHAT ANYONE SAYS, VERY FEW PEOPLE ATTENDED the earliest DFA parties. The history books will likely get that part wrong. Though those history books will say—correctly—that those events started something: a party that became a label that became a *thing* and ultimately vaulted LCD Soundsystem into the Top Ten and onto the stage of a sold-out Madison Square Garden. Here's what I remember: before one early DFA party a pal assembled a bulk order of ecstasy. He called E "the Ambassador" and sent everyone an e-mail. Subject line: THE AMBASSADOR'S KEYNOTE ADDRESS. It informed us that the Ambassador would be speaking the following weekend; tickets were $25 and could be picked up at his apartment. I maneuvered into his cramped kitchen for mine and saw baggies full of pills piled on the table. It looked like a mobile narcotics lab. It looked like pictures from a pamphlet published in the seventies that warned parents about drugs. The phone kept ringing, and people came and went.

It was very good E. Later, at the party, a friend's girlfriend passed out for a bit, and I watched him halfheartedly fanning her face with a T-shirt or a towel while continuing an animated conversation in the opposite direction. Shortly afterward I was on the dance floor, and Sigue Sigue Sputnik's "Love Missile F1-11" came on. A band, and a song, I always hated. But tonight it sounded insistent, speedy, early-digital: *brilliant*. And I thought, *THIS IS THE GREATEST SONG OF ALL TIME!*

Then I thought, *Wow. I must be tripping my balls off.*

Like I said, it was *very* good E.

BOOK 3

What Was It?

In May of 2006 Coptic Light returned to Japan to play Osaka, Kobe, Nagoya, and three shows in Tokyo. In Nagoya we played with a band from San Francisco called Why? A terrible name, and a terrible band—and, worse, a *very earnest* one—equally beholden to white rap and polite collegiate indie rock. It was also a terrible day in Nagoya, pouring rain, unseasonably cold, and back then American smartphones didn't work in Japan, so when Why? started soundchecking, I darted through the downpour to find somewhere I could check my e-mail. I finally found a place to rent the Internet, but soon discovered it was where guys came to watch porn and jack off. My private room looked remarkably like a dentist's office—the exact same chair, but the tiny metal tray where a dentist keeps his tools instead bore a tube of lubricant and some wipes. I logged in, read and answered e-mail, and washed my hands very thoroughly at the first opportunity. I was still in a bad mood when I returned to the club, where Why? was still soundchecking, and I hated their name and I hated their band and I started to really hate their singer, who seemed as precious as the most annoying kid in a gifted-and-talented program. Then he stepped down from the stage and started doing *cartwheels*.

Coptic Light had been together five and a half years. What began as a lark in my early thirties was now the longest-running band of my life, and our original lineup was still intact. Maybe that's why we were all a little tired of each other. In Tokyo the three of us shared one small hotel room, as always, and in close quarters idiosyncrasies chafed. Our drummer, Kevin—how to put this?—lived like he drummed, and thus was not the most structured and organized individual in the world. The smart thing to do, on our upcoming day off, would be for Jeff or me to hang out with him to make sure that he didn't run off, or get lost, or join the circus. But Jeff and I each had our own lists of Tokyo things we itched to do—having both gone crazy for the city the last time we were there—and after being on tour for a week, we desperately needed time alone, and on that day we split in opposite directions before breakfast. Kevin didn't return to our hotel that night or the next morning. He got utterly lost and, after wandering for hours, was finally taken in by two sympathetic young women who spoke no English. He didn't really sleep, and reappeared just a few hours before our big Tokyo show with Gang Gang Dance, spent and fried, as anyone watching could tell. So that show sucked.

I started repeating a dangerous sentence to myself: *I'm too old for this.* Not for rock. For being in a band with someone who still required babysitting.

That thought led to others: *We're in Japan. This should be more fun.* And: *We've recorded, and released, all our songs.* And: *We can't do anything cool—like tour Japan again—until we write and record another album. Which, given how we work, will require eighteen months. And be torturous.*

Which led to this conclusion: *I guess we're done.*

Really?

Yeah. We're done.

A sign of aging: quality of life within a band mattered. Twenty years ago I could grit my teeth through any shitty interpersonal jive if the music was good enough—if there was any music at all. Now I couldn't. After the tour we had one show scheduled in Brooklyn at North Six, opening for Yura Yura Teikoku, and I promised myself that would be it.

A few weeks after we returned from Japan, after straggling through another unproductive rehearsal, Jeff and I left the practice space together. As we walked toward McCarren Park I turned to him and said, "I don't think I can play with him anymore."

Jeff paused. "Yeah," he finally admitted. "I've been meaning to tell you that, too." I don't want to get into how we told Kevin after that show that we were breaking up, except to say that we—I—handled it badly, which led to a torrent of hurt and infuriated e-mails, and I don't entirely blame Kevin for his response, and that, after all of it ended, it horrified me to realize that, at thirty-eight, I still didn't know how to communicate with people I'd played with for years.

That night after Jeff and I quietly broke up the band, I detoured to Barcade, the bar closest to my apartment and, as you might guess, one known for its vintage video games. There I drank three or four beers, alone, and played Centipede for an hour. Visual comfort food—a few forms of old and familiar. Something was messing with my inner weather, but I didn't know what.

I always believed that each band would be my last. When I got kicked out of Bitch Magnet, I thought I was finished with music at twenty-one. But now forty was approaching. There was no music inside, burning to get out. Just thinking about the mechanics of starting up again—taking out ads, finding other musicians, the awfulness of endless auditions—exhausted me. I went to Barcade because I felt bad that I didn't feel worse, because I walked away from Coptic Light with only a twinge of melancholy, not a crushing sense of the end of the world. *That,* I suddenly understood, was the sad part: once all this had mattered so much more. A photographer friend shot us at that last show. I felt disconnected, but not much worse than that. But not one picture caught me smiling. And with Coptic Light I actually smiled onstage.

The notion of mellowing with age kind of makes me want to vomit, so I won't say that's what happened. But I no longer needed to fill a bottomless hole. I was now a columnist for *BusinessWeek*, writing about media and technology, which, once you factored out certain unavoidable bullshit, was interesting and gratifying and paid reasonably well. In 2002 I'd met Laurel Touby, a brainy entrepreneur once described in the press—accurately—as a tiny blond bombshell, and very quickly realized that I'd finally met someone I could spend forever with. (Luckily she shared this opinion.) Funnily enough, she knew very little about music, and what she knew and liked was *exactly* what most gave me hives: the most egregious forms of top-forty dance music. All those years I spent chasing sallow art chicks who hid behind long dyed hair and guitars and basses, and the one for me was absolutely bewildered by the music I most treasured. But I was over seeking women based on their record collections.

I'd spent my entire life absolutely obsessed with music. What the Brits politely call "a specialist." One eventually able to discuss music only with those as afflicted, and ultimately not even with them, because no one else could share the precise contours of the idiosyncratic taste you honed through years of solitary listening and thinking about rock. That obsession shaped me. Through it I found my place in the world. Because of it I've spent much of this book vociferously defending an aesthetic I'm not at all 100 percent behind anymore, unless an outsider attacks it. But what a relief it was when the fever finally broke.

Through various strokes of late-bloomer's luck, mine was a very good life: a happy marriage, a challenging and rewarding job—all that crap grown-ups say! but I meant it! not like everyone else who secretly doesn't!—that brought a sort of public profile, thus scratching, somewhat, that youngest child's itch for attention. In 2007 Laurel sold the company she founded, enabling us to live far more grandly than I'd ever dreamed, since my biggest financial move involved graduating from playing noisy punk rock to typing sentences for a living. Like I said: lucky. Really, really lucky. A late transition to real life turned out amazingly well. I landed a regular gig as a commentator for CNBC and found that some aspects of live TV were a passable replacement for being in a band—the acting out, the fix and rush of performance. Though I had to learn to remain still, after all those years jumping around onstage, and project energy rather than enact it, while staring into a camera, alone in a tiny over-air-conditioned studio room, with the show just voices in your earpiece. When you spotted your opening or the anchor threw it to you, you soloed—well, argued—with all the smarts and fire you could summon. You learned to speak fast when you cut in on someone else. Each show had its own rhythm, which I often tapped out with my fingers to make sure my motor was tuned to the right speed. In a few minutes it was all over, and the producer in your earpiece thanked you and said they'd have you back. (One way TV is like indie rock: no one ever tells you that you suck. Even if you do.) A black town car waited for you at the curb—TV networks really like spending money—in which you glided to your next destination. My mom always called, as I lounged in the back of the new-smelling car, full of the joy American parents feel when they see their kids on TV.

Even then it seemed like a scene from a different and earlier New York: gilded, privileged, all the men wearing hats, the day's work over, drinks awaiting at the bar. I'd be lying if I said I didn't love this. It also wasn't enough.

The closest I got to performing for a live audience was speaking at media and tech conferences. Which, of course, is not very close at all. At one event at Moscone Center in San Francisco, I found myself waiting backstage—or the conference equivalent of backstage—with the other panelists. A crowd awaited us in the enormous room nearby, and from it I heard some small hubbub rising, and old associations sent adrenaline into my bloodstream. But when I looked at the other panelists' faces and body language, I saw only tension, discomfort, a grim sense of duty. No one else felt an old tingle. No cues shot fire across their synapses. None of them knew from *showtime*. No one else had the performer's urge, and in fact it was totally out of place here. On these stages you had to sit still and be polite. I'd roasted under hot white lights at 120 decibels too many times to be fooled into thinking that these settings substituted for the real thing.

I hid my history in music from co-workers and bosses, because hiding it is always easier than explaining it. (Though I wasn't as obsessive about it as one friend, who thought out loud, apparently seriously, about whether he should use a pseudonym in his new band.) But the past never stays entirely past. Not in the William Faulkner sense, but in the sense that every morsel of information eventually ends up on the Internet. I worked among journalists, who by trade want to know too much, and as more data turned up online I could no longer conceal this part of my life.

One holiday season everyone from my section at *BusinessWeek* went out to a celebratory lunch. Like most such gatherings, it was fine, if a bit manic and awkward. Then my editor turned to me and asked the question you never want to hear.

"You know, Jon, I read about your band on Wikipedia. What was math-rock?"

Well. It refers to underground bands that played songs written in odd time signatures. Such bands were aggressive, generally too smart for hardcore or rote forms of heavy metal, and often featured downplayed vocals, if they had vocals at all. But, you know, I never liked that term at all, because . . . Oh, never mind. Forget I said anything.

What was it?

Much more fun than *this*.

192

I Wouldn't Be
Averse Either

Sing it like the Buzzcocks song: Every band gets back together now. But there's actually a long history of underground bands reuniting. Wire was the first, in 1985, though they'd only broken up in 1980. Stiff Little Fingers got back together in 1987. Patti Smith released her first new record in almost a decade in 1988. The Buzzcocks reunited in 1989, Television in 1991, the Velvet Underground in 1993, and the Sex Pistols in 1996. When Mission of Burma got back together in 2002, they kicked off the reunions of a next generation's bands. It didn't seem possible that Burma could reunite, since they broke up in 1983 when Roger Miller's tinnitus became unbearable. But he continued being a musician, and even though none of his other bands was as loud as Burma, smart folk could have realized that he hadn't wholly forsaken volume and amplification and that a Burma reunion was at least thinkable. (Though I don't know anyone who thought it.) Anyway, *après* Burma, *le déluge*. A trickle of reunions soon became a torrent. There are many ways in which punk rock bands are not like big-deal rock bands, but shunning reunions isn't one of them. Today the list of underground American bands that *haven't* reunited is likely shorter than the list of those that have.

Why?

The Label Asked. Most—though not all—important and longest-lasting labels in the American independent underground were generally beloved by their bands. (In the case of Sub Pop, the better verb is "forgiven," given the label's multiple near-death experiences and, in its early days, a very casual approach to paying royalties.) Let's say such a label plans to celebrate its fifteenth or twentieth or twenty-fifth anniversary with a weekend-long festival. Let's say you were on that label early on, when the people behind it were overworked adolescents scrambling to make something happen. You took a chance on them, as they did on you. You made a few records together, laughed, cried, shared triumph and tragedy and that uniquely memorable state of *being young together.* Twenty years later, when the phone rings or the in-box pings and those label guys are asking your band to get back together for this massive event—are you really going to just say no?

This kind of bond absolutely does not exist between bands and major labels. Capitol could *never* get the Beatles back together, and it was Live Aid, not Atlantic, that lured the surviving members of Led Zeppelin back onstage. But it's why Corey Rusk of Touch and Go convinced Scratch Acid and Seam and Killdozer and the Didjits and Negative Approach to reunite for that label's twenty-fifth-anniversary festival, in 2006. (Corey even got Big Black back together for a couple of songs; Steve Albini essentially said onstage that they only did it out of respect for him.) It's why Jonathan Poneman got Green River back together for Sub Pop's twentieth anniversary, in 2008. It's why Matador's Gerard Cosloy and Chris Lombardi got Guided by Voices and Chavez and Come to reunite for its twenty-first-anniversary weekend, in 2010. The people who ran your old label were a very special kind of old friend. A stranger wasn't calling. It was your brother.

The Golden Era of All Tomorrow's Parties, 1999–2013. The first

All Tomorrow's Parties, in 1999, immediately established ATP as the rock festival for people who, sensibly, detest rock festivals. The best versions were held at the peculiar British institution of a holiday camp—though ATPs have since taken place in America, Japan, Iceland, and Australia—where families go for a cheap getaway in a sort of rural English setting, albeit one crammed with water parks and small grocery stores and pubs and fast-food outlets and other amusements and conveniences. The entire ATP experience was assembled by and for indie rockers, and for good or ill—and more on that shortly—ATP held fast to the way the founding indie generation kept art and commerce separate. Unlike most every other recently created music festival, it shunned sponsorships, even while newer generations of indie rockers proved far less doctrinaire about such arrangements.

In rock-festival terms ATP was small—6,000 people instead of 20,000 or 60,000. Convening them at holiday camps meant that, unlike at various Woodstocks, an attendee was never far from all mod cons, and you were never charged ten quid for a bottle of water if you were parched or for a cup of coffee if you were freezing. The British ATP festivals became beloved for the minimal barriers they erected between performers and audience. Everyone stayed in the same complexes of cramped apartments, drank at the same bars, went to the same restaurants, and stood together at the same shows. There were no VIP areas. (Theoretically there are no celebrities in indie rock.) Most important, ATP felt like ours, another secret treasured among music freaks and kept from the rest of the world. I won't be the first to describe the old ATPs as summer camp reunions for superannuated indie kids.

The bands were chosen—in ATP-speak, the festivals were "curated"—by a luminary headlining band, and the bands ATP most wanted and chose as curators were actually among the vanguard of interesting music from the past twenty years, as opposed to those that headlined, say, Lollapalooza. Some of ATP's favored bands I liked and some I didn't, but if Shellac or Sonic Youth or Mogwai or Melvins or Pavement choose the performers, then chances are the festival will be interesting. And Barry Hogan, ATP's founder and guiding spirit, figured out quickly that reunions made his festivals much more of an event. ATP offered generally unheard-of sums—in indie rock terms—to the bands it most wanted to appear: mid-five figures, and sometimes more if they wanted you bad enough, to musicians accustomed to getting far less. Among the bands ATP effectively reunited: Slint, the Jesus Lizard, Sleep, My Bloody Valentine, and Neutral Milk Hotel.

ATP's reunions also enabled many bands to briefly reenter the bloodstream of the international touring circuit, because if you reunited for an ATP, it made sense to play London while you were over there. (Barry lives in London and often tendered a nice offer to play there, too.) Since you were traveling so far, why not a few dates on the Continent? Also, since we'll be rehearsing in the States, we might as well . . .

In most cases the tensions that broke up bands eased long ago. It had been decades since you and your band, barely old enough to drink, threw yourselves into vans and drove toward indifferent or hostile weeknight audiences. And if those old tensions still existed—well, it was just a commitment for a week or two. This was no months-long suicide mission of a tour. You could only play the places where people cared. How bad could it be?

Over the years, though, ATP's finances grew increasingly precarious. (Maybe there was a downside to offering tens of thousands of dollars to bands that never sold more than a few thousand records.) Its parent company went through receivership—British bankruptcy—in the summer of 2012, listing debts of over £2.6 million, and three of its American festivals lost a total of £520,000, according to documents filed at the time. Many strains were already evident when Bitch Magnet played ATP in December 2011. ATP had started canceling festivals, sometimes on very short notice, when tickets sold poorly. Many bands reported that just getting paid was becoming an arduous, months-long process—or longer. It was for us. Although we did get paid, after around five months, unlike some bands I know who were owed money for far longer. Me being a loudmouth may have bummed out Sooyoung and Orestes, but it had its uses.

ATP put on its last holiday-camp festival in December 2013. (Though as I write this, it's planning a major event in Iceland in the summer of 2015, despite canceling a planned East London festival on three days' notice in the summer of 2014.) A cultural moment built around remining eighties and nineties indie rock could last only so long, as even Barry recognized. "The bubble is kind of bursting for reunited bands," he told me in the fall of that year. Partly, he explained, because almost every band that *could* get back together *had*. Perfectly understandable, in business terms, but it hurt when ATP's paychecks vanished. It marked the end of a brief era in which fan interest and financial means came together to make it especially possible—even profitable—for many bands like ours to reunite. And even if ATP were to come back in full force, given all its recent shenanigans there are now bands that won't work with Barry. As for me, I'll probably hug him the next time I see him. Bitch Magnet likely would never have gotten back together were it not for ATP. Even though— or maybe because—Barry and ATP were so much like indie rock itself: promising so much, sometimes delivering, but often falling far short.

The Fans. In the late eighties and early nineties a left-of-mainstream American cohort graduated college and moved to cities, settling in neighborhoods bearing names we're now tired of hearing. There, in a fashion, they grew up. But unlike hippies—a peripatetic tribe—to a remarkable degree these aging creative types stayed in their cities as they aged. Indie rock's opposition to the mainstream, it turned out, was still congruent with real jobs in software and technology and law and media and teaching, those last two being long-standing destinations for smart misfits. And indie rock's fuzzy line between participant and fan meant that virtually everyone involved was more stakeholder than spectator. You may have a complicated emotional relationship with the culture that unorphaned you, but it isn't easily forgotten. Performers from this subculture were not the distant rock stars of previous generations. If you met them, there was a good chance you'd end up friends.

Also, our bands were often short-lived and broke up before many fans could see them play. Bitch Magnet played fewer than 150 shows. Scratch Acid played only a few more. Slint performed fewer than 30 times in their four-year existence and broke up before their landmark second album, *Spiderland*, was released, in 1991. While *Spiderland* was a major secret-handshake album in the nineties, it didn't get much press when it came out. Slint's fantastic debut, *Tweez,* got even less. I saw Slint twice in the late eighties, once at New York's Pyramid Club and once when Bitch Magnet played with them in Chicago at Club Dreamerz. At both, they played to tiny audiences. In 2005 I saw the reunited Slint during its sold-out three-night stand at New York's Irving Plaza, which holds well over a thousand people. The crowd from any one of those shows may have been larger than the *aggregate* audiences Slint played to while an active band. Even better-known bands found bigger crowds when they reunited. When My Bloody Valentine headlined shows in their heyday in their native Britain, they played halls that held around two thousand people. When the band got back together in 2008, they sold out five nights at London's Roundhouse. Its capacity: three thousand.

The Internet hollowed out the music business, we are told, but maybe it's more accurate to say the Internet hollowed out the business that depended on major labels. Because in many ways it made things better for bands like ours. The Web provided a central place—more precisely, a decentralized place—where many small campfires could be tended, around which widely dispersed but unusually ardent audiences traded tales and live recordings. Such audiences still cherished these bands and had been waiting a long time to see them play. While it's often hard getting fortysomething hipsters to come out to shows—they have real jobs and sore feet, and nights out often require a babysitter— they will respond to an *event*. A reunion of a band they still love. A night where they'll see others just like them, thus taking away the social anxiety an older person feels at a show. (Old age becomes childhood, and show-going fears in your forties mimic those of teenagers: you're entering an unfamiliar world, peopled by unfamiliar natives who know the rules that you don't.) And reunited bands' part-time endeavors are easily supported by such part-time fans.

Audience Realities. There was negligible interest in Ed Roeser's post–Urge Overkill bands. Nash Kato's solo album *The Debutante*, released in 2000 on a Sony-affiliated label, sold fewer than five thousand copies. But even after their ignominious mid-nineties implosion, there is still an audience for Urge. Sebadoh's draw collapsed at the end of the nineties, and J. Mascis's post–Dinosaur Jr. shows drew smaller crowds than the band that made him famous. So it was that J.'s manager called Lou Barlow one day in 2005, laying out the proposition for reuniting Dinosaur's original trio lineup. Musicians kept learning that their old band's popularity wasn't transferable to their new projects— but if they got their old band back together, there was actual money to be made, sometimes for the first time. For lifers it was a simple calculation: it beat finding a real job.

And, of course: **Do Bands Ever Really Break Up?** Yes, the world may have ignored your band and its records while you were around. Yes, hardly anyone may have noticed when your band finally slipped beneath the waves. But now a musician never knows when some music supervisor might choose one of his songs for some TV ad or video game and catapult him from obscurity to . . . if not fame, then at least nonobscurity and a half-decent check. Some real-world examples of rediscovery are the stuff of Hollywood: here's the part where we trot out Sixto Rodriguez, the subject of the 2012 Oscar-winning documentary *Searching for Sugar Man*. A singer-songwriter from Detroit from the late sixties who released two albums (which initially sold about as well as Vineland and Freshkills) and about whom only the barest facts were known, Rodriguez somehow became iconic in South Africa—a country in which he'd never set foot. In 1998 he flew there to play sold-out arenas, a jubilant occasion memorialized in the movie. *Searching for Sugar Man* omitted some key facts, chief among them that Rodriguez had his records reissued in Australia to significant acclaim and toured that country in 1979 and 1981, the latter with the (inexplicably) huge Oz band Midnight Oil, when it was exceedingly rare for smaller American bands to get to that part of the world. That aside, the documentary parlayed Rodriguez's freakish fame far from home into something much bigger in America: sold-out shows at New York's Town Hall; appearances on Letterman and Leno. Somewhat similar is the tale of Anvil's heroic, if baffling, thirty-year commitment to a very mediocre Canadian version of eighties metal, despite decidedly limited rewards, which was recounted in the fabulous documentary *Anvil! The Story of Anvil*. When that movie became a surprise hit, Anvil suddenly started selling out venues worldwide, more or less for the first time in its existence.

Chances are no one will ever make a movie about your forgotten band. (Though people made—or are making, while I type this— documentaries about Tad, Silkworm, Mudhoney, Mission of Burma, SNFU, Slint, Walt Mink, and venues like Memphis's Antenna Club and Trenton's shithole hardcore warehouse City Gardens, and that's just what I know off the top off my head.) But none of us required a movie or sold-out shows at an arena in Cape Town to make us reunite. Kind words and a few small rooms full of transfixed faces were often enough. It's all we ever really wanted in the first place.

* * *

BY THE EARLY 2000S A FEW LABELS HAD CONTACTED ME OR Sooyoung about reissuing Bitch Magnet's catalog. We ignored them or put them all off: *We haven't been in touch, it's too much trouble, we don't know where that stuff is.* Then, in 2008, during the final summer of the second Bush administration, Jeremy DeVine of Temporary Residence started courting us and in his quiet and persistent way ultimately won us over.

Jeremy is blue-eyed, wavy-haired, and atypically kind and level-headed for someone in the music business. It's easier to imagine him as the proprietor of a small family-run company than as the guy running his thriving label. (Explosions in the Sky is the marquee band, but Jeremy has had a remarkable streak of signing other acts that still sell in the mid-five figures: big numbers for a company with a full-time staff of three, including Jeremy, all of whom work in about five hundred square feet in Brooklyn.) Jeremy doesn't drink, is a vegetarian, and in conversation it's impossible to hurry his Kentucky drawl. He lacks the chip on his shoulder common among ex-hardcore kids, myself included. If his idealism about the power and nobility of indie and community is decidedly earnest and unblinking, it's because the label he more or less built single-handedly is a rare place where such idealism actually works.

Before we could make any final decision, though, we needed to find Orestes. Sooyoung and Orestes had always swapped the status of most reluctant member, but Orestes held it last. He could never hide how much he disliked rock clubs and smoky dives, always had unreadable motives—though Sooyoung's often seemed as obscure—and left the band abruptly. More to the point, after all these years, neither Sooyoung nor I knew how to find him. I knew that Orestes had taken his father's surname of Morfín in the nineties after attending college under his stepfather's last name, Delatorre. I thought he was living in Tucson, but neither he nor his wife—the girlfriend he spent that summer with in Atlanta—had a listed phone number. He was on Facebook briefly, but then his profile disappeared. I found a couple of academic citations for grad work he'd done years earlier, but there were no more recent traces on the Internet. He was not active in any band, or at least in any band mentioned on the Web. He did not appear to exist, though of course he did. Believing you can find everyone and everything through Google is another narcissism of the tech-y crowd.

One day, though, I was killing time at work watching a clip of a live Laughing Hyenas show in Germany, and when the song ended, the location suddenly changed, and Orestes's face filled the screen, talking into the camera, looking directly at me. (His friend had recorded that show.) *He had to be out there somewhere*, I thought. I kept trying. Some time afterward, I Googled him again, and his name popped up on LinkedIn. I doubted that anyone else in the world could share both his uncommon Greek first name and his uncommon Mexican last name. But there's always that instant when you can't be sure.

We hadn't spoken in at least twelve years. When I was prompted to "add a message" when I "invited him to connect on LinkedIn," I stared at the empty text box, and all I could come up with was:

> Hi Orestes. How have you been?
> —Jon Fine

Within an hour I received a reply:

> I'm well, thanks. And you?

I thought a bit and sent him a longer response. I said I was visiting Los Angeles. I said it was colder than anyone would want it to be. I said I'd just seen Sooyoung in New York. Then I got to the point.

> A label on the East Coast—Temporary Residence—has been after us to do BM reissues. No $$ up front but a profit split. Sooyoung and I both think it's a good idea. You? I know the guy behind the label and he's a good and solid dude who will do a good job w/it.

He said yes immediately, and we kept e-mailing. Two hours later, after two more exchanges, he wrote:

> Is there any possibility we would re-convene to support the re-issues?

Son of a bitch. Did the guy who I was certain would never want to play again just say that? At the bottom of my next response, I asked:

"reconvene" means what?

At the bottom of *his* next response:

Reconvene. Would we need to get back together and play a few shows, or does Temporary Residence not care?

To steal someone else's line, I wanted reunion shows so badly you could see the stains on my pants from across the street. But our band dynamic had always been me being too eager and everyone else being ambivalent, and I couldn't tell if I'd entered the reality distortion field you can slip into when you want to hear something. Orestes could well be asking, eyes rolling and prefatigued, *Oh, Jesus, are they really going to ask me to do this?* I flashed back to the summer of 1990, during one of our last rehearsals, when I told him about some new development brewing as he screwed felts onto his cymbal stands, and he sort of smiled or winced and asked, "But what would that *entail?*"

I deliberated for a bit and then wrote back.

No one's mentioned anything about playing shows, so I strongly doubt that's a prerequisite. Were you asking because you'd like to?

Ten minutes later:

I ask because there is usually some talk of playing out with this kind of thing. I hadn't thought about it, but I certainly wouldn't be averse if that was part of the deal.

So we were heavy petting. Or at least talking dirty. But I still wanted to be cautious. So I lied.

> I hadn't thought of playing out as part of this, and haven't discussed it at all with Sooyoung. But I wouldn't be averse either. Have you been playing at all?

Thirty seconds later:

> I haven't sat down with it on a regular basis since early 2008, but I played out a few times this past Fall and was not disappointed.

He still had that same red Yamaha kit, the one that sounded like God to me, which as far as I was concerned all but sealed it. A few months later I flew out to Tucson to play with him, but I knew going in that this was just a formality. On my second day there Orestes woke at 6 a.m., met the group of guys he cycled with, and pedaled his racing bike fifty miles in the desert. Then we loaded his drums into his car, drove to a practice space, set all the gear up, and played for six hours. He'd always been a fucking ox. Still was.

* * *

WHEN SIGNING A RECORD CONTRACT WITH AN INDEPENDENT label, the smart move is to license your recordings for a specific term, such as five or seven years, so that when that term expires, all rights revert to you. (Certain indie labels—hello, Restless!—sometimes signed less-savvy bands to fuck-you-we-own-this-forever deals.) While visiting San Francisco in May 2010, I contacted Gary Held, whose label, Communion, had released Bitch Magnet's records in America. From our old contracts I knew that the rights to those recordings had been ours for a decade. But Gary was still selling Bitch Magnet on iTunes, even though he hadn't the legal standing to do so. We wanted him to stop. Also, I wanted him to cough up the royalties we were surely owed, since he last paid us around 1995.

It was a brilliant spring day in San Francisco, and, like a tourist, I met Gary at the Ferry Building, and we walked to the end of a pier to see the Bay Bridge and Oakland's hills and all the gorgeousness in the distance. But the meeting was as passive-aggressive as any indie rock business discussion could be. In a polite and almost kind way, Gary said there was no way we'd get royalties out of him, and in any case, he had no paperwork whatsoever documenting how much he owed us. He mentioned he had a small stash of a few hundred old Bitch Magnet CDs lying around, and afterward I made a few fruitless attempts to take them off his hands. He did agree to take our songs down from iTunes, and made good on this a few weeks later. He also promised to send over an accounting of iTunes sales, for which I am still waiting.

Evidently I'd learned nothing in all my years of dealing with remote and soft indie rockers and still couldn't cajole them into anything. As I started to stew, a curious Gary asked me if Bitch Magnet would reunite for a few shows, given the upcoming reissues. Normally I admitted nothing in response to such questions, but I thought, *What the hell, it's not that much of a secret,* and said that, while it was by no means certain, I really wanted to.

"You guys are lucky," he said.

I didn't understand what he meant.

He explained that he'd grown accustomed to running into guys who played in some band and, amid backslaps and reminiscences, asking whatever happened to this or that member. And suddenly everyone is silent, tight-lipped, looking down. Musicians died young, from misadventure, from illness. They disappeared into hardcore drugging or drinking, especially around San Francisco and Portland and Seattle. They wrecked their cars and rolled their vans. When Gary called us *lucky,* he meant that we were all still around, and healthy.

Several hours later I called Sooyoung, ostensibly to tell him about meeting Gary, but really to discuss getting back together, while I paced in front of Hayes Castle, an oddball theme restaurant that had gone belly-up, leaving behind its fake-castle carcass and some bewildered reviews on Yelp. One argument I made was: *People die.* I said it with some levity—with as much levity as you can say something like that—but I was serious. Jerry Fuchs had died six months earlier. I'd been lucky, until then, never to lose someone around my own age, someone with whom I was in mid-conversation. I didn't bring up Jerry with Sooyoung, because he knew what had happened, and anyway, what do you say about that? (This, I guess: A bunch of us played hooky from our lives and went on an epic weeklong bender, it was terrible, it was amazing, I sobbed and howled and laughed and drank until the bars closed every night, my ribs got bruised from endless crushing hugs, I danced on tables and did drugs in bathrooms and terrified my wife.) Anyway, Sooyoung always responded to persuasion and logic, not a hard sell. He was unconvinced. But Orestes and I would keep working on him.

* * *

JEREMY WAS REMARKABLY PATIENT WITH HOW LONG IT TOOK us to assemble the Bitch Magnet reissues: forever, basically. The master tapes were spread among four locations in California, New York, and New Jersey, and Sooyoung and I weren't certain what was where, and none of us lived within easy distance of California, except for Orestes, who, as a father of two young boys, had even less free time than the rest of us to travel and knock on doors and scour half-forgotten closets. Shortly after Orestes signed on, Jeremy assigned us the catalog number TR150. The triple LP and triple CD finally came out three years later, just after Temporary Residence released TR203.

One night in March of 2011, as the reissues slowly made their way toward a December release date, Laurel and I met Ian Williams of Battles and his fiancée, Kate, for dinner. At some point during the main course Ian mentioned that Battles was curating All Tomorrow's Parties'

Nightmare Before Christmas festival in early December. Then Kate blurted out, "Hey, Ian, why don't you have Bitch Magnet play?"

Ian and I looked at each other.

I was opposed to the entire idea of rock festivals, or as much as you could be without ever having attended one, but I knew ATP would be as good an offer as we'd get.

The next day Ian told me to expect a call from Barry Hogan, and Barry reached me while I paced one of the grimy blocks in north Chelsea that defiantly, even gloriously, resist gentrification. Barry was charming. Barry was practiced at his spiel. The Nightmare Before Christmas would be held the weekend of December 10 at a Butlins (*Butlins!*) holiday camp in Minehead, an English coastal town ninety minutes southwest of Bristol. Bitch Magnet was guaranteed a prime-time slot. Rooms at the festival for the band and crew were included. Meals and flights were extra. Also, Barry said, he could book us a show in London and maybe even throw in practice space at Butlin's if we needed it. Then he named a pretty generous fee. I named another. After a day or so of negotiation, he put everything in writing.

All that remained was selling Sooyoung on it.

* * *

THE OFFER FROM BARRY IN HAND, ORESTES AS ANXIOUS AS I was to get back together, both of us confident we could do it without embarrassing ourselves, we started war-gaming various scenarios with Jeremy—who was paying us attention far out of proportion to how many records we'd likely sell—and set up a conference call in mid-March with him and the three of us in Bitch Magnet. I'd stamped into my brain *Sooyoung responds to logic and persuasion,* so, in as steady and unaffected a voice as I could manage, I mentioned that we had received an offer to reunite and dispassionately read off the terms. I had Jeremy on hand to chime in with how singular an opportunity this was, but it wasn't even necessary. I don't remember when, or if, Sooyoung actually said yes, but the conversation shifted almost instantly from "will we?" to "how do we?" Several months later, in an interview in Asia or Europe, Sooyoung explained we had presented ATP's offer while he was several drinks into a night at a pub in Singapore, so his defenses were down. But, hey, if that's what it took.

Through March and April we started working out details and scheduling practice weekends in Canada—because Orestes was moving to Calgary—and New York, and Sooyoung asked if we could practice in Asia as well. Then he said, "I can get us a show in Seoul," and—because there's always competition within bands, I guess—I said, "I can get us a show in Tokyo," and we began planning our first reunion appearances, and our first Asian shows ever, for November 2011. Spring was coming on slowly in New York, and my days were pleasantly distracted by the logistics of plane tickets and finding practice space and lodging in distant cities, as well as by a low-grade rush always buzzing in my blood because *we were doing this*.

Jeremy was almost as thrilled about the reunion as I was. But he was also sensible enough to wave a yellow flag. A few days after our conference call, he and I had lunch near his office, at the godhead pioneering Bushwick restaurant Roberta's, and after we finished our pizza he made it clear that Bitch Magnet was best off reuniting only for a short and defined time. Play the biggest cities once, put it all back on the shelf, and don't linger. And *don't* make a new record. (Though he did graciously hint that he'd put it out on his label if we did.) He reminded me that Mission of Burma had just been dropped by Matador—and then got turned down by every other prominent independent label. I've said this before, but it's worth repeating: In our sandbox, everyone adored Burma. Everyone came of age idolizing them. In 2011, though, no one could afford to put out their records. And Jeremy didn't have to point out that Burma was a hell of a lot more famous than Bitch Magnet.

All right. So we were still doomed. So the clock started ticking as soon as we said yes. So what?

Don't you feel tears welling up at the end of *This Is Spinal Tap*—that love story about two old friends, dim-witted as they may be—when Nigel climbs onstage to rejoin the band? (And inexplicably finds his guitar there, plugged into an amp and ready to play, which would *never* happen in real life?) Or when Rodriguez walks slowly onstage in South Africa in *Searching for Sugar Man*? Or when Anvil takes the stage in Japan at the end of their movie—old guys fearful that everyone has forgotten, suddenly blinking in disbelief at the crowd that's gathered? Their stunned faces as they take it all in, and their looks of dumb surprise?

I had no illusions that involved arenas. What I wanted was another shot at our story. To stop feeling like an outsider in a band I co-created. To write a different and better ending for Bitch Magnet, and with these guys.

Calgary Metal

Like all rock reunions, ours started in earnest on the outskirts of Calgary at a rent-a-rehearsal-room joint called Slaughterhouse Studios, and driving there from downtown was like watching a movie of the city's development run backward. You first passed the blue-glass curvilinear swoop of the newest and tallest building in town, The Bow, an atypically loud monument to the city's new oil money. You passed the grim grandeur of the concrete Brutalist buildings erected in the seventies. Then you left the central core, passing feed and fertilizer businesses, a creamery, a scrap yard with a huge sign screaming CALGARY METAL, which never failed to make my heart happy, until you finally arrived at a cluster of absolutely unremarkable industrial parks, where businesses sold tractors and obscure parts for machines I'd never comprehend. Despite the oil boom, Calgary is still a cow town at heart. In its past life Slaughterhouse Studios had been a meat locker. Our practice room was behind the door of a giant walk-in refrigerator, one built for storing the cow and pig carcasses that had once hung there.

We started rehearsing at Slaughterhouse in April 2011, but practically nothing there suggested that the twenty-first century had happened. Hell, not much at Slaughterhouse suggested that the late *nineties* had happened. I started hanging out in places like this in the eighties, and what a relief to find one where nothing had changed at all. In our practice space were three defunct and decrepit seventies suburban-piano-teacher organs: fake wood, complicated speaker grilles, multicolored buttons to nowhere. Also a mysterious Peavey tape deck that promised to strip vocals from cassettes, a useful technology for a previous era. I plugged into a mutant Marshall half stack that coughed out a nasally, trebly shit-metal tone no matter how much you fiddled with the dials. In the lounge, cans of Canadian beer chilled in a vending machine, across the room from the smeary-screened Asteroids game or the sad, faded pool table. Cold concrete floors and unadorned Sheetrock walls in the narrow and claustrophobic hallway. The bathroom, back by the office, was appropriately disgusting. Years-old posters everywhere for a local Iron Maiden cover band that was named after Maiden's mascot: Eddie the Great, of course. And that slightly pickled scent, again, the one instantly familiar to anyone who's spent time in practice pads or recording studios run by not particularly fastidious guys. But we weren't looking to play somewhere sanitized. When it's time to create some culture, I like to have a little native yeast floating in the air.

On nice weekends Slaughterhouse's owner, Bob, rolled a grill into the cement yard and offered free hot dogs and hamburgers. Bob sported a drinker's reddened capillaries, an inveterate stoner's blown-out gaze, and the uptalk and heavy Canadian accent that always makes Americans giggle, eh? He was tall and thin and big-headed, like Big Bird, a mop of a mustache spreading above his upper lip and a wad of brown-green-hazel hair flopping over his forehead. Some late afternoons it started to smell very skunky up front, where Bob and his friends gathered. It was such a boy's clubhouse that it was hard to imagine any woman ever stopping by, but Bob's girlfriend sometimes did, to throw back beers and get roasted with Bob and his pals.

By now I'd known for a long time that the entire idea of performing this kind of rock music was inherently awkward and dorky-looking:

grown men standing around, clutching instruments, making organized loud crashing noises. (Turn off the sound on many older rock
videos and squint a bit, and it looks like a bunch of thirtysomething
fieldhands, slightly stiff from age and overwork, grimly performing
farm chores.) But the vibe and gear at Slaughterhouse and the fact that
no one younger than their late thirties was ever present often made me
wonder if the entire idea of a rock band was a fossil from another epoch,
something younger people no longer thought about, like doo-wop or
electric typewriters. I knew hip-hop now occupied a lot of the cultural
space that rock once had, but was rock really this dead?

Still: fuck it. We were doing this again. The last time the three of us
had played together was almost exactly twenty-one years earlier. And
though Calgary seemed a supremely random meeting place, the location actually made sense. Orestes had just moved here from Tucson,
and because I lived in New York and Sooyoung lived in Singapore,
Calgary was as good a middle ground as any. We knew no one in this
city, so it was a forgiving and private place to see if we could get into
these old clothes without shredding any seams. There were no distractions, and there was no one to meet. Nothing to do but rehearse each
day, then get dinner, and begin to warm to one another again, drink by
drink, conversation by conversation.

Orestes and I had both been practicing on our own and came ready
to rip into our whole repertoire. Sooyoung hadn't, and was far more
tentative. His idea was to drill five songs, over and over again. I thought
this had to do with his discipline, but he admitted to me much later that
it was more about his fear. He hadn't played bass in over fifteen years—
he'd sold his years ago and only bought a replacement a few days before
he arrived—and knew he had a lot of work to do.

* * *

WE'D GATHERED IN THE SAME ROOM FOR THE FIRST TIME IN A
long time several months earlier, in October 2010, when we met in

Dallas to mix some unreleased songs for our reissues. That weekend went smashingly well, and we all got along, which was important, because playing in a band on this lower rung of rock means being around each other all the time. I still felt like the only talkative one, and was definitely the only one who talked with his hands, and, as always, their reserve and stillness made me a little more frantic around the edges. But it felt good, working with them and dining with them and drinking with them and crashing the Texas State Fair, where only I was brave enough to eat the fried beer. (Their caution was well founded.)

Orestes was now an environmental scientist. He had those two sons and recently finalized his divorce. He still dressed like a rugby player, absolutely innocent of any style, and was a bit chunkier, with a lot of gray flecking his short black hair. The passing years and fatherhood and all that desert sun had aged him in an appropriate and appealing way. Sooyoung looked almost exactly the same. He'd founded a software and programming company just as the world economy went into the toilet in 2008, and though he worked constantly and always talked about how much of a struggle it was to build his business and keep it going, by now it seemed on a much better footing. Somehow he had become even skinnier while learning to drink like a Russian. Sooyoung also flew around 200,000 miles a year, since his clients were spread across the globe, and he and I started swapping nerdy frequent-flier tips. All our airline miles would come in handy for this midlife caper we were planning, the first stop of which brought us to the rehearsal room in Calgary. Where, despite the decades, and the rust on the gears, and Sooyoung's struggles to relearn bass and needing to hear Bitch Magnet MP3s to transcribe the lyrics he'd written but no longer remembered, an old feeling started stirring almost immediately.

One day when we broke for lunch, one of Bob's beefy and slightly stupefied friends stopped me as I rushed out the door and said, "Dude. Sounds great down there."

You never knew, in these practice-space exchanges, if someone was being sincere or merely being kind. But I stopped for a moment and turned to him.

"Thanks," I said. "We haven't played together in twenty-one years."

"*Ehhh?*" the guy replied.

Which could mean a million different things. But why worry which?

 Bitch Magnet
May 3, 2011 · 🌐

so last weekend, at an undisclosed non-US location, Bitch Magnet practiced for the first time since 1990. Went well, too!

Like · Comment · 👍 42 💬 8

Magnet, Bitch

slept on people's floors well into my thirties whenever I was on tour. But you make certain concessions to age, and we quickly decided that, during the reunion, it was crazy-talk to consider couch-crashing with friends or fans. For rehearsals in December 2011 for our European tour, we rented a small house in Stoke Newington in London, for the three of us and Matthew Barnhart, our driver/tour manager/soundman/one-man road crew. I've never gotten along particularly well with England, and its skies darken far too early this time of year, but Stoke Newington is disarmingly neighborhoody, and each day we walked to rehearsal past shops and pubs and young couples and children at play, and it was really quite pleasant. After practice we sat in pubs for hours. If we had to do anything in the morning, our five or eight pints each night would be a mistake. But we were on rock time now, so mornings were an afterthought, and this, too, was lovely.

House and apartment rentals are way less rock-star than hotels, because doing dishes is not very rock and roll and because you don't get to stride through a busy lobby gripping a guitar case, hungover and wearing shades. But they're much more practical. At a house there's breakfast no matter how late you sleep. You have your own room—so: privacy—and a washing machine, both major blessings when you're on the road. Instead of a lobby, you hang out in an actual living room. Where we all sat, under comfortably dimmed lights, the night before our first show in Europe.

A nice moment, this. Even domestic, if temporarily. There's a fake fireplace, with design books piled on the mantel. Chairs next to the window, through which we glimpse the patterns of streetlight and row house and shadow. Though the house is cold, of course, because it's December in England, and apparently, even in the twenty-first century, no one in this entire country understands *heating*.

I'm playing my black Les Paul and surreptitiously recording song ideas on my phone. Orestes and Sooyoung are on their computers. Sometimes I wonder if they feel a similar amazement at the strange coalescences that landed us in the same room, back on tour all these years later.

By now we've gathered for practice weekends in Calgary, Vancouver, New York, and Seoul—on so many levels it's amazing to be able to type that phrase—and hanging out is remarkably comfortable, and our roles are growing familiar. I'm the worrier, and handle logistics. Sooyoung is cool—medium cool, not hipster cool—and reserved. Orestes is the most genial, and almost always upbeat, and that part is new. Still, tonight this room is very quiet, because it takes us a few drinks, at least, to really start talking. If this were some sitting-room drama on the BBC, a grandfather clock solemnly sounding its hushed *bongs* would be all you could hear.

Orestes looks up from his laptop: "Did we talk before we had computers?"

I say, "No. We didn't talk. Except for me, so I always thought I was talking too much."

He says, "You were."

So I give him a bit of a look and say, "Well, *someone* had to talk."

(Sooyoung, gazing into his computer, says nothing at all.)

But tonight, after all these years, it's okay. Soon we'll head to the pub. On our way out, we'll squeeze past the half wall of stacked boxes in the entry hall that contain the T-shirts, records, and CDs we'll sell at our shows. Matthew picked up the van today. Tomorrow we'll get back in it for our three shows on the Continent—in Belgium, the Netherlands, and Germany—then three more in England. It's unclear how much longer this reunion will go on, or even if it *will* go on, since we haven't discussed it. Though an hour ago Orestes mentioned the prospect of playing the Primavera festival in Spain in June, and started thinking out loud about playing Brazil, where none of our bands have ever performed. In response, Sooyoung said nothing. (To be fair, neither did I.) But Orestes's ideas aren't nuts. You can do almost anything in this culture, if you have any sort of following, and one superfan in Brazil could set up shows in São Paulo and Rio, once we found said superfan. But just because we could doesn't mean we should, because playing to twenty-five people in Brazil would mean losing thousands of dollars. I know the real reason why Orestes brought those shows up: he doesn't want this to end. Neither do I. Though Sooyoung is mulish at the prospect of long practices, I'm ready to spend eight hours each day rehearsing, as is Orestes. This is *fun*. I find myself smiling a lot during practice—lasting, daffy, face-splitting grins. The buzz these songs still provide, even if many were written before I could drink legally. (If our songs were people, all of them could drink legally now, too.) Orestes and I have talked about how we both keep finding new nuances in the music. I'm finally nailing the parts that I've heard in my head forever but that never sounded right when I tried to play them. "Big Pining" had been a staple of our live sets even before our first album came out, but not until these rehearsals did I really figure out how to play the bridge. But in deference to Sooyoung's definitively reclaiming Most Reluctant Member status, neither Orestes nor I have discussed any of this with him. Although we know Sooyoung is getting an itch to write songs again. As am I. Maybe there is another record to make, after all.

* * *

FORTY HOURS LATER WE'RE IN A VAN FULL OF GEAR CRUISING up the A27 in the Netherlands after crossing the border from Belgium, passing flat, grassy fields that, even on this cold and rainy December day, are an alarmingly bright green, bisected by neatly cut irrigation ditches in which still water shimmers. Last night we played Brussels. Matthew is driving, no one is talking, and I'm in the middle row, alone with my secret: I'm as happy as I've been in years. I could go from show to show forever. Simple scenes on this featureless highway shine with beauty. Sheep graze. A farmer plods along the roadside, leading a horse draped with a maroon blanket to ward off the chill.

We arrived at the club last night later than we should have, which drives me insane even when it's not the first show of the tour. (I've had nightmares about missing soundcheck since I was a teenager.) Ancienne Belgique, which everyone calls the AB, is so huge and complicated that it doesn't take someone as confused as Spinal Tap or Ozzy Osbourne to get lost going from the loading dock to the stage. Luckily the club had painted color-coded lines in the hallways—trail markers—and kind and capable men instantly appeared to get us and our gear to the stage and set up. As Orestes started assembling his kit and Sooyoung and I shoved amps and cabinets into place, Matthew started his system check, for which he mouths wordless noises into mikes and checks the PA's output against an app on his iPhone, seeking frequencies that either feed back or sound too prominent in the room, which he'll then tweak on the soundboard. Matthew is from Dallas but lacks any regional accent, is a music nerd through and through—he's doing this tour for love, not money, so he's cutting us a great deal—and is stocky, sandy-haired, and always clad in the road-dog uniform of loose jeans and a hoodie. He's cool-headed and very thorough, which are major virtues for someone who does what he does. He has also toured Europe enough to toggle fearlessly between driving on the left and right sides of the road.

After soundcheck an in-house mess hall served dinner. The back-stage was spacious and quiet—I'd forgotten how peaceful clubs are during off-hours—and included an excellent private bathroom with its own shower. Welcome back to touring Europe, boys. I learned that Sooyoung had showered by blundering in and glimpsing his bare ass as he toweled off. If you're in a touring band on our level, you're all but guaranteed to see one another naked, but it had been a while. All other inevitable road intimacies, like sharing beds with your bandmates and seeing them cry, also grow less common as you age.

Just before showtime—the room was filling nicely, I saw, relieved—I began my routine: check an iPhone photo to make sure my pedal and amp settings haven't changed since soundcheck. Tune the black Les Paul. Tune the red Les Paul. Tune the black Les Paul again, because I use it for our first songs. Thwack the muffled strings to make sure the pedals and amp are working, recheck looping pedal settings, insert extra picks into the microphone clip, and head backstage, even if only for a minute or two. It took me years to understand certain things about performance, but by now I know: *Never walk onstage alone.* Or wait up there, after checking your rig, for the rest of your band to join you. (Only acceptable exception: if someone's starting the show with a solo piece.) Walking on together as a group looks so much tighter than if musicians straggle on individually.

Some nights things just feel off and every verse is a trudge uphill, and then you start anticipating what might go wrong, fearing that each downstroke will invite disaster, which makes fuck-ups far more likely. Some nights you know everything will be all right from the first note. We opened the show with a long version of "Dragoon," the ten-minute song from our last album, *Ben Hur,* and during the intro I jammed my guitar hard up against the speaker cabinet, to have the feedback come up just right, and the notes melted into feedback and hung in the air with perfect correctness, and I felt the way a surfer must feel after he catches a wave at the right moment and knows all he has to do is stay upright and let it carry him home.

In Brussels the first few rows—they're the only ones you can really see with stage lights shining in your eyes—were almost all guys, many bulky and fortyish. (That Soundgarden *Louder Than Love* tour shirt one very enthused dude wore definitely fit better back when he bought it.) There were, thankfully, some cute girls up front, too, including one thirtyish black-haired fan in a skirt and white boots, who bounced up and down by my side of the stage. She stayed there for the entire show. I locked eyes with her a few times, until she looked down. At one point my slide accidentally bounced offstage—I have to get rid of it very quickly between the introduction and the verse of "Motor," and the only way to do so is to fling it off my left ring finger—and afterward, while I stood tuning for the next song, she placed it at my feet. Obedient. I liked that.

In sum—no shit—the best show I'd played with this band, ever. Which I needed, after the show we played in Tokyo a month earlier.

Guitarists constantly struggle with their instruments, and the procession of knobs and devices and cords and amps and speakers required to transmit sound to the audience. Tube amps sound different each night. Dying batteries change how your pedals behave. My Les Paul is heavy enough to push your shoulder blade a few inches south, if you wear it long enough, and is solid enough to crack open a skull, but it's still a fickle and finicky assemblage of wood, and changes in temperature and humidity knock it hopelessly out of tune. The collective body heat of a crowd drastically alters any room's weather, and the extremes of cold and depressurization on long plane flights can affect guitar necks and make them impossible to tune, which is exactly what happened when I flew to Japan.

I'll spare you the technical explanation, in part because I'm not sure

I understand it myself, but when a guitar's neck is screwed up, it doesn't just go out of tune—anomalies occur up and down the fretboard that defy logic. So it was that at soundcheck in Tokyo the notes I struck on the third fret were wildly sharp, while notes on those *open* strings were perfectly in tune. Through some strange magic, this was happening on both guitars, and as luck would have it, in several songs I play delicate, quiet passages around the third fret. I've flown with guitars forever, and always take precautions: detuning each string one full step, loosely packing underwear or a T-shirt around the headstock as padding and talisman. Never before had anything like this occurred. I soundchecked in a quietly mounting panic, knowing that as soon as we were done I'd have to break out precision screwdrivers and diddle with the string saddles and intonation, trying whatever I could to coax the open string and the third fret closer in tune. But the problems remained, and I was left to await showtime with jangling nerves. I knew our set would suck, and it would be my fault, because my tuning was a mess.

I was mistaken. So many *other* things went wrong, too.

Different countries use different voltages—Japan runs on 100 volts while America uses 120—and I forgot to run my looping pedal through a voltage transformer, resulting in a momentary blinding flash that toasted the pedal and spread the homey scent of electrical fire throughout the club. My amp kept cutting out because, I thought, low-frequency vibrations were shaking the speaker cable loose. A stagehand kept leaping toward my amp mid-song—this country treats touring musicians ridiculously well—to help, but her English was bad and my Japanese doesn't exist, and of course it was deafeningly loud onstage, so very quickly I was barking at her in frustration. An asshole thing for me to do, and I'd also made a wrong diagnosis: even after she helped me switch amps, the sound kept dropping out.

Then my guitar strap came off mid-song, forcing me to play pancaked on my back while the same kind stagehand frantically tried to reattach it. It is a bad feeling to be prone onstage, staring straight up into the stage lights, horribly aware of the crowd, while strange hands fumble about your shoulder and waist. Though not as bad as it felt when the strap came off again a song or two later. I even got completely lost, somehow, during "Motor," a staple of our live set since we'd written it, and a song that, by now, I should be able to play in a coma.

Katoman, the Tokyo promoter who put on our show and the kind of guy legendary enough to be known by one name worldwide, stood by my side of the stage, looking more and more bewildered as the night went on.

Near the end of the set Sooyoung got on the mike to deadpan that we needed a new guitarist. Not a great thing to hear from the guy who once kicked me out of the band.

When we finished, I dashed backstage and blurted apologies to Orestes and Sooyoung. Despite everything, the crowd was still cheering. "What do you want to do?" asked Sooyoung. I said we should play our encores. Big mistake. When we finished, I jammed my guitar down on its stand and lurched backstage. From there I saw people staring strangely at my side of the stage, some clicking away on camera phones. Then Katoman dashed over, looking sheepish, and told me to check out my guitar.

It had fallen from the stand and now lay on the stage, its headstock split right down the middle. I took one look and thought: *Unfixable.* Second thought: *What the fuck?* I never knew guitars could crack like that. I wasn't even upset. On a night like this? It made perfect sense.

The crowd cleared out to an upstairs bar. I made my way to the stagehand I'd berated, iPhone in hand, translator app on. I punched in things like I APOLOGIZE, I WAS VERY RUDE, I AM SO SORRY. She nodded, smiled, pulled out her own phone, tapped onto it, and showed a screen saying, PLEASE COME BACK AND PLAY AGAIN NEXT YEAR.

I choked up a little. Sometimes you don't deserve the kind things people say.

I forced myself to join everyone at the bar. It's one thing, after a show, if people slap you on the back and thank you. It's another thing if they fumble for a polite way to say you stunk. It's another thing entirely if they fix you with a look of grave sympathy, put a hand on your shoulder, and say, "Man, I'm *really* sorry about that." That hadn't happened in a very long time.

Then a thought occurred to me. I slipped downstairs to the stage, grabbed the busted guitar, and jogged back up to the bar. Sliding sideways through the crowd, I strode toward an empty patch of floor, held the guitar up as high as I could, and waved it back and forth, back and forth, back and forth.

This was my gorgeous cherry sunburst Yamaha SG 3000. Shaped like a Gibson SG—those lovely symmetrical dual cutaways—but built like a Les Paul, from a thick slab of mahogany and a thinner maple cap. I'd bought it in 1993, just before a Vineland tour. A true seventies relic, this Yamaha. It had a brass block built into its body, which allegedly enhanced its sustain. I loved it, though it weighed a freaking ton. My Les Paul weighs more than ten pounds, and the Yamaha was heavier still.

But when I started slamming it into the floor, it came apart as easily as a toothpick.

People really like it when you smash a guitar. Here they howled and scrambled for smartphones and started snatching up the big pieces. In a blink or two only a few scattered matchsticks remained. A longhair who'd stood up front all night, headbanging through the entire show, immediately pounced on the body, which was more or less intact. His friend grabbed the strap and immediately improvised a properly knotted tie from it. Two guys came up to me with stray chunks and Sharpies, wanting autographs on the wreckage. (I obliged.)

Isn't it a common impulse to want to smash something to bits? Some agitation in the basal ganglia, the bit of our brains where we're no better than snakes, that place beyond the reach of words. Sometimes demolishing everything at the end of a show seems like the only proper finale. A very severe form of punctuation. Though I'd generally pictured it happening after a *good* show, like a very definitive last word.

The Yamaha was the third guitar I'd destroyed, but only the first *intentionally* demolished. Early on in Bitch Magnet we ended our sets with "Cantaloupe," a song whose ending always begged me to throw my guitar around. Which is how I broke my Peavey T-60—the one accessorized with stickers of shitty hardcore bands and Garbage Pail Kids and blood and the bitten-off logo from a can of Carling's Black Label—at the end of our first show at CBGB in 1987. We recorded that show, and that version of "Cantaloupe" ended up on *Star Booty*, and at the very end of it you can hear the guitar disintegrate, the feedback detuning a few half steps, after the neck snapped and the strings went slack.

The second was somewhere in Germany in late 1990, on the tour with Doctor Rock when all my gear was stolen, after which I paid an inflated British price for a Gibson SG from the sixties. Damn thing was *way* too delicate. I cracked its neck one night during the mildest bit of onstage roughhousing. At least it was fixable. I broke another guitar while recording *Star Booty*. Simple idiot luck: picked up the guitar by its strap, the strap slipped, the guitar fell, headstock cracked on a ceramic-tile floor, and then dangled like an unstrung marionette. Done. Though it probably didn't help that I started bashing it into said floor afterward.

After I annihilated the guitar in Tokyo and stood idly snapping the last few long bits, one guy cornered me with a video camera, asking why I'd done it. I told him it was the least I could do. That Tokyo, and my bandmates, deserved better. I told him I saw how the headstock had split and knew there was no way it could be brought back to life.

I didn't mention that I'd kind of been waiting forever to do it. I also didn't tell him that the comedown of a shitty performance sometimes involves a pit of self-loathing so black and relentless that only an explosion can make it go away. I broke my hand once, punching a wall after a bad Vineland show in Pittsburgh, and it wasn't the first time I'd bruised and bloodied knuckles that way.

At least, in Tokyo, I didn't do that.

* * *

BUT IN THE VAN SPEEDING THROUGH THE NETHERLANDS, ALL that feels very far away. Even the way the night ended in Brussels was perfect. When we got to the hotel after the show, the desk clerk slid our keys at us, attached to a sheet of paper with MAGNET, BITCH scrawled at the top. I always loved it when that happened.

But what's better is that I could breathe again. The fears were gone. We're all back within the roar I've been hearing in my head since I was a teenager, and it sounds exactly as it should. Even after all these years. Alone in the middle row of the van, I have the rare feeling that everything is going to be fine. We can play as well as we ever did.

Hell, maybe we can even play better.

I Hope We Don't Suck

Atour is a parallel world in which all citizens basically only talk about rock, and once we got back on the road after being away so long, I started struggling through those conversations. Despite those decades feeding an encyclopedic knowledge of all current bands, I'd stopped following music obsessively and now knew so little about what was going on. At least I wasn't the only one who wasn't keeping up. When I mentioned to Sooyoung that someone from *MOJO*, the very smart British music magazine, would interview us in London, he looked at me blankly and asked, "What's *MOJO*?"

Then we saw our old friends Superchunk play La Scala in London. They encored with "Slack Motherfucker," and the crowd sang along, so loud you couldn't hear the band. Because Superchunk, surprisingly, *weren't* loud. Clubs now posted and enforced volume restrictions. Our first time around, almost none did. (When I heard in the nineties that New York's Bowery Ballroom insisted that bands not exceed a certain decibel count, I was outraged, and vowed my bands would never play there. Of course, Bowery Ballroom never asked.)

Onstage, Superchunk dressed more or less exactly as I remembered.

I'd gone onstage in jeans and T-shirts since I was a teenager, but this tour I knew I just couldn't anymore. I couldn't stand looking like something dragged from the attic, dusted off, and sent out to play, slightly moth-eaten around the edges. Also, the ridiculous T-shirts in which I'd always performed—a Thompson Twins shirt silkscreened with garish new wave peaches, pinks, and blues; a three-quarter-sleeve 1981 Rolling Stones tour jersey featuring some giant serpent belipped with their logo; the blue-green one proclaiming, GOD BLESS DETROIT, ROCK & ROLL CAPITOL OF EARTH; that Grim Reaper shitty-cities tour shirt—were now fashion clichés, often seen stretched across the chests of models and starlets. For the Bitch Magnet reunion tour I wore my favorite white oxford button-downs onstage: Thom Browne. Super-slim, perfect fit, and look great rumpled, which means they travel well. (I quickly got over the fact that the younger me would totally snarl at the thought of wearing such a shirt.) And tight pants, because I'm short, have no hair, and skinny's all I got. I wanted to wear a suit jacket, too, but people who've tried that assured me: bad idea. I'd *shvitz*; it would restrict movement and look misshapen and lumpy mashed under my guitar strap.

This time around I also had to learn to keep my head still when I played. As much as I had a stage presence on our early tours, it was built on whipping my long hair around, which is why several old friends asked if I planned to wear a wig for these shows. (Ha-ha. Thanks, dicks.) That long hair made headbanging dramatic—because it made almost anything you did onstage look dramatic, a curtain of curls waggling back and forth, amplifying every gesture and movement. But when you're bald, headbanging doesn't look good. It looks like convulsions. Before this round of shows I sometimes practiced while looking in a mirror—a pro-rock vanity move I forever found repugnant—trying to unlearn old instincts to telegraph each chord, tempo change, or dramatic downstroke with a quick headsnap: *Stop twitching!*

Also, we decided it was cool for wives and girlfriends to come along. In the past I was always against allowing spouses or equivalents in the

227

van. Not because tours are don't-ask-don't-tell trips for dudes—the no-mates rule held for tours I did with women bandmates, too, because I wanted tours to be band-only bonding experiences, and I didn't want any outsiders in the van making musicians peel off from the rest of the gang or, worse, introducing their own emotional valences and complications. Band chemistry is delicate in the best of times. Now, though? Why not? And we thought it would be nice to have our women witness this weirdness, too.

We still played primarily to overly intense guys in glasses, all of whom are still clad in familiar clothing: Chuck Taylors or cheap low-rise Adidas, band T-shirts, formless jeans, a flannel or hoodie. But at least the gender breakdowns were now often better than the brutal ninety-ten ratio we routinely experienced when we were an active band. Though some nights it was worse. I knew there were women at our headline show in London, but you wouldn't from the photos. At our show in Cologne I sat at our merch table, across from the entrance, watching the people stream in. The first hundred attendees were all guys. By the end of the night I think there were five women, one of whom booked the show. If success is playing to a crowd that looks exactly like me, Cologne was our best show ever—but it *was* a great crowd, even if, during the set, we couldn't make our blood run redder by eyeballing the women in the audience. And we were absolutely mobbed at the merch booth afterward, because our merch sales were suddenly twenty times better than they'd ever been. At some shows basically everyone who showed up bought something, sometimes also asking us for autographs for their kids.

What got me thinking, though, was that there weren't many younger fans at our European and American shows. After the show in Brussels one did ask me a question about *Umber*. I did some quick math and realized he was two when that record came out. Then I met the gray-haired guy who explained he'd loved us forever but had to sit for much of the show, because he had bad feet.

And here comes the part about How the Internet Has Changed It All. Everything is recorded now, and all of it is visible, because shows get posted to YouTube almost immediately. (The one song I fucked up badly always went online first. *Always*.) Online translation engines helped me through minimalist Twitter conversations with fans in Asia, and with my apology to that kind stagehand in Tokyo. We dealt with nine different currencies during an eighteen-month-long reunion and quickly developed an iron-lung-like dependency on the exchange rate site and app xe.com. And you saw all reviews immediately. In the old days it took months to see the coverage of overseas shows, if you saw it at all. The day after our show in Brussels—the one that made me so happy—we read one review that contended that Sooyoung's performance slipped up at times, and quoted his backstage observation that relearning the songs had been hard. Also: e-mail, not faxes and transoceanic phone calls! Twitter and Facebook interactions with fans! Cell phones, so no more desperate searches for rest stops or gas stations when you were lost! Though you were never lost anymore, thanks to GPS and Google Maps! And in America you no longer worried about the cost of long-distance calls—so touring bands no longer had to use stolen credit cards or phone phreakers' red boxes! Thank you. Moving on.

Were we different, too? I wasn't sure. In 1990, after a riot of a show in Belgium or the Netherlands or Germany, I ended up at our hotel bar with a gaggle of fans, still wound up from the performance. I naturally vibrated at a very high frequency back then, so I'm hanging out, animated and wired even at that advanced hour, doing the thing where you talk with your hands, because, you know, *Jewish*, and a woman— Ellen—nodded seriously after I unleashed some spiel and said, in a thick accent, quite carefully and quite out of nowhere, "You know, you are really like—ehhhhhh—Woody Allen?"

So I wasn't getting laid by anyone that night.

Twenty-one years later she and her husband saw us in Brussels. After the show I ducked away from the merch table to talk to her. This time she said, "You guys were great tonight. And you seem much more relaxed than you were in 1990."

Low bar, Ellen. But thanks.

* * *

AND YET SO MUCH REMAINED THE SAME. ON TOUR YOU FUNC-tioned effectively on half as much sleep and twice as much drinking. You had four or five beers each night before you *really* started drinking. You didn't tolerate the long dead stretches in the van, you welcomed them and their crucial salve to sanity: hours of quiet with no demands beyond simple forward motion. You woke, dazed from a nap in the van, no longer concerned about whether this landmarkless stretch of highway was in Austria or Germany or Belgium or the Netherlands, because you finally understood that, in that moment, it didn't really matter at all.

After playing our three shows in Europe, we arrived at the Butlins holiday camp in Minehead for All Tomorrow's Parties in full-on tour mode. Getting there, of course, was a particularly British nightmare: sliding through an ink-black night and pouring rain, the sky seemingly six inches above the roof of the van, and a series of towns one can legitimately call "villages," with roads slightly too small for a van. Matthew scraped overgrown hedges and narrowly evaded ancient stone roadside walls. If I'd driven, at least one mirror would be lying on the side of the road somewhere, if not a bumper and door, too. We pulled into Butlins just as the festival was starting on a Friday night, and immediately beached in an impressive clot of traffic at the check-in. My room key came taped to a piece of paper that had Stuart Braithwaite's name crossed out and mine in its place, leaving me terrified for days that I'd bump into a naked member of Mogwai stepping out of the shower.

A festival has its own momentum, and if you arrive late and road-weary, it can be hard to catch up. That night I saw the last fifteen seconds of Wild Flag—nothing but some feedback squalls and Mary

Timony muttering "Thanks"—and left annoyed that I didn't see more. Mini-gangs of fortyish, anorak-clad overgrown indie kids, mostly British, were everywhere, and all seemed to know each other. They moved from building to building, happy and chatting and hunching against the wind and rain. It felt like attending someone else's college reunion. Albeit a very efficient one. Bands started their sets on time at ATP, which was great, unless you were sluggish and a step behind, as I was. Luckily I came across a gaggle of friends—the guys in Battles and a bunch of mutual pals, all of us joined later that evening by Laurel—which was enormously comforting, because there were something like six thousand people there, and fans were already coming up to us: *We came from Macedonia to see you. I came from Dubai to see you. I came from Australia to see you.*

The only possible response, which I found myself repeating over and over, was "Wow. Thanks. I hope we don't suck."

That scene in *Body Heat* when Mickey Rourke does the there's-fifty-ways-to-fuck-up-any-decent-crime thing? There's at least as many ways to fuck up onstage. (See: Tokyo.) By the time I was in Coptic Light I no longer suffered from preshow nerves. But here they were again, as bad as ever: the undefinable floating deep dread that *something would go wrong*, terribly wrong, and then the horrible shaming sense of failure would descend. A feeling made all the worse given how long I had waited for this show. The culmination of our reunion so far. The meal ticket that made it all happen, after all these years. Here. *Now*. At an off-season holiday camp on a cold coast of England, of all places. Amid several thousand people like us, whose existences I couldn't imagine when I was in high school, even though they'd all been out there, somewhere, stumbling upon records, wading each day through schoolmates' indifference or contempt, waiting for their lives to begin.

The day of a show flings you onto a conveyor belt and trundles you through the tunnel that leads inexorably to showtime: travel, arrival, unloading, soundcheck, dead time, doors open, onstage. But we woke up in Butlins on the day of our show, and I'd never played a festival before, so the rhythms were unfamiliar. I watched Battles and then Nissenenmondai destroy an early-afternoon crowd, but afterward bands washed over me without making any impression. A few times I choked up, realizing I'd never be able to tell Jerry Fuchs about any of this or hear him make fun of us for reuniting, as he surely would have, before coming to see us anyway.

At the merch booth we met a few more people who came a long way or said they'd been waiting a long time to see us.

I hope we don't suck. I hope we don't suck. I hope we don't suck.

The bands ate at a mess hall. A high school cafeteria, just about: an oversized kitchen, buffets of cold and hot foods in an underoccupied and giant institutional room. But this was our water cooler and green room, and I saw people I hadn't seen since college, and I loved it instantly. I found Bob Weston—bassist in Shellac, soundman for Mission of Burma, all-around excellent human—and his wife, Carrie. Pharoah Sanders sat at the head of another table; stupidly, I didn't introduce myself. Dinner was a blessing, a normal interval on a day in which I was gradually losing my mind. I mean, just *writing* this makes me nervous, bowels rumbling, like a junkie watching bubbles break the surface in the spoon.

For a while we thought All Tomorrow's Parties was going to be our first reunion show. Good God, what were we thinking? *Hey, let's play live for the first time in twenty-one years to our biggest crowd ever!* Bad idea. The stakes are way too high, and no matter how much you've played together beforehand in a practice space, you can't replicate showtime: confronting the fear, riding the adrenaline, understanding the spectacle of it, relating to your bandmates naturally while unnaturally being on display, dealing with the X factor any audience introduces. Onstage chemistry for the first reunion shows is always unstable and uncertain, and even the best performers can get pretty hinky about it. The Jesus Lizard's first reunion show was a headline slot at ATP, and David Yow, one of rock's most natural frontmen and the veteran of over a thousand shows, recalled, "I always get nervous before shows, but I was fucking *shaking*. I was so terrified."

After I ate, I headed back to our apartment to grab my guitars and get ready. Change strings, take a dump, breathe—all the preshow essentials—and then I told Laurel I was leaving. The late nights and late mornings of ATP ran counter to her biorhythms, but she still ran with the rest of our crew and did gangbusters business whenever she worked the merch stand.

Big smile. Big hug. "Aren't you excited?" she asked.

"No. I'm completely out of my fucking mind," I told her.

Backstage at Butlins was a holding pen, all cement and steel, as cold and echoing as the bowels of some great, hideous arena in the American Midwest, not that I'd know from experience. Block-printed band names were taped to dressing room doors above the legend "Fire door—keep shut." (So British, all that lowercase.) The three of us had to stand to fit comfortably in ours. A few mirrors took up one wall, all artifacts, with round bulbs running around their borders, the kind seen only in movies. These made me smile: showbiz! Cases of bottled water and skunky lukewarm Peroni and Corona. And no cell phone reception, but that was fine. It was time to shut off the rest of the world.

I stretched the new guitar strings, and tuned and retuned. Sooyoung fiddled with a camera. Orestes languorously laid into his warmup. Normally steady before a show, tonight he turned oddly obnoxious backstage, referring loudly to Cults—the band playing before us, whom we hadn't yet met—as *CAHHHNNTS*, in a fake English accent. But he calmed as soon as his sticks started moving on the shallow white Formica shelf beneath the showbiz mirrors. Always slightly mesmerizing, that mantra. Or at least it gave us something to look at and listen to: *Rat-a-tat-a-rat-a-tat-a-tat-a-rat-a-tat-a-tat-a* . . .

We congratulated Cults after their set when they passed us backstage, though in truth we couldn't hear anything in our dressing room.

Once onstage, I started to tune one guitar again but got no reading on the digital tuner at my feet. *Oh, Christ.* Then I noticed I wasn't plugged in. The lighting woman sauntered over to ask what we wanted. "More blues and whites than reds," I told her, glad to be asked. Reds make a stage look smeary. Blues and whites look sharp and distinct.

Sets are staggered among the different rooms at ATP, so there's a stretch of dead time in each venue after every performance, and the crowd quickly filed out after Cults' set. Thirty minutes to showtime, and we were setting up to a distressingly empty room that could hold a couple thousand people. Twenty minutes to showtime: still empty. Fifteen minutes to showtime: empty but for twenty diehards pressed up against the barrier separating them from the stage, and maybe twenty more people scattered elsewhere in the room. *I don't care*, I told myself, and continued the preshow ritual: check the tuning on my guitars again, thwack the muffled strings, recheck amp and pedal settings. I jammed a few picks into the microphone clip and went back to the dressing room for the last ten minutes, resigned to play to a lonely crowd in a huge hall. Orestes's girlfriend, Rosi, was there with her camera. *Click. Click.* That and Orestes's *rat-a-tat-tat*ing drumsticks were the only sounds. Then I heard a familiar voice and looked up to see Laurel in the doorway, clutching a camera, a big smile on her face, flashing all of us a thumbs-up. For a long moment I stared at her blankly, lost in thought.

Then: showtime. Sooyoung and I walked down that chilly hallway, through the stage door and onto the stage lit a crystalline blue, passing the stagehands and the gear, and only then did we see that somehow— somehow—the room had filled.

Grim-faced bouncers in orange shirts settled into position on either side of the stage. Sooyoung grabbed his bass. Scattered applause. I hefted the black Les Paul—the one detuned to D—settled the strap onto my left shoulder, flicked the standby switch on the Hiwatt, tapped on the guitar a few times to get a drone going, turned to face the crowd, then hit the three opening notes to "Dragoon" and spun around to belly up to the speaker stack, guitar body pressed hard against the top speaker cabinet, the notes hanging in the air just so.

Sooyoung—deadpan and still, as he always was onstage—glanced my way. We nodded, hit the C-to-D change that ends the opening riff, then I shoved the guitar hard against the speaker cabinet again, this time slowly running it up and around the edge. A gratuitous and totally phallic move, and I will never tire of it. Also a showy way to keep the guitar up against the cabinet and let sound waves and sheer volume make the three bottom strings vibrate a flawless, endless open D chord, all fifths and octaves. We let that chord roar for a while.

Three more notes, ending on a ringing, unresolved interval, and Orestes bounded onstage to shouts and cheers, settled on the drum stool, turned my way, mouthed "One-two," and we all slammed into the next three notes, and after the last I wheeled to face my amp, gripped the guitar with both hands and raised it overhead, the neck pointing straight up, shaking it furiously, catching a feedback note that shook along, exquisitely in sync—*Yessssssss*—and I saw Orestes looking hungry and intent, and I instantly knew he'd take us wherever we needed to go.

I was holding on to myself so tightly through "Dragoon"—the song has several different tempos, many gradations of soft and loud, and those delicate parts for which I forever fear being out of tune—that I ended the song out of breath, even though I hadn't run around at all, and during the set I understood that I'd played better shows on the tour. But I also understood that it didn't matter, because the event took over. The looks on some faces in the front row were so intense that glancing at them felt like getting shocked. The guys from Macedonia, standing directly in front of Sooyoung, hopped up and down, singing along with every song, eyes closed, faces contorted—watching them made me feel I was intruding. Chavez's Clay Tarver once told me about the difference between pretend shows and real shows. At a pretend show the crowd is sluggish and the band has to supply all the energy, while at a real show the audience provides the juice. This was a real show. An energy current whipped around the room without the least resistance: sound to crowd, crowd to us, amplify and repeat. There's a sheer sexual power when you fill a huge room with glorious, massive noise, playing through a guitar rig that behaves exactly as you want it. There's a magical feeling when you believe—no, when you *know*—you can wave your hands or a guitar at the amp and the electrons inside instantly respond. Even after all these years it's still the closest feeling to God that I know. And every time I got the tiniest taste of it, I understood why so many willingly ruin their lives for it.

After "Sea of Pearls"—likely our most baby-splitting compromise between Sooyoung's pop sense and my secret wish to go metal—and thank-you-good-night, we ambled backstage. (Something else it took me years to learn: exit all stages *slowly*, savoring.) I grabbed another beer, took a piss, and when I returned to the stage, the room was empty again but for stagehands and spent cups and smells. Then someone called out, and I saw Bob and Carrie Weston standing alone in the middle of the room, huge smiles, Bob flashing a thumbs-up. Like I said, in indie rock almost no one will tell you that you sucked, especially friends. But my heart still leapt out of my chest a little at that sight.

After 4 a.m. our crew that night—us and Rosi, Battles and Ian's fiancée, Kate, Nathan and Madeleine from Cults, our friends Pedje and Anya, all our chemistries still blazing with post-performance highs—ended up at one of Battles' apartments, where Pedje methodically broke out excellent bread, geeky cheese, a case of natural wine, and the entire side of a smoked salmon. To plastic knives—the only ones around—salmon skin may as well be barbed wire, so soon we just yanked off unruly chunks, mashed them onto hunks of bread, and shoved the whole mess mouthward. I watched the fish and cheese sweat in the dim and crowded room, knowing exactly how gross it would smell in the morning and how much grosser it would smell with a severe hangover, toward which each of us was sprinting. Cults had a 6 a.m. van call for their three-hour drive to Heathrow. Their tour manager was a classic British road dog, bald and soft-bellied in a loose gray hoodie, who showed up precisely five minutes early to shepherd them out. Being escorted from the afterparty to the van that takes you straight to the airport is rock-star stuff. But I was unbelievably grateful not to be them.

Were there drugs at ATP? There had to be, though, except for a little pot, I saw none. A few women working for a well-known record label offered us E. But entering the Decemberian gloom of London while coming down hard and short on serotonin would make any man sui-cidal, and we declined. (One undernoticed reason for indie rock anhe-donia: it's almost impossible to explore rock's druggy sideshows when touring without a road crew. There's too much crap to do each day.) I'm sure some colorful, rock festival-y things happened that weekend. The chilly morning after our show I saw muddy footprints—as in, from someone's bare feet—describing a winding path on the walkways. Guess someone had an interesting night.

* * *

OUR EUROPEAN TOUR ENDED IN LONDON, OPENING FOR HOT Snakes at the Garage, a show more addendum than a climax. The opening-band problem is that you don't play to your crowd. The appeal is that you play to people who otherwise wouldn't see you, but convert-ing new fans is useless for an old band reuniting for just a few shows. Anyway, we were never an easy opening band—too weird to go well with aggressive bands, too aggressive to go well with weird bands, and definitely a sore thumb for something as straightforward as Hot Snakes. As I hit the first notes of the show, a good-looking woman standing by my side of the stage winced and went for her ears, eyebrows knitting together in dismay. *How dare you*, I thought. I moved to the lip of the stage—an actual stage, six feet tall; there was real hierarchy in standing on it—and stared straight through her eyes for several minutes as I played. Towering above her, with a guitar and amplification on my side, so it was not a very fair fight.

But halfway into "Dragoon" I realized my guitar had gone slightly out of tune. A very bad thing to discover when five minutes remain in a song. Then Orestes had some problems, which never happens. People talked through the quiet parts. Everything I said between songs sounded rushed, and even though I knew it did, I couldn't slow myself down. At the end of our last song I went hip to hip with the amp stack, making big Leatherface motions with the guitar, and when I threw it down in front of the amp, I destroyed a patch cord. Better that than breaking another guitar, I guess.

Bartenders at the Garage pour bottles of beer into plastic cups—having spent time among drunk Brits, I endorse any policy that separates them from potential weapons—so after the show I crunched my way across a huge dance floor calf-deep in crushed and empty cups to chat with a few fans still sticking around, like Phil. Phil was about forty, but it was his first time seeing us, he explained, because when we'd last toured Britain, his parents wouldn't let him go. That cracked me up. He snapped a pic of us together and begged us to return. "I hope your parents let you come next time, too," I told him, pleased he'd set up the punchline so perfectly.

Our headline show in London the night before, at the Lexington— that would have made the better ending. Though that evening didn't start out so well. Andrew Male from *MOJO* was there and began his interview by asking a perfunctory question about reuniting, to which Sooyoung matter-of-factly replied, "For the record, I was against it." Which would have been the lead quote, were I writing the article. But I wasn't, and luckily, when the piece was published, it wasn't.

The Lexington is tiny, and the show was oversold, and there was a ludicrous volume restriction of 101 decibels. (I can *burp* louder than that.) Backstage was yet another dingy room in yellowed paint with cleaning supplies on open shelves, walls and ceiling displaying endless

Magic Markered dicks and balls, monkeys with mysteriously enormous testicles, and baroque instructions concerning what to do with all the genitalia. But the opening bands, Former Utopia and smallgang, were the crew we'd gone to pubs with each night in London, and the show became a homecoming to a city we'd never really bonded with before. When the club opened the doors, one of the first entrants bounded up to the merch booth to confess how anxious *he* felt. The room was so excruciatingly well lit that from the stage you could see the face of everyone in the audience, which is always nerve-racking, But everyone was pulling so hard for us, we could have crapped our pants and it would have been fine. This was a Monday night, and some people told us they were calling in sick tomorrow, because they'd driven 250 miles from Liverpool or 300 miles from Newcastle. The Lexington is an excellent whiskey bar, and people stuck around to drink until very late. Just before closing time someone clapped me on the back in the men's room and stuck out a hand to shake while I stood at a urinal, peeing.

More than anything, I want to remember meeting Allan, who, like most everyone else there, was burly and bearded and balding and forty-ish. Allan, though, came with a minder. He has a severe seizure disorder, typically experiences several each day, and lives at an assisted-living facility. He's also a huge Bitch Magnet fan, and even though loud music triggers his episodes, he insisted he absolutely had to see our show, and whoever decides such things finally consented. He had several seizures during our set, he told me afterward, a huge post-show grin on his face. Then his smile widened and he added, "So, when people say that your music is *convulsive* . . ."

Hearts, Allan. You made it all worth it.

Bitch Magnet
March 29, 2012 · 🌐

BITCH MAGNET, ASIA, APRIL 2012:
4/13: Singapore (Home Club)
4/14: Hong Kong (Hidden Agenda)
4/17: Manila, Philippines (Saguijo)
4/21: Tokyo, Japan (Kaikoo Popwave Festival)

Like · Comment

 Bitch Magnet
March 30, 2012 · 🌐

April Asia Tour, Mach 2: We just confirmed one more Tokyo show. Friday, April 20 at Shibuya O-East, with doseone, and Ningen OK

Like · Comment

Burutaru Desu

Noon in Tokyo. Late April 2012, but it feels like March: partly cloudy, quite windy, a tinge of winter you can't ignore. Sooyoung and I stand on a paved expanse outside the Museum of Maritime Science, a six-story building shaped like an ocean liner. We're at the Kaikoo Popwave Festival, during our second run through Asia. Batcave is onstage, proving there's no metal like old metal. The members of Batcave—dear God! what a name!—are all middle-aged, with waistlines that would make any Hell's Angel proud. Before their set we watched them rip open beers backstage, a move wholly unremarkable were it not for the fact that everyone else was still eating breakfast.

We're on next. Set time: 1:30. Sooyoung has recovered amazingly from another epic night out. (I started falling asleep at the bar around two—thank you, jet lag—and went back to the hotel.) He was late and semi-responsive for van call and breakfasted on a microwaved cup of convenience-store noodle soup as we sped to the festival. To approximate something David Chang once said, in Tokyo even the shitty food is great, and you can throw together a shockingly good meal from prepared foods available at any 7-11 or Lawson's. I still winced at

Sooyoung's choice, but it worked, and he's identifiably human again. Today, thankfully, won't be like that day in Seoul last fall when his bedroom door was still closed at noon and Orestes and I thought he might still be out from the night before. Then my phone rang, and I heard Sooyoung croak, "I can't move," and I got all Florence Nightingale and brought him water and a fistful of Advil, which got him well enough to rise and lead us to a restaurant known for steaming bowls of a rejuvenative chicken-and-ginseng soup.

The thing about outdoor festivals isn't just that you sometimes play at lunchtime in weather that begs for a sweater, and maybe mittens, too. Playing outside, broadly speaking, sucks. Sound dissipates no matter how huge the speaker rig is, so you never attain the good sonic density common to any half-decent club. At Kaikoo we are playing on the festival's Grand Master stage, and after seeing Batcave, I start to grasp the retirement-community overtone to "Grand Master." On top of everything, Orestes is brutally sick. Bedridden our entire time in Tokyo, wracked by fever and chills and cramps and shakes. I'd stopped by his hotel room every few hours with water and medication, and to monitor his general condition. Before the set I ply him with bananas: easy on the stomach! calories! potassium!

When Batcave lumbers offstage, our friend Carl, who speaks fluent Japanese, hears someone compliment a Batcaver on his band, to which Batcave guy says, *"Burutaru desu,"* which translates to "It is brutal," a phrase that immediately enters our lexicon. ("How's the pizza?" *"Burutaru desu."*) Our songs seem slow onstage, which made me crazy when I was twenty and still does now. But we get through the set. Decent crowd, subpar performance. Though it is miraculous that Orestes can play at all, let alone as solidly as he does. At our previous Tokyo show he was even sicker, and I told him backstage that he'd carried me for many shows and tonight I'd carry him, so I stayed close to him onstage, jumping up and down, locking eyes, urging him along. I had to do something to get the energy level up, so when a photographer was shooting me at the end of one song, I charged right at him, jumping off the stage—still playing—making extravagant faces into his lens, licking his cheek when I finally caught up with him. He kept clicking like mad as he backpedaled. (I wish I could find him now and see those photos.) Tokyo is one of my favorite cities, and I love playing there, but for us it feels cursed. We played three shows there during our reunion, and not one went well. At least at Kaikoo the guy who'd interviewed me after I'd smashed my guitar the last time we were in town showed up at our merch booth and handed me a DVD of that interview. I thanked him—and discovered much later that he'd missed recording the actual guitar-smash.

I ALMOST PULLED THE PLUG ON THIS ASIAN TOUR. SETTING IT up was an unusually large pain in the ass, and I had to absorb almost all of the ass-pain. The costs were brutal, and there was no way to avoid losing thousands of dollars. But we had a cash cushion left over from Europe, and eventually the choice became binary: go on tour, or go to work for two weeks. Not a hard call when framed like that. Even less so when framed like this: We're old. When else would we do this? So we got ambitious. Maybe too ambitious: Singapore, Hong Kong, Manila, and those two shows in Tokyo. A tour in which we had to clear passport control and customs in a new country every day, with lies about why we were visiting, since most countries demand work permits for performers. A frisson of tension always came with crossing borders, especially since I was lugging my guitars in two enormous flight cases that kept getting mistaken for something in which you'd stash an assault rifle. Most smaller bands half-sneak across borders this way, but everyone knew at least one that had been denied entry into some country or other. Two bands I know—Red Scare and Storm & Stress—got turned away from Canada. (*Canada.* That's gotta sting.) For their first Japanese tour in the nineties, Tortoise learned about work permits only when authorities at Narita Airport wouldn't let them into the country—so they flew to Seoul, did the paperwork at the American embassy, secured the permits, and made it into Japan without missing a single show. I'm really glad I never had to deal with anything like that after an endless flight from America to Tokyo.

Orestes and I arrived at Singapore's Changi Airport in early April, mildly deranged after flying roughly twenty hours, for a few days' practice and our first show. How nice an airport is Changi? There's a fucking *swimming pool* atop Terminal One. Singapore is hot and equatorial. Also, basically an upscale outdoor shopping mall extrapolated to an entire country. Much of it looks like it was built in the eighties. These parts are considered historic. (I'm joking. Somewhat.) Everything works. Sit-down restaurants are exorbitant, since almost every ingredient is imported, but hawker centers are crammed with small stalls purveying cheap and variegated Asian grub, the stuff of food bloggers' wet dreams, and Orestes and I gorged ourselves in them daily.

I'd found a practice space called Four Tones—a reference to Mandarin pronunciation, I learned—and reserved time well in advance of our arrival by corresponding with someone who signed e-mails THE WALL. All caps. We found Four Tones on a surprisingly sketchy block. ("Sketchy" in Singapore is relative, but there was no mistaking the prostitutional vibe there and in an often abandoned bar just downstairs from Four Tones.) In person The Wall was a friendly, wavy-haired Malay in his late twenties or early thirties, neither hulking nor freakishly tall. His feet splayed in the way of people who are barefoot all the time: Four Tones is a shoe-free practice space. You stepped out of your sneakers in the hallway and padded into your carpeted rehearsal room, and when you glanced down during rehearsal, you saw your stupid socked feet alongside your effects pedals and suddenly felt twelve again, in a friend's fancy suburban basement rec room—the friend whose parents were humorless hard-asses and banned footwear in their new-carpet-smelling house.

That sight didn't make you feel as if you were grasping pure power with both hands, and the gear at Four Tones was semi-functional and sounded terrible, but things still clicked once we started rehearsing. In our first reunion shows Sooyoung wore his bass higher on his body than he did our first time around, because some sense memory made him wear it as high as the guitar he played in Seam. But you don't strum a bass gently, all wrist, as you can a guitar. In Singapore he adjusted his strap, shifting his bass maybe three inches lower, a minor change that made a huge difference. Now he got his shoulder into every downstroke and started playing with much more muscle and authority, and despite the bad amps and toy drums and overall sock-rock vibe, we sounded *good*. Noticeably better than we had in Europe.

During the day Sooyoung went to work at his company's office. He invited us to stop by, and we met his staff, though he generally kept the band a secret, and I don't know how many of them really knew why we were there. Orestes and I stayed in an apartment complex near Fort Canning Park, popular with expat European and American families, where we sort of worked, too, on our laptops, but lunch took a huge bite out of our afternoons, and we spent a lot of time lounging around the giant outdoor pool, sometimes catching each other's gaze and cracking up. Our first time around hadn't been anything like this.

Each morning at our apartment building, everyone crammed into the too-small breakfast room and attacked a free buffet until everything was gone. Once, still reeking of booze and fried food and the very late night before—the kind of morning when you feel the need to apologize for your appearance, if not your scent—I squeezed into the tiny elevator alongside a fresh-faced American family, whose young children regarded me with one glance and instinctively moved closer to their parents.

Sorry, folks. We came to Singapore for rock. You remember rock, don't you, ma'am? Though, who knows, it may be gone by the time your kids grow up.

The Singapore show was at the Home Club, which sits in a mall across from a cement river channel, or maybe it was just a ditch to catch the runoff from heavy rainstorms. We'd never played in a mall before, but in Singapore it kind of made sense. There we met Phil, an Australian superfan who'd told us through Facebook that he was burning a lifetime's worth of frequent-flier miles to make the show. *(Great to meet you, Phil. I hope we don't suck.)* The club had concrete walls and concrete floors and concrete steps leading up to the stage, which is not exactly the zenith of acoustic design. But after our set we came offstage, looked at one another, and realized no one had made any mistakes. Nothing had gone wrong at all. The strange dawning hit all of us at the same time: we'd probably just played our best show ever. A young band called Amateur Takes Control opened and played incredibly elaborate instrumentals. Each guitarist had a pedal board maybe three feet square, as jammed as a city parking lot with effects boxes. As he'd done at our show in Seoul, Sooyoung enlisted someone from their band to play bass on our encore—on this tour the Hard-Ons' one great song, "All Set to Go"—and then he watched us all from the audience. In this case, being drafted last-minute to play on a song you've never heard sounds much more intimidating than it actually was, because "All Set to Go" is a single two-chord progression, endlessly repeated, and after Sooyoung big-brothered this guy onstage and handed him his bass, I taught him the song in roughly fifteen seconds:

It's four bars of straight eighth notes on A: da da da da da da da da da da da da da da da da da da da da da da da da da da da da da da da.

And then four bars of straight eighth notes on D: da da da da etc.

Got that? Great. Just keep repeating it.

It's a hard song to screw up, especially if you can play as well as any member of Amateur Takes Control.

Afterward we went to a large private room in a karaoke joint, where an endless procession of new arrivals meant that, soon enough, there was nowhere to sit and not many places to stand. Platters of fried chicken (excellent) and bottles of whiskey (cheap) kept appearing. Eventually I kept a full plastic cup of whiskey nearby at all times so Soo-young's wife, Fiona, wouldn't refill it and insist I drink more. Certain details are fuzzy, but I remember singing "Hungry Like the Wolf" with her. And that at one point Sooyoung tried to get me to sing something but I kept refusing, and when he tried to force the mike on me, we got into a weird, shovey standoff for a few seconds. What was *that* about?

* * *

NOTE TO MIDDLE-AGED TOURING BANDS: IN HONG KONG, PAY whatever is necessary to avoid guesthouses and hostels like ours, on a crowded, commercial strip in Tsim Sha Tsui. Imagine a grimy building that takes up an entire city block on all four sides, so crammed with people and stuff and activity and everything that, unfortunately, the only word to use is "teeming" and the only thing to say is that a Wes Anderson fantasia played out within its walls, endlessly. The building was centered on a courtyard, across which residents hung laundry. To get to the elevator, you passed through a long and dense arcade of small, grubby shops until you found travelers lined up, waiting beside their giant backpacks. At each floor, as you ascended in the lift, people streamed on and off, clutching their microcosm of everything: guys rolling handtrucks stacked with bags of cement mix, women carrying count-less plastic sacks, people staggering under statuary. After a few floors you wouldn't be surprised to see someone ride in on a motorcycle.

To get to our tiny room, you traversed an interior hallway, passing a few more "hostels"—a few equally tiny rooms off other obscure hallway passages—keyed open a door that led into a narrow passageway, and *then* opened the first door on the right. When we first walked that nar-row passage, we squeezed past a woman eating soup on a tiny shelf next to our door. When we came back that night, after the show and drinks, the same woman was sleeping peacefully and remarkably compactly on that same shelf. Our room was just big enough to hold a bunk bed and a single, and it made you want to avoid the shower and keep your socks on at all times. I was all for being budget-conscious on a tour already destined to lose money, but on the way to the show I made a reservation at the Holiday Inn across the street for our second night. Rooms there were done up in slightly stomach-turning eighties tones of peach and beige and marbled brown, and a night cost something like $250, but it felt like money spent very wisely. Johns and hookers met in the parking lot. You'd see a dolled-up woman leaning against a wall. A few minutes later she'd be gone, replaced by some ferrety-looking and fidgety guy. Waiting. Though probably not for long.

Our show was at a venue far more punk rock than I'd ever been, one called Hidden Agenda, tucked away on a high floor in an anonymous building in a deeply industrial part of town. There was some kind of auto shop on the ground floor, though the totally stripped Smart car skeleton out front made me wonder about its legitimacy. Filmmakers who seek the dystopia that looming gray cityscapes signify would do well to shoot in this neighborhood on a cloudy day. Or any day. I'm not sure sunlight ever made it to street level there. I mean: *Burutaru desu.*

Hidden Agenda regularly butted heads with local authorities over real or perceived infractions, the latest of which meant the club couldn't serve alcohol. We snuck some in, but I winced to think what that ruling would do to turnout. One guy in the audience had flown in from Taiwan, though someone else had to explain that to us, because he didn't speak any English. He just stood there nodding during that conversation, and I hope our translator got across how thrilling and crazy that was to us. Another showed up with an original copy of our first record—from our self-released first pressing of a thousand—wanting autographs. Amazing to see how that record ended up so far from home.

But we were already tour-weary and dispirited, even on our day off, when Orestes and I roamed the city while Sooyoung traveled for work. We did manage to eat well, an overweening concern of all bands, and ours in particular: an amazing meal at Mak's Noodles—delightful dense and springy noodles, finer than angel hair—where the waiters were so actively unpleasant it was hilarious. On Sooyoung's recommendation Orestes and I also went to a Korean place in Kowloon: Won Pung Won. At first the badass *halumni*—Korean grandmas—running the joint treated us indifferently. Then Orestes spoke to them in Korean—ever the language savant, he picked up quite a bit in our five days in Seoul—and it became a glorious meal. Afterward Orestes and I each did the inevitable asshole-American-tourist thing and took pics of a sign we liked, which he spotted emblazoned on an awning:

FOOK KIU MANSION.

* * *

I'D NEVER PLAYED AT A VENUE WHERE LIZARDS CRAWL THE walls until we played the saGuijo Café in Manila. A bar in the tropics, with a loose division between indoors and outdoors. We spent just enough time in Manila to begin to appreciate its size and troubles: the air is smoggy enough to hurt, traffic jams are epic and constant, and the people under the elevated expressway aren't just hanging out—they live there. But saGuijo is in Makati, on a side street where you wouldn't expect to find it, and it was quiet around the club. Before the show I walked the neighborhood, past scenes stolen from someone's imagining of how a place like this might look: Guys hanging out on white plastic chairs, obscured by the night, nursing beers. One grilling meat in the street, in front of a satay stand. Sleepy open-air bars where a few solitary figures sat, slouching in front of their drinks. A woman sobbing quietly into a pay phone. A few hundred meters ahead, in the main street, taxis drifted past. The air still felt hot and wet but with a welcoming hint of a breeze. Night, and its great sense of relief, had descended. The only things missing were dogs lolling, half-conscious, in the street or chasing each other around the venue's microscopic dirt yard, where we drank cold cans of San Miguel with the audience after the show.

Inside the club there was a huge Virgin Mary mural—a punk rock club, perhaps, but nonetheless one in a Catholic country—and an old Caballero skate deck, under glass. (Sooyoung photographed the latter. I went for the former.) A tiny blue drum kit with SAGUIJO emblazoned on the top of the kick drum and SUPPORT PINOY ROCK just below it, which is how I learned that Pinoy = Filipino. The stage, too, was tiny, and during the set I stood close enough to Sooyoung to do the homoerotic back-to-back thing for the first time since sophomore year in college. But the beer was ice cold and dirt cheap, and the audience was thrilled, and one of the other bands, Wilderness, was one of the best bands that opened for us anywhere, ever. Wilderness—what a lovely and fitting name they chose—are an eight-piece, three of whom drum or play percussion. I imagine every review of them will inevitably include the word "tribal," because there are congas and a kind of primal swampy, pounding repetitiveness. They spilled over the edges of the stage and into the audience, playing a sort of shake-your-ass psych that, I thought, was rooted in Filipino or Polynesian records from the sixties and seventies that I suddenly needed to find *right now*. After the show their percussionist Pat Ing pressed a CD in a handpainted and cracked case into my hands. "Made with love," she said, smiling, and refused my money. People smiled in Manila. A relief, after Hong Kong.

IF YOU'RE LUCKY, WHEN YOU'RE A BAND FAR FROM HOME, A DE facto ambassador and chaperone materializes and takes you in. In Manila it was Diego Castillo, who plays guitar in Sandwich. He took us out for *sisig*—fried pig's face—one night. (He also arranged for friends to bring us a sack full of *balut*—fertilized duck eggs—after dinner, but sadly we were too stuffed to try any.) In his apartment he played us a bunch of local funk and hard rock from the seventies, and I wish I'd taken notes. He drove us around in his new Honda, playing American indie stuff from the nineties and aughts that even I hadn't heard. Diego loved a certain strain of sappy indie rock—minimal, soft to loud, heart on the sleeve, pop sweetening sprinkled over the top. A part of me likes it, too, in very small doses, but it's primarily nostalgia for a particular time of my life, because I generally find both that music and that part of me weak and despicable. A group of old friends you forsook, after they disappointed you too many times, or the sad boy you no longer wish to be, alone in his room with his record player, his one true friend.

The living room in Diego's apartment was dominated by his massive wall of records, and there he told us how much effort it took for him to track down music on small American independent labels in the pre-Internet nineties. He had to find addresses for the record labels, scrounge in Manila for American cash to send to those labels, pen an appropriately obsequious letter, throw in extra cash for shipping, and cross his fingers, because not everyone sent records in return. Like all collections, his was built laboriously, and with an antlike determination, just more so than almost anyone else's. It was easy to get disgusted with this little indie world: its incestuousness, its essential fecklessness, the way it always crumbled when you most needed it to be solid. But then you would run into people who still held on to its artifacts for dear life. And in 2012—years after these records were made, and probably years after rock last really mattered—I found myself standing in front of a wall of such records in Diego's apartment, eight and a half thousand miles from home, shaking my head. Because people actually cared. People really worked for this stuff. They did whatever it took to track down your message in a bottle. And then they held on to it, throughout all these years.

Many Thoughts About Underwear and Rock-Related Maladies

T hen you're standing outside a locked hotel room at 3 a.m., without a key and naked but for a pair of briefs, and as much as you might wish for another solution, there's really only one.

Luckily the elevator was empty when it arrived, and after it chimed and sighed to a stop in the lobby, I marched toward the front desk, trying to act dignified and business-casual about everything.

When the guy on duty looked up, he didn't even blink. Just stood, poker-faced, waiting. "The less said about this the better," I told him, "but I've locked myself out of room 1012."

He nodded and called the bellman.

This was during a practice weekend in Calgary in September 2011, and I'd gone barhopping with Orestes after rehearsal. He's twice my size and can drink like an elephant, but no night with him had ever ended this stupidly. I mean, after our last stop I was drunk enough to lose the willpower required to keep a slurriness out of my voice. But not *that* drunk. Still, when I woke needing to pee and walked through the heavy door to the right, it slammed shut behind me, and I could see, even without my glasses, that things were not right. But understanding the problem was a very gradual process. I knocked on the door and called through the crack at the bottom. Neither of which did any good, because I was the only person staying in the room. Or had been, before I became the only person standing in the hallway.

In the elevator back up to my floor, the very young bellman asked me how my night was going. "Really good until about five minutes ago," I said. He nodded, we arrived, and he used his magic key card to get me back into my room. *Thank god I didn't have a hard-on,* I thought, and settled back beneath the covers.

During and after any rock-related travel during the eighties and nineties, I only needed to blink a few times after waking up to remember where I was. Now travel left me all harebrained and sleepwalky. One night in late April 2012, back home after two weeks of shows in Asia, suffering from jetlag and a bad case of the bends from a rough reentry into workaday life, I went to bed at nine. Our last hotel room in Tokyo had wedged the three of us into another space barely big enough for the beds, and I was grateful to be back in my own room. But just after 10:30 I bolted upright, panicked with the realization that I went to bed *sans* underwear and fearing that my bandmates would be freaked out in the morning when they saw me with my man-parts dangling. Even though neither bandmate was in my bedroom. Or the rest of the apartment. Or even in America, because both had returned to their homes in *entirely different countries.* But somehow that didn't register at all. I looked around the room, which I didn't recognize. Laurel was still watching TV in the living room, so she wasn't there to remind me that the tour was over. I saw a door with a hint of light behind it and cracked it open. A bathroom. Finally I remembered: home. I opened a drawer, grabbed a pair of underwear, and—triumphant!—went back to bed.

A few days earlier I staggered onto my flight home from Tokyo, utterly spent, bit off a chunk of a Xanax, shoved in earplugs, and crashed for about eight hours. But I woke up halfway through, in sudden terror because I didn't know where our gear was, and it took a good thirty seconds to figure it out.

Sleep aids had something to do with this, though I used only Xanax to beat jetlag, never Ambien, which, as many people have discovered, can be quasi-hallucinogenic. All the flying had something to do with it, too. On van tours you can feel every mile accumulate, which keeps you somewhat situated geographically, but up in the air it's easier to lose the thread. Still, sometime during our yearlong reunion I started to think that going crazy on tour was not just part of the deal but sort of the entire point. To go purely beast for days on end, running on adrenaline and anxiety and fear and volume and power. To be absolutely immoderate for a while. A middle-aged man is so rarely permitted to get so *glandular*, to throw himself to the point of derangement into the ups and downs of any situation and reach the state where it's not merely acceptable but even expected to be walking the streets, head down, jabbering to yourself, still reeling from the previous night's hangover, jonesing openly for the next onstage fix, praying that the madness ends quickly, hoping it lasts forever. As I found myself doing in London and New York and Seattle and Tokyo and San Francisco and Hong Kong and, well, everywhere, basically. Peak crazy was often set off by incredibly minor complications and always came during the afternoon scramble just before we entered the tunnel and its familiar rhythm. Thus the Three O'Clocks, which gripped me while dashing around London just before an early dusk, hours before the last show of the tour: constantly forgetting to look the wrong way when crossing the street so cars scared the shit out of me and vice versa, trying to take direction from the sound guy by text to find the precise obscure connecting cable his computer required to record the show. The Three O'Clocks came while I was standing on the sidewalk in Seoul alongside all the gear, searching desperately for a taxicab that refused to appear, running late for the first show of our reunion, for which I was not at all certain the band was ready. Nervous that my back would lock up again, as it had two days ago out of nowhere, for the first time ever. Come to think of it, my back seized up just as we arrived for an afternoon rehearsal, which started around . . .

The Three O'Clocks hit in Manila's Ninoy Aquino airport, when I was exhausted because the operator had called three hours early for my wake-up call and I'd barely slept, before or after, and the fucking Wi-Fi wasn't working, and there were a million things I needed to check, and the show in Manila had been terribly promoted, and I had just learned that Sooyoung would miss soundcheck in Tokyo. The Three O'Clocks in New York: racing around the city, trying to finish every idiot errand before soundcheck as traffic thickened and slowed, each extra minute making the eventual arrival at the club exponentially later. And that moment a day or two later, standing in the middle of the street, both guitar cases leaning against my shins and both middle fingers raised, screaming, "Fuck you!" at the top of my lungs, over and over, at a taxi disappearing down the street, because the driver refused to take us to the airport. One afternoon I walked around Tokyo—one of my favorite things to do in the world—with nothing more strenuous to accomplish than to find a pair of sneakers, and I felt some bolus of horror rise for no reason whatsoever. I stopped and checked the phone: five minutes after three.

One day on tour in Asia, feeling exhausted and very Three O'Clocky, I skyped with Laurel. She sometimes gets booze-induced insomnia, and thought I might, too, so she asked, "Are you drinking?"

"How could I *possibly* get through this without drinking?" I demanded.

* * *

SOMETIMES I'D GET A TEXT LIKE THIS FROM ORESTES:

Easy there. We're in the subway.

So then I'd have to reply:

Why "easy there"?

He'd text back:

Because I know you.

Point taken. Or, as the tension rose just before a tour, I'd get an e-mail from him:

All I need is for you to stay out of jail for another two weeks.

Yeah. I think I can manage that. Can you, Orestes? Can you keep the beast in the cage until then?

But the real problems started after a tour, when you still hadn't rehinged and readjusted to civilian life. Recovering from anything— illness, drinking, the annual dalliance with mushrooms or E or coke— takes longer when you're older, and post-tour whiplash, too, was now far more savage. Several days after returning from our second Asian tour, badly sleep-deprived and depressed, I caught myself thinking, *There has to be something more than moping around the house, waiting for a socially acceptable hour to start drinking.* The latest version of a very old jam: nothing felt nearly as good as music. Everything else seemed so watery and pale. The rock hangover in full flower, a condition characterized by fatigue, malaise, difficulty concentrating, and an overweening desire to do it all again. I braced for depression to descend a few days after each tour ended, in the way that weekend ecstasy freaks gird themselves for the Tuesday blues. You returned to reality with your endorphins tapped out and your pleasure centers suddenly and stubbornly resistant to milder buzzes. Sleep patterns stayed upside down for weeks. And no one understood what you were feeling unless they'd been there, too.

Yes, the buzz of performance was as strong as ever. But what was the price—in time, in attention, in money? And where would it lead?

With each leg the reunion seemed less like an art project than a drug problem. Being in a band whose members lived in three different countries was complicated enough, and we were all already chin-deep in full-time commitments demanding adult-sized chunks of attention: families, real jobs, lives. You only play that first round of reunions once, after which audiences and pay envelopes almost always get thinner. And we weren't about to do this as cynically as the Pixies: cashing a decade's worth of reunion-tour checks while having written exactly one new song. Though we, of course, hadn't even written *that*.

So we were doing it for the same reason a dog licks its balls: because we could. For the fun of it, and it was great fun. For the experience and the weirdness of it. Turn any of that down? Never. I'd say it would take a toll, but the truth was, in many ways, it already had.

* * *

WHAT DO YOU HEAR WHEN THERE'S NOTHING TO HEAR? SERI-ously. I want to know what that's like, for normal people, because the decades spent playing in bands and going to shows are permanently inscribed in my middle ear. My ears stay noisy, even through the most profound hush, and constantly send certain tones to my brain. Why are old musicians never alone? Tinnitus! Our ears never stop ringing, thanks to how we've damaged the tiny hair cells in the ear that transmit sound, from sonic overexposure. A pretty steady A plays in my left ear—makes sense where that drone settled, I guess, since I was obsessed for years with that huge, droning one-note chord, played across multiple octaves and multiple strings—while a more variable note rings in the other. I live in the city and wear earplugs when I sleep, and when I wake in the quiet of the morning, the tinnitus is most noticeable and my right ear is doing its auditory roulette. Sometimes that ear oscillates between two tones, a full step or so apart from each other. Sometimes there's a main drone and another quieter tone or two, seemingly somewhere off in the distance. Once I woke to it quietly playing something like a seventies synth sample-and-hold solo of randomized notes. Which sounds like complete madness, I know, but it was actually sort of cool.

A few years ago I started noticing that I needed to lean in, really far, to hear anything at noisy restaurants or bars. A meal or a drink in such places now means I shred my vocal cords, especially if Laurel isn't there to remind me, gently or not, that I'm shouting. But sometimes that's what it takes to hear myself. It's also why my voice sounds so Jewy and nasal: I hear myself much better when I push it from my adenoids and sinuses. I know it sounds better, and causes far less vocal strain, if I project from my diaphragm—but then I don't really *hear* it.

Not good. So I went to an audiologist: Dr. Andrew Resnick, a guitarist who specializes in treating musicians. He asked whether I had trouble hearing—left ear, right ear, both ears? (In places with background noise, both.) Ringing in my ears? (Yes. But it doesn't bother me too much.) How many hours a week did I listen to music on headphones? (Maybe four.) Did I have a history of exposure to loud noise? (Heh. Yes. Lots.)

He pointed me toward a soundproof booth—so old-school it could have come from a movie about the golden age of radio—and directed me to strap on headphones. The room was dead quiet. The never-ending orchestra in my ears wasn't. *This won't work,* I thought nervously, *I'll never hear anything over this ringing.* He ran a series of tones, low to high, quiet and quieter, until they began to fade beneath my constant din. Then I heard the kind of background noise you'd hear at a restaurant or cocktail party, and the doctor played voices against it, fiddling with the volume until the conversation disappeared into the clatter.

There it goes, I thought, *for all us aging punkers.*

* * *

MUSIC IS FOREVER, IF YOU TURN IT UP LOUD ENOUGH, AND, viewed from the perch of middle age, it seems absolutely inevitable that most older musicians would have fucked-up ears. It's hard to describe this without invoking sexual terms like "penetration" and "insertion," because we all wanted to get deeply inside the music and have it deeply inside us. When Mudhoney's Mark Arm was in junior high, he'd put on a favorite record, turn the stereo all the way up, and plant an ear directly against a speaker.

Wait. *What?*

"I was trying to get the most out of it," he explained.

But I understood. When Bitch Magnet was starting out, I liked leaning my forehead on my cranked-up amp when I played, because I loved how that sent vibrations straight into my skull. Mid-song during early practices, I sometimes stuck my head in Orestes's bass drum. Proximity to extreme sound produces interesting physical sensations, though they're not always pleasant. During Bitch Magnet's last European tour, I ended "Big Pining" each night by getting within inches of my speaker cabinet to produce feedback. But many times, instead of hearing a distorted chord melt into a pure single note, my rented rig instead produced incredibly piercing shrieks and squeals: microphonic feedback, an entirely different beast. These sudden blasts of high treble, so loud and at such close range, made me stumble, dizzied, and sometimes I felt myself gag, as if I were having a sudden attack of vertigo or had otherwise briefly deranged the intricate whorls of inner-ear plumbing that govern balance. Onstage while touring with Panthers, Justin Chearno recalled, "I stood next to the crash cymbal, and our drummer fucking hammered it. I saw white multiple times, just from the sound."

"All my life I've been interested in the idea of getting overwhelmed by sound," Mission of Burma's Roger Miller said. "Even when I was in ninth grade I would stand right in front of the amps and just do feedback for hours. Varying the sounds of the world exploding really appealed to me. It's pretty reasonable I would get tinnitus."

Was Roger wearing earplugs back then? Of course not. Nor was Justin when his drummer was bashing the crash cymbal, nor was I on that European tour or at many of the several thousand shows I attended

or played. We all wanted sound to be a physical as well as aural phe-
nomenon. To *feel* it. LOUD, like 120 decibels. Like a jet engine in a small
room. To quote the band NME:

> *Louder than hell is what we are*
> *You say that we take it just too damn far*
> *You can't understand a thing that we say*
> *But we don't care, it's the way that we play*
> *We play loud*
> *Louder than hell*
> *Fucking loud*
> *Louder than hell.*

Yes. *Exactly.* Thus, the ears go first. More specifically, your ability to
hear silence goes first. "We were in Italy, and some guy took us to the
forest," Andee Connors from A Minor Forest recalled. But no soothing
sounds of nature awaited him. "All I could hear was this high-pitched
whine. I had a total panic attack. I bought earplugs the next day."
Though the damage, of course, had already been done.

In 2013 Laura Ballance quit touring with Superchunk—the band
she'd played bass for since 1990—because of mounting hearing loss
and increased sensitivity to loud noise. "I can't hear that well, and I'm
always saying, 'What? What?'" she told me. "Then all of a sudden I'll
be like, 'Stop yelling!'" And an audiologist once told David Yow that
many people with hearing aids heard trebly frequencies better than
Yow did—when they took their hearing aids *out.*

We were all chasing abandon—animal, grunting, feral abandon—
and our ears were the route of administration for something that filled
the body as well as the head. Did we have any notion that losing silence
might be the price of admission? Not really. Even though, as early as
the eighties, Pete Townshend was warning everyone within earshot
(sorry) that they, too, could end up deaf. I'm surprised at how many of

us *don't* have severe hearing problems, given how loud we all routinely worked and the hundreds of shows we attended that were just massacres of volume. But you have no idea how good it felt, playing the music you centered your life on *that* loud. It made the air seem suffused with electricity. It lit you up like a city at night. People in thrall to a lesser rush end up turning tricks to afford it. Chasing ours made us slam onto our guitar or bass or the drum kit harder, push voices into higher and higher registers, scream longer, jump higher. Messing up our ears was one obvious outcome, but there was other cumulative wear and tear: we attacked our instruments and music with so much more aggression than, well, pretty much anyone else. (Look at how gently, how *politely*, dullards like Eric Clapton and Mark Knopfler play their guitars.) Many of us also developed various chronic injuries, from hurling ourselves and our bodies at the music as hard as we could, over and over again, until our knees or backs or elbows or necks told us, *Now stop.* When James Murphy drummed in his old band Pony, he recounted matter-of-factly, "I used to throw up at every gig. I played with marching sticks"—which are very heavy—"and I had no efficiency of movement, and I would just play until I barfed."

In general, talking to middle-aged drummers is often like talking to old wrestlers or stuntmen. "I've probably broken the front knuckle on my left hand—which constantly hits the edge of the snare drum—thirty or forty times," said Andee Connors. "I'd split it open every show, and there'd be blood all over." Over time he developed a large floating bone chip on his left index finger, which now restricts movement. A Minor Forest toured again in 2014, and after many shows, Andee posted on Facebook fresh pictures of that bloody and brutalized finger.

"I've got carpal tunnel in both wrists. I've got a pinched nerve in one elbow. My hands often go numb when we're playing," said Mudhoney drummer Dan Peters, running down his list. Dan recently had his ears checked. It will surprise no one that the doctor told him to get hearing aids immediately. Another common drummer injury is epicondylitis, or tennis elbow, which can sometimes get so bad that it requires surgery, as it did for Six Finger Satellite's Rick Pelletier.

Rock has always been a contact sport. Patti Smith once broke her neck when she spun herself offstage. When Frank Zappa was in the Mothers of Invention, he was pushed into an orchestra pit, and broke his neck so badly that, at first, his bandmates thought he was dead. Imprecise pyrotechnics set Metallica's James Hetfield and Michael Jackson on fire. Our freak accidents were different. Void's extremely gymnastic singer, John Weiffenbach, destroyed his knee—blew out his ACL—in the middle of one show, forcing a quick visit to an emergency room. David Yow made a habit of diving into the crowd, which didn't always work out so well. "My longest-lasting injury—I call them by the city where they happened—is my 'St. Louis,'" from the early nineties, he recalled. "I got thrown back on the stage by the crowd, and I couldn't catch my fall. I landed right on my spine, right about where your belt goes. The next day I could barely walk, and it's been a problem ever since."

I know from experience it was a desire to transcend, as well as a fundamental masochism, that led us to dive into crowds and contort our bodies until they broke: *This is how crazy you, the audience, make me, and this is how far I will go for you.* So can we now, in middle age, learn how to perform in less joint-destroying ways? Not really. Though you knew your creaking body couldn't take much more, and you made so many promises to it, once it was showtime the old excitement kicked in, and like a weak ex-lover you went right back to *the exact same fucking thing* that hurt you. "Before you start playing, it just feels ridiculous and impossible that you will be jumping up and down at any point," said Laura Ballance, whose knees are battered from doing just that. "But then it happens. You just can't help it." She also has arthritis in her neck from headbanging her way through two decades of Superchunk shows. "I've been advised that I should not be doing that," she said. "But I still do."

Eventually, though, you just physically can't play anymore, or at least play in a way that you'd recognize. In 2013 I asked Roger Miller, when he was sixty-one, how much longer he thought Burma could keep going, given the limitations of the mortal frame. "You grow older and either you figure out a way to do it or you don't. If you sit at your computer, you get carpal tunnel. If you're a football player, you get concussions." He shrugged. "And I'm not trying to be fatalistic or negative, but you're gonna die anyway."

* * *

HERE IS WHERE I'M SUPPOSED TO SAY I'M SORRY. HERE IS WHERE I'm supposed to say I realized, too late, that we should be careful with guitars and amps and drums and earbuds. Here is where I'm supposed to say we must *respect* the delicate tissue that makes sense of the sounds around us. Here is where I should beg everyone, in simpering and cloying tones, to *please teach the children to learn from our mistakes.*

Screw it. I don't regret a thing. Sure, I did some stupid stuff. (It doesn't sound so great when you stick your head into a bass drum.) But everyone who did equally stupid stuff was transported to places most people will never know. The old athlete walks tenderly on his aching knees. My ears ring. And—along with Mark Arm and Dan Peters and Laura Ballance and Andee Connors and Roger Miller and God knows how many more—I can't hear anything you're saying in this noisy bar. But so what?

I ended up getting a relatively clean bill of health from the audiologist, though he found my left ear is weaker at picking up mid-range frequencies. Ear doctors sometimes call this a "noise notch," because it often appears among those steadily exposed to loud sound. (For many years of practice and performance, that ear was closest to my amplifier.) I was told that my hearing against background noise was actually passable. Neither Laurel nor I believe this finding, for what it's worth, and Dr. Resnick later conceded that real-world conditions are impossible to simulate. Still, that's what his test showed.

Some months after my visit I called Dr. Resnick to interview him for an article in *The Atlantic*, and at the end of our conversation I asked him if he had worn earplugs when he was an active musician. "Ah," he said—and here he paused deliciously—"more often than not, no. I found it a little difficult to wear them while performing, especially if you're doing any singing."

I guess he'll understand, then, if we all keep treating our ears the way old drunks treat their livers, always wanting one last spree, always hoping, each time we play too loud, that they don't go kablooey. Because, really. We're just gonna *quit*?

When Bitch Magnet played our reunion show in San Francisco, Andee Connors lent us a speaker cabinet, and we met him at his practice space to grab it for soundcheck. As we drove up I saw him leaning against his truck, stooped over and plainly in pain. His back had gone out the day before, he told me. He has arthritis and related maladies, for which he blames his bad posture while drumming.

Andee's new band, ImPeRiLs, opened for us that night, and when I ran into him backstage, he was clearly still hurting, bent over and wincing. It hurt your own back just to see him. Once onstage, though, he was gleeful, grinning, beaming, joyful, looking years younger. As long as you're up there, you don't feel a thing.

Bitch Magnet
October 8, 2012

our tour dates once again:
10/21: SEATTLE, Neumo's
10/23: SF, Rickshaw Stop (w Life Coach, Gold Medalists, Imperils)
10/25: NEW YORK, Le Poisson Rouge (w Moss Icon)
10/26: BROOKLYN, Knitting Factory (w Turing Machine and Violent Bullsh*t)
10/28: CHICAGO, Empty Bottle (w Electric Hawk)

Goodnight to the Rock and Roll Era

A Korean, a Mexican, and a Jew walked into a bar in Vancouver on a Saturday night in late October 2012, not far from the weekend shitshow of Gastown and the vacant-eyed junkies zombie-ing down Hastings, and, once the drinks were served, Sooyoung raised his glass. "I'm glad you guys talked me into this," he said. Tomorrow we would play Seattle, the first night of our American tour. But I took him to mean the entire reunion adventure.

I always liked touring in the fall. Cooler, clear days, night coming on earlier, breaking out sweaters and heavier jackets for the first time since March. Once, October meant fall break and bombing eastward on Route 80 in a rattling old American car full of gear with Sooyoung, en route to play New York and Boston, talking all the way about the future and the band. Not this time. We knew, going in, that these shows would be the end. That was the key to selling them to Sooyoung. We crammed as many shows as we could into the time each of us could carve from his schedule, and since the dates wound up being in Seattle, San Francisco, Chicago, and two in New York, we had to fly to each one, as we had in Asia in April. Jimmy Page was really into how flying to each show injected urgency into touring, and you don't need to travel on your band's private jet to feel it, too. But I felt pangs of regret over losing one last time in the van and the sound of those tires turning on pavement, a music in itself, one long ago bound to *this* music in my mind.

There was symmetry and logic to ending the band after these shows in America, or there was once I got past the horrible, poignant, aching back-to-school-and-things-are-dying autumn-of-the-soul feeling I inevitably got at this time of year anyway, made worse by the looming conclusion to a very delayed extension of my early twenties. But I'd tired of the logistics and persuasion required to make it all happen: mapping itineraries, arranging transport and lodging, dealing with promoters and equipment rental. I'd tired of the complications associated with disappearing from work for long stretches. I'd tired of how crazy the run-ups to touring were and how harsh the rock hangovers were afterward and the effects my mood swings had on the people around me. I'd even tired of a couple of the songs in our set. (Though only a couple.)

After years and years of living with barely any structure at all, I'd discovered that the routines of marriage and adult life were strangely comforting, but there was little template for what would happen on the road, and that chaos—the sheer density of events jammed into such a short stretch of time—was still so seductive. The foreknowledge of each approaching tour took up much mental space, tugged at me endlessly, and could never be properly explained to civilians. And describing the musician's transition to normal life, once the touring is over, was even harder. "I don't mean to make light, but I really would liken it to a soldier in active duty coming home," Rick Pelletier of Six Finger Satellite said. "Suddenly you're a civilian. You have to act excited when you're going out to dinner with friends." Even though you're used to much stronger stuff at night.

Peter Mengede, who played guitar in Helmet and Handsome, portrayed homecoming in even starker terms: "You find yourself without that thing that you've been focused on, that you looked forward to, that you found satisfaction in, that got rid of all the horrible, ugly stuff inside you. All of a sudden you're sitting at home. No band. Nothing to do and nowhere to go. It's time to grow up and retrain yourself. Try to find a way into the real world. But then, once you do get in the real world, it is fucking boring. The work thing, apart from the money—it's absolutely pointless. I've got a band now. It's minor leagues. But it gives me something to do. Without that it would just be suburbs. It would just be fucking shopping malls, and getting on the train with all these fucking diabetics going out to buy a flat screen or Kentucky Fried."

The night after I returned from touring Europe in December 2011, I dragged my reluctant and severely sleep-deprived carcass to a work-related event in a landmark building uptown. I didn't want to go, but I thought, *I have to get back to normal life.* Even though the other life was still so present: severe fatigue, ringing ears, the sensations from the crowds and volume fading only slightly after traveling those thousands of miles. I walked in, confused from jetlag and feeling very out of place beneath the carved and gilded ceilings, so intricate that in my addled state they made me think of looking up at the circuitry underneath the spaceship in *Close Encounters.* I grabbed a glass of wine off the first waiter's tray I saw, tried to focus, ran into someone I knew, and casually asked what's up. This person went into an excruciatingly detailed description of a something-something and then went into an equally colonoscopic analysis of a deal that something-something was considering. You know how you find yourself in a conversation and try to find the polite way to end it, or see someone over a person's shoulder so you can disappear as quickly as possible, but can't? That. The ennui and jetlag made me feel weightless. I looked up and imagined myself floating above this dazzling room. Quite a setting, this. Real nineteenth-century robber baron shit. Old-money eccentric, incredibly ornate, even slightly deranged in its details. Everyone else here seemed so happy. But it was just people walking around. Some rock-damaged circuit in my brain kept asking, *This is it?* I was both bored and overmatched, feeling like I understood nothing outside the ritual of driving and load-in and setup and soundcheck, the tension of waiting for the venue to fill and the relief when it did, slowly at first and then very quickly. But this event, tonight? What was the point?

The people around me were good people, but they had no idea how wrung out I felt, how my head was still slightly blown off, how that feeling was fading, and while I knew far too well that it was a crazy and unsustainable way to live, especially now, I was still desperate to fan its dying embers. That I was slowly waking up from the dream, and the contours of everyday life were only starting to come into focus. The closeted husband can't talk about his boy toy downtown. The functional junkie doesn't tell co-workers about his weekend nodding off in a motel room amid needles and spoons and people he would normally never see in daylight. Those guys can only share those things with others who've been there themselves. There was no one like that here this night. Or on most other nights.

Sometimes at a work-related gathering it comes out that I've played in bands for over twenty years, and that one of them recently reunited to perform in Europe and Asia and America. And necks inevitably straighten and heads tilt, and a fiftyish fund manager or lawyer or media executive or management consultant will ask the name of that band, and sometimes, as soon as I say "Bitch Magnet," the gravity shifts, and any power of being this specimen—an actual rock musician who actually toured and put out actual records and CDs, back when people actually did that!—diminishes. You see it register, and then see mirth.

This is what it sounds like: *What?*

Oh.

Oh! Ohhhh! Ha ha ha ha ha ha ha. Ha ha ha ha ha ha ha!

Bitch Magnet? Bitch? Magnet?

Ha ha ha ha ha ha ha! Ha ha ha ha ha ha ha ha ha ha ha ha ha!!

After all these years of playing music, and as a grown man now myself, I understand this reaction. Bitch Magnet is kind of a silly name! But the person who laughs isn't laughing like a pal who had *also* been a teenage punk rocker and, as such, laughs from knowing. This person who laughs doesn't understand. This person who laughs is laughing because—briefly—this person feels superior. In Passover seder terms, this is the son who doesn't even know how to ask a question: *What is this?* As such, the Haggadah instructs us, he should be treated with patience.

But sometimes I feel like, enough already. And what I want to do more than anything is smile through my anger, maybe chuckling a little bit myself—*Heh heh heh heh heh*—then say to the person who laughs:

I wish you'd seen, and heard, the amazing things I did because I was in bands.

I wish you'd seen, and heard, the amazing things I did because I spent all those years in punk rock clubs.

I'm sorry you never had a moment in which the dim candle flare of discovery suddenly became apparent to a few musicians locked away from the rest of the world in a soundproofed practice studio. Or a moment like the ones I glimpsed alone, at home in my tiny studio apartment in 1993 or 1994, kneeling on the carpet next to my 4-track—its red RECORD light blazing—singing quietly so the neighbors couldn't hear, into a microphone clutched hard in both hands, suddenly dead certain, after groping blindly for hours, that I'd picked the lock and stepped through a doorway to a moment of pure glory.

I wish, at least once, you'd known how it felt when people pulled you aside urgently to tell you how much they loved your records. I wish you knew what it was like to stumble on a stage, stoned with exhaustion, congested and sluggish and woozy from a mid-tour flu, and then feel some switch flip, and take you from earthbound to flying. I wish you'd been there and we'd run around together in our little underground— punk rock or indie rock or whatever we called it—because it was, you should know, one of the more important cultural movements to happen in your lifetime.

It's clear, though, you weren't there, because you're laughing about *a fucking band name.*

That's why, laughing guy, we need to leave this party or dinner right now, rush back to my apartment, flick on the lights, fire up a computer . . . No. To *really* do this, I have to dig through boxes of old flyers and tour itineraries and clippings from music magazines that no longer exist, and fanzines made with the jarring look and terrible fonts from the earliest days of what was then called desktop publishing. And tell you about Wire and Stooges and This Heat and Mission of Burma. Wipers and Sleepers and Swans. About Melvins and Void and Green River and Meat Puppets, and how Black Flag got even better once they slowed down. Naked Raygun and feedtime and High Rise, and Laughing Hyenas and Scrawl. Die Kreuzen and Squirrel Bait and Honor Role. Drunks with Guns and My Dad Is Dead. Glenn Branca and Smash-chords and Gore. About seeing Butthole Surfers and Boredoms and Suckdog and Caroliner, and Pavement with their first drummer and Live Skull with their last singer. Watching Sonic Youth on *Night Music* in 1989, and the Minutemen on MTV in 1985. About college radio and record stores, and how fanzine editors were either the quietest or most annoying people in town. About finding original Electro-Harmonix pedals and Moog synths and Travis Bean guitars, and Orange or Hiwatt or Ampeg amps long before eBay made all their prices skyrocket, thanks in part to how we sought them out and talked them up. Drinking at the Rainbow and Max Fish. Combing through the new-arrivals bin at Pier Platters and Oar Folk and Reckless and Olsson's and Newbury Comics and Fallout and Aquarius and Amoeba and Wuxtry, and scanning the racks of fanzines at See Hear. About Homestead and SST and Touch and Go and Sub Pop and Drag City and Matador, of course, but also Amphetamine Reptile and Neutral and Rabid Cat and Treehouse and Ruthless and Reflex and 99 and Ecstatic Peace.

But whatever you do, laughing guy, please don't start talking about your cousin who *plays in a band, too!* if that means he plays classic rock covers in a bar sometimes, or in a "blues" band that performs in the gazebo in a town square once every summer. I don't really expect you to know that we invented our music to destroy that stuff. But I'd still rather chop off a finger than take you up on your offer to introduce us so we can jam sometime.

And allow me to make this one nagging and exquisitely subtle point: your cousin and I *do* have a few things in common, having both spent time on the lowest rungs of the music business, a truth I cannot escape even if I believe in my aesthetic and spent my entire adult life scorning his.

And, yes, since you asked, you can find my band on Spotify and Pandora and iTunes and Amazon and YouTube.

Oh, and one last thing?

Fuck you.

* * *

IN 1998, WHEN I WAS THIRTY AND BROKE, A GOOD FRIEND GOT married in Manhattan, at the kind of wedding romantics call *magical*: the vows were exchanged at the Church of the Ascension on lower Fifth Avenue, and the reception was held in a gilded space nearby, where a few of us music freaks found each other. Though all the men wore suits and ties and all the women looked ravishing in evening dresses, we could still smell the subculture on each other.

One of us seemed slightly more off than the others: older than the rest of us, tall, quiet, wearing institutional glasses and an ill-fitting suit, awkward-looking in an almost alarming way. His name was Ray. Somehow the subject of high school came up, and awkward Ray started talking.

"Man, I was the uncoolest kid in my high school," he began, and I immediately and uncharitably thought, *Yeah, we could tell.* But, he continued, after high school he joined a band, which toured and put out some records, and after years of that he finally thought he might be, at last, sort of cool. He attended a high school reunion, believing this music thing would make him less outcast. "But," he concluded, "you know what? No one cared. They all still thought I was the biggest loser there." Nods of agreement and murmurs of sympathy all around. I broke the subsequent silence by asking, "Hey, Ray, what was the name of your band?"

And Ray answered, "I was in a band called the Dead Kennedys."

Holy shit! We're talking to East Bay Ray!

I told him that if we'd had this conversation when I was sixteen, I would have just peed my pants. But set that aside, because no matter that you think what you're doing with your band is the coolest thing in the world, no matter, Ray, that you are a founding member of *one of the biggest and most important punk rock bands ever*—the straight world will never understand a thing about it. Or care. As the world will be quick to remind you, should you ever fail to remember.

Hence the delicate dance in handling The Conversation when people in your normal workaday existence—the decent, interested people who have absolutely no idea about this world—find out about your alternate life as a musician. One smart strategy is simply to explain nothing. "I usually say, 'We really like a lot of krautrock,' and then they're like, 'huh?'" said Andrew Beaujon, the Eggs front man who now plays guitar in Talk It. "Once you share that with most people, they really don't want to talk about it anymore." Make obscurity work for you: one of the first lessons in Indie Rock 101, still.

✳ ✳ ✳

OUR FIRST AMERICAN SHOW WAS IN SEATTLE, ON A RAINY AND dreary Sunday in October, though perhaps all I need to say is "October in Seattle." It was the most lightly attended show of the tour, and by no means our best performance, but diehards still came out, and we saw several old friends, including Linc, my best pal from college, who flew in from Los Angeles. But I will forever cherish that show, because Mark Arm hopped onstage to sing our encore—Minor Threat's "Filler"—and Jesus, did he peel the paint off the back wall. That show kept me buzzing through the night, into the next morning over breakfast, on the drive to the airport during which we did an interview with the *Village Voice*, and all the way through our flight to San Francisco and the rest of the day's travel. No show that night. Laurel had already flown to San Francisco, where she helped organize a party. Our flight was late, and getting out of the airport took forever, and Laurel kept texting me about the party. I told her I was filthy—I was, not having showered since the show—and she texted back, PLEASE COME FILTHY, which honestly is the best and hottest sentence any woman ever communicated to me on tour, ever.

But, as with that event in New York just after I got back from Europe, I was still too present in the world I had just left. Scanning the room made me keenly aware that the previous night would be impossible to convey to anyone, so, fairly or not, I was disappointed immediately. Someone I know sidled over, sat near me, disgorged his update, asked me what was up, and went facedown into his phone before I even started talking.

Say what you will about annoying and oversensitive indie rockers: *they* never pulled shit like that.

* * *

THE RICKSHAW STOP, WHERE WE WERE PLAYING IN SAN FRAN-cisco, is (fortuitously) within walking distance of the food-nerd destina-tion Zuni Café, but during dinner I realized I might miss Andee Connors's new band, ImPeRiLs, who were playing first. When I called him in a panic, he said there was nothing he could do about their set time but reminded me, "*You* can do this. Not me." A realization dawned: *Yes, sometimes a headliner can.* I made another call, to the club, and pushed everyone's set back fifteen minutes.

That kind of night: back among friends, and those who understood. There was even excellent wine backstage, sent by my winemaker pal Fred Scherrer, of Scherrer Vineyards. In case any of this sounds the least bit rock-starish, I manned the merch table with Laurel before the show, and, judging from the questions I fielded ("What time are *they*"— gesturing toward our records and CDs—"going on tonight?"), it was clear that few people realized I was actually part of "they." And, late into our set, I looked past the crowd toward the lit-up merch booth and saw Laurel sprawled out on a couch, asleep. Still, there is nothing wrong with being a king frog in a small pond, playing a real show for a few hundred people pouring off so much energy that all we had to do was feast on it and reflect it back to them. Halfway through the set, with people in the crowd yelling for different songs, I stepped up to the mike: "Hey, this is San Francisco, people. Can't we come to some CON-SEN-SUS?" Sometimes you make jokes onstage just to amuse your own damn self.

* * *

WHEN LAUREL WOKE IN OUR HOTEL ROOM THE MORNING after that show, she was exhausted and crabby. I wasn't, though I'd slept much less, because the rhythms of the road made perfect sense to me. I also knew, as she did not, that sleep is postponable on tour. Sometimes for a very long time. But Laurel wasn't getting that nightly performance rush—the touring musician's crucial chemical advantage. I felt bad for her as I watched her stumble, half-awake, to throw on clothes and get coffee. But I also thought, *The difference between you and me is that I can do this for weeks.*

There was little time to reflect on that, though, because we had to dash immediately to the airport to drop off the rental car and fly to the next show in New York, and of course we ran late and of course missed the exit from the expressway, and of course I only remembered to detune my guitars while on the AirTrain, to the bewilderment of all the other passengers, and of course we had to sprint while pushing a tottering baggage cart across the entire terminal before barely skidding to a stop in front of a wordless Orestes—whose expression nonetheless screamed, *I've seen this too many times before.* I turned my sleep-deprived, red-rimmed gaze toward him and demanded, "Isn't this *fun?*" and he replied, without smiling, "No."

He was right, he was wrong, this was awful, it was tremendous. I was sick of Orestes—he and I spent practically every waking moment together on tour—and I was sick of Sooyoung, and I didn't want to spend time apart from them. It had to end, and I wanted it to last forever.

At home in New York the next morning, I lazed in bed, dicking around with the multitudes of any band's online communications: retweeting and replying to mentions and shoutouts on Twitter and on Facebook, answering texts and e-mails. There is a special room in hell for people who send day-of-show texts asking, HEY, WHEN DO YOU GUYS GO ON TONIGHT? Especially if you've already told them. When my brother e-mailed asking that very question, I painstakingly tapped out a response gently reminding him to JESUS CHRIST LOOK UP OUR PREVIOUS FUCKING E-MAIL EXCHANGE. Then a nasty burr of realization: the day was over. Orestes and I were guest-hosting a show on East Village Radio shortly, and, according to my calculations, we should have left twenty minutes ago to start the sprint to showtime.

FUCK.

After that radio show, the day went like this: Pick up my 2002 Subaru Forester. Hand Orestes keys. Text Andy, the guitarist from Violent Bullshit, to arrange pickup of his Marshall cabinet. Direct Orestes to my practice space in Bushwick to pick up my amp. Dash up two flights to our room. Unlock the three locks on the door, marvel at the squalor, disassemble the tangled boneyard of synths and amps and basses and road cases and guitars and cords and amps and mike stands, locate my amp, realize that said amp in its road case weighs more than eighty pounds and is too bulky to carry. Drag it carefully down the stairs, hoping no rats appear, heft amp into car, jog over to Main Drag Music, next door to the practice space, for just-in-case supplies: picks, strings, a long patch cord. Head to Temporary Residence headquarters to pick up more records and CDs. Text the entire staff—all three of them—begging for someone to meet us on the sidewalk with our stuff when we arrive. Alfie waits for us outside the office, we screech to a halt, jam records and CDs in car. Thanks, Alfie. Head to pick up the next batch of T-shirts at the absolute ass end of Greenpoint, hard by Newtown Creek. Arrive and run into large warehouse building. Buzz the elevator. No response. Seconds, then several minutes, pass. Elevator finally appears, and the large Jamaican elevator guy runs me upstairs and—crucially, *brilliantly*—offers to hold the lift for me. Run into screen-printer's space and spot head guy Carl, whom I'd met back when we both had long hair. Carl hoists a box and hands it over. Ride back down in elevator, then dart to the car. Head to the Queens Midtown Tunnel but take several wrong turns, each of which gives me a minor heart attack. Then home, where Sooyoung calmly stands by the kitchen island, in front of his computer. It's unclear whether he even noticed me burst into the room, sweating and panting. Orestes grabs a pair of shorts, still wet from the washing machine, pulls them on, and points a hair dryer at his crotch. I gather every merch box. Everyone moves much more languidly than I do, as always, but in time we're on the way to Le Poisson Rouge. As we load in I eyeball the area where bands sell merch, calculate how people flow past it, see where the light is bright-est, and cover the best place to set up with boxes of records and T-shirts. Location and real estate are crucial everywhere, but a little more so in New York.

Though it has a private shitter, the dressing room is too small to accommodate two bands and everyone else who finds their way back here. After our soundcheck I come back to change strings, taking a seat across a low table from a guy I don't recognize in a white button-down shirt, who's chatting with friends far too loudly for the room. He is impossible to ignore, and very quickly I decide I have to throw him out. A simple matter: *Dude, I'm sorry. But this room is for bands, and you gotta go.* Just before I can, he leaves. It would have been awkward if he hadn't, because when the opening band, Moss Icon, starts their set, he strides onstage and starts singing.

My mom and dad come in from New Jersey. My brother and his wife, Sharlene, come, too, bringing my niece and nephew, Edie and Zeke. (It took a few e-mails to ensure that the club would let in a nine-year-old girl and a twelve-year-old boy, but in the end all goes so swimmingly I should have asked for drink tickets.) Poisson Rouge is a far more professional club than the shitholes we typically play, and the staff kindly set aside a few tables for them in the seated section. I meet them all at the entrance, show them to the tables, and start to chat, but the club is filling, and I can't ignore the tide pulling me back to the dressing room, which, when I return, is jammed with friends. The downside to knowing lots of musicians is that they all end up backstage. I have to change my shirt and briefly consider ducking into the bathroom but instead announce, "This is a dressing room. And I'm gonna take my clothes off."

When Moss Icon start their set, the dressing room empties but for Orestes, warming up, and his friend Mark, peacefully tapping on his phone. I take my preshow dump. I don't know if *calm* is the right word, but I'm nearing the end of the tunnel without too much fear or excitement or tension. Moss Icon finishes, and once again I bound onstage to set up far too soon, before they have a chance to break down their gear. Another upside to the pro rock club experience: there is help. Stagehands in black T-shirts shove Moss Icon's equipment to the side of the stage and grunt my cabinets into place. Matthew Barnhart is running sound for us on this tour, and I'd told him to play Rush's "Red Barchetta" over the PA right after Moss Icon's set, and when it begins, I walk through the club, air-drumming and miming guitar lines into some faces I know and some that I don't. Maybe I'm more revved up than I think. When I bump into Moss Icon, I can't stop throwing out overeffusive praise. I saw about thirty seconds of their set, tops.

I arrange two beers, two bottles of water, and our set list by my mike stand and set up my pedals. One extremely excited guy keeps shouting up at me while I tune the Les Pauls, but I keep a tight smile on my face, averting my gaze, saying nothing. A lot of people have come out tonight. I took pictures at soundcheck of the empty room and now snap two more from roughly the same angles. We'll open with "Douglas Leader," a slow and quiet song Sooyoung starts with unaccompanied bass and vocals. Orestes and I will come onstage mid-song, just before the drums and guitar come in. I go to the farthest end of the stage, past the amps, to lurk and wait on the steps, guitar strapped on. A woman comes up to ask if I'm Orestes. I tell her I'm not. She says she knew him in fifth grade and hasn't seen him in a very long time. I say: evidently. She says she has a guitar pick for me, which I'm too surprised to decline, hands me a flyer, and then starts describing the project detailed on the flyer, which is called . . . well, why mention it here? I thank her, though I don't want to, and slide the pick and flyer between some speaker cabinets, marveling at her brass to pitch me while I stood onstage in a crowded club, thirty seconds before showtime.

I totally fuck up the solo in "Douglas Leader," thanks to some glitch in my setup, but the crowd is with us from the first note. They cheer loudly, shout when we launch into favorites, and stay dead silent during the quiet parts. We end with "Filler," this time drafting my friend Jay Green, who sings for Violent Bullshit, on vocals. I drop my pick on one of its first chords and have to speed-strum the rest of it with my middle finger, convinced I'm flaying it to bits. Then my guitar strap breaks and there's nothing to do but play the rest of the song on the ground. Someone gets a great photo of Jay bent over and screaming down at my head just before Jay shoves the mike into the face of someone in the front row, perfectly timed for the dude to yell out, "FILLER!" during the chorus. At the end of the song I toss my guitar skyward, catch it, then slam it pickup-side down atop my amp, more or less on beat. *Good night.*

At the merch booth Laurel rips open boxes of T-shirts and records and CDs and shoves shirts at people and loudly calls the name of someone who's left his credit card. Edie is the first to appear, and I bend down to hug her, even though I'm a sweaty mess. I ask her if it was really loud, and when she says no, I make a mental note to ask Matthew why. Clusters of people stick around: old friends and old fans, people waiting to talk to us. Everyone is smiling, flushed, and sweaty from the happy, wrung-out feeling that follows a good show. Generally I prefer shitholes to pro rock clubs, but tonight everything clicked. Though Poisson Rouge also took 15 percent of the merch sales, as its standard contract insists, which I could have done without.

We end up at a horrid bar nearby, in the no-man's-land near NYU, with a bunch of people who went to the show, and stay for hours. I finally leave around 3:15 a.m., the taxi floats me home down trafficless streets, and I collapse into bed next to Laurel, home at last, stinking of drink and show sweat and my post-show halal-cart sandwich and everything else that had happened since I left our bedroom this morning.

* * *

WE PLAY BROOKLYN THE FOLLOWING NIGHT WITH VIOLENT Bullshit and Turing Machine. Orestes and I again drive the Forester, jammed with gear, to the club. Idling at a stoplight near the Williamsburg Bridge while I'm staring at my phone—cranky from the flood of texts and e-mails, impatient because *the light is still red*—Orestes excitedly nudges me and nods at the next car over. At first I hear indeterminate thuds and muttering and assume it's hip-hop. But the dude is blasting our song "Lookin' at the Devil." And headbanging. This has been a grouchy, hungover, and stressed-out day, but now we're in a good mood all the way to the club.

The Knitting Factory is a shoebox turned sideways, primarily composed of concrete. In terms of acoustics, that's strike one and strike two. It's painted a sickly, sticky-looking red that, now that I think about it, reminds me of Kokie's walls circa 1999. (Strike three, for looks.) The club's soundman, Bob, paces the room, wearing shorts and a face well-creased by rock and carousing, endlessly stressed out. He greets each request with a series of compulsive headshakes and dark mutterings about how impossible it is, then disappears and returns with whatever we need.

Before the show two guys wave me over to tell me they flew in from Atlanta for last night's show and changed their flights to stick around for tonight's. *(I hope we don't suck.)* Jerry Fuchs's younger brother, Adam, also came up from Georgia, and his sister, Erica, from North Carolina. Jerry should have seen this. I'm enormously touched that his siblings will. Besides its bad acoustics, the room is too shallow and the stage height is weirdly out of proportion with the space, and it isn't the best show of the tour. But somewhere during the loud part of "Ducks and Drakes," I close my eyes, turn my face up toward the stage lights, and behind my eyelids everything goes orange and I feel something I'll never properly describe, and I can't stop myself from laughing out loud, tickled by something, I'll never know what. During the long sustained A after the first verse in "Valmead," I turn the feedbacking note down, bend down to gulp a beer, stand upright, turn my volume back up, then launch into the next bit, perfectly timed and on beat. From your perch inside the song, you imagine that its intervals sound staggeringly cool, though these little dramas are far too inside baseball for almost anyone else to notice.

Then an afterparty where a bunch of us DJ, and when that bar closes its doors and turns up the lights, we stay for one more drink. Afterward Sooyoung takes us to a place he knows in Koreatown that is still serving food and, perhaps more important, pitchers of beer. It's not as if we're celebrating and bro-hugging all over the place—that never was our style—but none of us wants any of these final nights to end. We get home around 6 a.m. That afternoon we fly to Chicago for our last show.

* * *

THAT FINAL SHOW BROUGHT US TO AN INCREDIBLY EXALTED and appropriate venue, by which I mean a shithole made comfortable by years of familiarity. The Empty Bottle. The kind of place that every band, ever, has played at least once, and though I hadn't been there in years, it was instantly familiar once we stepped inside. Smaller and grottier than I remembered, perhaps, but its essentials hadn't changed at all. The couches backstage almost certainly hadn't. The main interior color was black, stickers covered virtually every surface—different ones than in 1996, but honestly that felt like a minor detail—and the backstage bathroom was still a riot of multicolored graffiti. Quality bourbons were available now, since its crowd was getting older and transferring its musical connoisseurship to food and drink, as well as a very good selection of beer, for what struck a New Yorker as shockingly low prices. The club was still a clumsy hodgepodge of three oddly connected rooms, with steps awkwardly and randomly placed throughout. I almost tripped, spectacularly, while getting offstage, and another time getting *to* the strangely shaped stage, which is situated where two rooms meet in the corner of a capital L. Bands usually set up their drums in the middle of the stage, then everyone else struggles to figure out where they should place and point their amps. I set up stage left, as always. From there, I was told, the local consensus was to aim the amp toward the men's room.

It was fitting that Bitch Magnet would end here. We remixed our first album and recorded much of our last album in Chicago, and Sooyoung lived there for years in the nineties. Also, the old Chicago rule still held: no matter how bad any tour was going, as you slogged through whatever dead and depressing stretch in the Great Plains or topmost tier of the South, you hung on until Chicago. It was your second hometown. Where everyone knew your name and understood your decades of accumulated indie rock bullshit.

281

I was unusually obsessed with selling merch, because I knew unless we had a huge crowd and sold a mountain of shirts and records and CDs, we'd lose money on the tour. I felt like a campaign manager who realizes, the night before Election Day, that his candidate needs a record turnout and a couple of other breaks to win. (And who doesn't share this insight with the candidate—or Sooyoung and Orestes.) Rose Marshack, the Poster Children bassist and another old friend, showed up early. She may have offered, but it's more likely I shamed or strong-armed her into running the merch table. Two people working merch is exponentially better than one, and—rock is sexist—for mostly-male crowds, women often sell better than men. I kept barking idiotic *Glengarry Glen Ross* jokes at her. But they worked. Soon Rose, a deeply kind, modest, and mild-mannered Midwestern mom, was all but grabbing people by the ear as they passed, demanding they buy something. One guy couldn't decide between a gray shirt and a brown one. "You should buy both!" she shot back. He picked brown. Three minutes later he returned, wearing an embarrassed grin, and bought the gray version, too.

Sooyoung's parents showed up, and I handed his dad a beer and two pairs of earplugs. Then, still playing host, I gave earplugs to Rose, my ex-girlfriend Martha, and my old friend Zoe. Martha and Zoe had been best friends at Oberlin and still seemed to be. I imagined such a thing was easier in Chicago than in New York or Los Angeles or London, cities where the currents of life and work dragged you into deeper and deeper water, so when you finally paused to look, all the people you'd known were dots on the horizon, paddling away from you, toward some other distant shore. I don't know if this is actually *true* of Chicago, but it's always been easy for me to idealize it as the road not taken.

The openers, Electric Hawk, were crushing and relentless and right up my alley: a very loud instrumental trio, all rock solid on their instruments, performing music at once elemental and complex. When they finished their set, Orestes and I paused alongside one of the awkwardly placed sets of steps. I scanned the room and said, "Good turnout." But he shook his head and replied, "No, it isn't," and he was right. Empty Bottle's capacity is four hundred. Only a couple hundred people were there. Said it before, but I'll say it again: when dealing with nightlife aimed at thirty- and fortysomethings, one has to accept that life complications can interfere with the best of intentions. I certainly did. But it still stung. It made me think, again, that we weren't good enough or important enough or *whatever* enough to get everyone off their couches. Still invisible. A too-secret handshake.

What Jeremy had implied—and what I'd suspected—at the beginning of the reunion, I now knew was true: we weren't going to get any bigger. I knew that we were out of step with this decade, in so many ways. To cite just one reason, the way we mixed our records was utterly unsuited for today. Too much ultra-low end, for starters. We also often avoided using compression on our records, because we wanted as wide as possible a range of soft and loud. Ultra-compressed production crushes those dynamics and makes EVERYTHING SOUND LOUDER. It's no coincidence it came into vogue in the twenty-first century, because ultra-compressed recordings sound good—or, more accurately, less bad—on the tiny cheap speakers in earbuds and computers and smartphones. Which is how most everyone hears music today. After our first reunion show in Japan, I went drinking with Katoman, and he told me he'd been thinking for days about how no current bands sounded like Bitch Magnet. He meant it as a compliment, and I was moved. But later I understood the secondary edge to that observation, one that cut in a far less complimentary way. "Unique today" could also mean "a relic from a time now gone."

When the familiar stomach rumbling came on, as it had for every reunion show, I looked for a moment toward the backstage bathroom, but there wasn't enough time. Twenty-five years since I started doing this, but with this band showtime still gave me the bowels of a coke fiend, drugs in hand, waiting. But then we were onstage, where it was dark and loud, and the crowd was crazy, or as crazy as a crowd of record nerds our age ever get. As with all the best shows, all I registered was snapshots. Boys and girls—well, men and women—headbanging down front, a few even pounding their fists on the stage. This night I played the closing solo in "Navajo Ace" and a certain end-of-verse flourish in "Sea of Pearls" just right. I don't think I'd ever played either entirely correctly before. And though I knew all along I was leaving all this, and there was something sad about that, nothing felt sad about the show. It felt correct. It felt complete. The proper finale to a very peculiar midlife foray.

One last night at the merch stand. It seemed that everyone who came bought something. In some cases, many things. My right back pocket held a burrito-sized wad of cash, until it grew too big to fit and I had to palm it like a small basketball. When I did the final tour accounting, I saw that, thanks to Rose and Chicago, we had turned a tiny profit in America after all.

The next day I drove over to see my old friend Bryan, the general manager of the mini-chain Reckless Records. Another musician was there, who'd also come to the show. He thanked me. Told me that his bucket list was now one item shorter. He also said he was surprised that certain people weren't there. I smiled, nodded, said: Me, too.

But no. No. I won't complain. It was beautiful. Nearly everyone in that crowd had a story. The ex-drummer from Hum—the same one who, in the nineties, tormented me every time our paths crossed with endless questions about Orestes—had driven three hundred miles from southern Indiana. The guitarist in Hum came up from Champaign. One guy came from Minneapolis; one woman, all the way from Los Angeles. An entire contingent drove from Louisville. Someone from St. Louis. Rose came from Bloomington, Illinois, which meant a two-hour drive to and from the show, followed by an early wakeup to teach her morning classes at the university. People we had met years ago in Pittsburgh, in New York, at school, in Europe. Looks of deep gratitude in familiar eyes, now set into older faces. A look that, I hope, was mirrored in mine.

* * *

IN THE IMMEDIATE AFTERMATH OF THE TOUR, VERY FEW PEO-ple I spoke with believed we'd really played our final shows. But I was not among them.

Bitch Magnet wasn't a band whose reunion would blossom into a second career, as had happened for bigger bands like Dinosaur Jr. or Mission of Burma or the fucking Pixies.

Bitch Magnet wasn't the kind of band for which a new generation of young fans would crowd into clubs.

With the possible exception of Orestes, none of us was that interested in keeping this going.

Though Bitch Magnet *was* the kind of band in which, during our year and a half of reunion rehearsals and shows, Sooyoung and I each wooed Orestes for new projects that excluded the other.

And we never even mentioned those projects to each other.

* * *

WE WERE STAYING WITH SOOYOUNG'S PARENTS IN CHICAGO, in their two apartments in a Gold Coast building. That company they started so many years ago in Charlotte, the one they'd worked so hard to build, had done very well. The three of us drank beer in the guest apartment until I couldn't keep my eyes open any longer. Someone woke me just after 7 a.m., and I went to my room.

I woke about three hours later, and, checking the circuits—weary eyes, bearable headache, no epic nausea—decided they were intact enough. Sooyoung's mom had thoughtfully left a basket of sweet rolls and muffins on the dining room table, around which the sun streamed in, beautifully if a bit painfully. Orestes had an early-afternoon flight home and already had his bags neatly stacked in the hallway, and Sooyoung, who'd slept in the other apartment, materialized to say goodbye.

I insisted that his dad take a few last pictures. Who knew when we'd be in the same room again?

Sooyoung and I both look pretty rough in those shots. We were facing the windows, and sunshine was a hard thing to take.

Then Orestes's phone rang: his cab was waiting outside. Sooyoung and I helped him hump his bags to the curb. Cars were speeding by, and we stood there, blinking in the sunlight. Always a little awkward, these goodbyes.

I hugged Orestes after maneuvering around his enormous pecs and traps and shoulders. In that clinch I managed to mutter, "We did it." Sooyoung and Orestes hugged, Orestes climbed in the backseat, and then he was gone.

I knew Sooyoung and Orestes's new band, Bored Spies, had recorded a single a few months ago, and in the upcoming year they'd play shows in America and Europe and Asia. Sooyoung and I had never talked about that before, and we didn't now. Instead, Sooyoung announced he was going back to bed.

Well, this was it.

What to say? We hugged, and once we stepped back from each other, I repeated what I'd told Orestes: "We did it."

Sooyoung nodded, smiling through his exhaustion. "And we did it *right*."

Maybe we had.

He suggested that Laurel and I come meet him and Fiona for a vacation in Indonesia sometime. I said, sure.

I quickly hustled in and out of the shower, taking care to keep the tidy bathroom as neat as it was. Sooyoung's dad appeared with a luggage cart, and after I loaded it, we wheeled it into the elevator and to the garage, where I hefted my bags and our merch boxes into the trunk of his car and carefully placed the guitar cases on the immaculate tan leather backseat. Then we headed east on Lakeshore Drive toward downtown. Sooyoung's dad had aged well. Still trim, with a good head of hair. He and his wife had been incredibly welcoming, and I was moved by their kindness. Twenty-five summers ago, when Sooyoung and I fled Charlotte for Atlanta, I'd left their home under much worse circumstances. I rarely sit on the kind of soft leather found in expensive cars, and I gratefully sank into my seat and looked toward the lake.

A winter-bright morning. December weather in October. A day where the wind turned your face red and whipped up whitecaps and real waves. You could imagine, briefly, that this was the shoreline of some sea. A few clouds scudded quickly in and out of sight. We arrived at my hotel, where I shook hands with Sooyoung's dad, thanking him once more, and followed a bellman into the hotel.

My room had amazing eighties wall switches for the lights and TV, with one button actually marked MOOD LIGHTING. State of the art, for the Atari age. It would take time to figure it all out. But I took the elevator to a great room downstairs, ordered tea, opened my laptop, and started writing.

The cement tones of downtown Chicago outside the window. Grand, but terribly monochromatic. A sad pile of pumpkins in a courtyard provided the only natural color. No place could underscore the late-autumn feelings of finale better than Chicago. Portlandia for this kind of music. Where there was an endless procession of bands like ours. As such, it was our culture's best argument for *careful what you wish for*. Nerdy, earnest boys, dressing badly, trying desperately to rewrite the rules of rock—and generally failing, often egregiously. I was always just one left turn from ending up here and being a part of it, too. I always resisted, and shit-talked and belittled this city instead. And yet, while I stayed in Chicago after we played the Bottle, people I hadn't spoken to in years showed me around, bought me drinks, waved me into their shows for free, refused to let me eat any meal alone. This town took me in whenever I showed up. I always forgot that part.

* * *

I HAVEN'T YET MENTIONED HOW THE BUILD, PEAK, AND AFTER-glow of any performance and tour is much more visible today. Preshow chatter on Facebook and Twitter is an effective early-alert system, so you can sense how much interest is building. (I knew, for instance, that Hong Kong would be bad, that Singapore would be pretty good, and that London and Tokyo and New York would be really good.) And, after each show, there would be a day or so of Twitter and Facebook comments before the crowd flitted on to the next thing.

It always hurt a bit, watching the vapor trail of any tour's final show fade. You knew that it was inevitable, but that didn't make the absence of chatter and noise and anticipation and showtime feel any better. Chicago's traces would disappear, too. But they had a longer half-life than most, and while they were still fresh, I marveled over the kind things people posted online.

Like this, from Jay Ryan, who played bass for Dianogah:

> Went to the Empty Bottle last night to see Bitch Magnet, a band whom I've loved for roughly 20 years, but whom I'd never seen before, as they broke up before I found them. They reunited for a handful of shows, and this was one of the best concerts I'd ever been to, ever. Insanely tight, especially for a bunch of old guys. The experience was only improved by being surrounded by friends I don't see nearly often enough, most of whom have made music which has been heavily influenced by this band.

Especially for a bunch of old guys?

Oh, the hell with it. He's right.

And this is where the story ends. A strange little band, oddly and briefly reunited two decades after it broke up. Kings of a few small clubhouses for a few more nights. Living a modest dream. But sometimes that's enough.

Almost nothing I'd hoped for twenty-five years ago had happened. The weirdos hadn't taken over. Our bands hadn't changed the world, or destroyed the big, bad major labels. (That was the Internet's job.) Or even changed the mainstream much. I'm not even going to get into how almost all of the places we most treasured, where we found each other and where we gathered—record stores, bookstores, mom-and-pop music shops, the dive bars and venues we all knew—long ago vanished. But believing that this culture's significance depends on fulfilling any ancient grandiose expectation is missing the point. Because, despite everything that happened and everything that didn't, we carved out—and nurtured and maintained—a place for bands like us.

Sometimes that's enough, too.

Sometimes.

And today, after all these years, when rock music means so much less than it once did, weird bands as different as Tortoise and Battles and Fucked Up and Swans and Shellac still play and thrive. In some cases, even make a living from music alone. A framework—a touring circuit and a culture—still stands for new generations of musicians like us. I haven't been paying attention, but I can feel them all out there, as the ocean feels the phases of the moon. As I can feel all those I've known forever who are still at it, like Ted Leo, Lightning Bolt, Yo La Tengo, the Ex, Will Oldham, Melvins, the Sea and Cake, Mudhoney, Uzeda . . . There are too many to list, and that's a small victory, too. I don't love all those bands, but that's not important. What's important is this: they're the people I recognized, long ago. The ones who made me realize I wasn't alone. Maybe they recognized me, too.

And sometimes that's enough.

No. It is enough. That's the happy ending. One far better than any of us ever dreamed, back when we crouched beside our parents' stereos, peeling shrink-wrap off the first record we bought by the Stooges or Wire or Black Flag or Hüsker Dü. Lonely, ignored, maybe even hated, but suddenly strangely excited.

"I ended up in a band that has a really small following. People with gigantic record collections. Who have socially maladapted lives because of their love for music," Mission of Burma's Clint Conley once told me. "But those are the people I wanted."

Those are the people I wanted, too.

Because those are the people we are.

Epilogue: Staying Off the Bus

After our second Asian tour I stayed in Tokyo and booked myself into a fancy hotel for two nights. It was exorbitant, even after I found a crazily discounted rate, and not in the slightest bit punk rock. But I couldn't resist going grand after the madness and bruisings of this tour. All of which started receding as the cabbie, dressed in a suit and white gloves, sprang from the right-side driver's seat and began Tetris-ing my gear and luggage into the minuscule trunk and backseat.

I settled in and gave him the name of my hotel. Soon we passed the O-East, where we'd played the night before last, and a few moments after that we left behind the parts of Shibuya that light up like a pinball machine every night, garishly, blaringly, neon-soaked.

An overcast day in April, under a weak and tired sun. Only barely spring. Our friends here told us we'd just missed the cherry blossoms. *But we always just miss the cherry blossoms*, I thought. Combining touring and tourism never really works out.

The VIP wristband from yesterday's festival was still on my wrist, and my body was a catalog of ache and malady. Half of my back was balled up and crying: in your mid-forties, wearing heavy guitars night after night messes you up. My feet and calves still throbbed from all that bouncing up and down onstage. A small constellation of angry-looking blood blisters dotted my right forearm, friction welts from up-and-downing too hard on my guitar. I clicked my teeth together, testing, and felt jolts of pain. During the encore in Singapore—was that ten days ago?—I lunged toward Sooyoung's bass, trying to bite the strings, but missed, and my top front teeth smashed into the pickguard instead. They hurt like hell the next morning, and I checked them in mirrors for the rest of the tour, convinced they'd start turning black, but they didn't. On top of everything, *Jesus,* was I fried. Exhausted and place-shifted. Returning to the hotel the night before around 4 a.m., I asked the desk attendant for my room key, by number, in approximate Japanese. *Roku zero roku.* But then unfathomably added *s'il vous plaît?*

I lolled against the white lace draped across the backseat to watch the order and correctness of Tokyo rolling by. The harmony of a thoughtfully designed city, especially on a quiet Sunday. When we arrived at the hotel, the driver pushed his magic button, and my door eased open. A small crowd of employees descended, all wearing suits. One asked the name on my reservation, two muscled the bags and guitars out of the car and onto a large luggage cart, and a fourth, speaking fluent unaccented English, escorted me in, through the entrance and into the teak-walled elevators that opened out into a grand vaulted space of the lobby bar and indoor bamboo garden. This was the kind of hotel where, once you stepped into the lobby, all the noise of the day falls away, submerging you in a deep, delicious, calming hush, a very expensive quiet for which I'll forever be a sucker, and never more so than after the strung-out extremes of a tour like this one. Every detail here was so thought-out that in the hallways the ceiling fixtures cast perfectly symmetrical round pools of light on the carpet. Ridiculous. But I loved it. As it was ridiculous I could even *be* here—that fortune had smiled on me so brightly that I could come to Asia for a wholly improbable ongoing reunion of my teenage punk rock band, and afterward sleep two nights in such a setting.

Just after I arrived in my room, the doorbell chimed—the bellman, who neatly propped open the door and hauled in everything, starting with the duffel bags and merch boxes. When he set the guitar cases down, he made his joke, asking whether or not they contained machine guns.

No, I told him. Guitars. But sometimes they're as *loud* as machine guns.

It wasn't funny, but he laughed anyway. We both bowed, and he left, gently closing the door behind him.

I looked out over the city. *So we'll do some shows in America this fall,* I thought, *and that'll be it.* Orestes and I were still talking about a new band, but nothing was coming of it, and I couldn't pretend I was dying to start all over again. Not even with him.

Some leftover tour anxiety fluttered, and I walked across the carpet to where the bellman had perfectly stacked the guitar cases atop one another. At the festival someone had packed up both Les Pauls for me—another first—and I wanted to check.

Each guitar was fine, nestled perfectly into a fake red velvet interior. But something tightened in my throat.

Every now and then I looked at one of my guitars, still marveling: *What a lovely thing.* Though this time it wasn't that. It was more like: *All the places we've been. Crazy.*

I strummed the open strings on the black Les Paul with my index finger. The D-A-D-G-A-D tuning that Sooyoung first showed me in late 1988, which I'd used off and on ever since, and the chord resonated in the case and through the body, hanging in the air for a long time, which is exactly what you want from a Les Paul:

Braaaaaaaannnnng.

How many times had I heard the gentle rise and fade of that open chord on an unamplified Les Paul and thought, *Wow. So beautiful.* No song—no recording—ever truly captured the subtleties and colors of its overtones sounding in a quiet room.

Braaaaaaaannnnng.

This magic wand that could dispel all bad feelings, turn the air electric, fill every empty space, be beautiful or brutal and every shade in between—and it all started with this unamplified, unadorned sound. A toddler would first play a parent's guitar like this: drawing a tiny, tentative finger across the open strings, amazed at the magic that follows.

Braaaaaaaannnnng.

* * *

IN MAY 2010 MY FRIENDS IN LCD SOUNDSYSTEM PLAYED FOUR sold-out shows at New York's Terminal 5. Everything about those nights was perfect. They were a hometown send-off before the band left on a long international tour. They'd just released *This Is Happening* and were absolutely on fire. The opening act, their labelmates Holy Ghost!, were friends with all of us, too. I went to every show. Each night the audience went bananas. Each night the afterparty went very late.

Backstage and VIP sections of rock clubs generally suck, but at these shows it was different. Not because it was decadent and everyone was crazy on drugs and fucking in the bathrooms and broom closets. Because it was all old friends. Many of whom were my favorite people. We'd all known each other forever. Our bands played together. We all dragged out our adolescence for as long as possible before growing up, late, together. Saw each other get married. Gathered, blotchy-faced and sobbing, to bury a close friend. Met their kids when they were born. The VIP section was filled with the people you most wanted to invite to the party—the crew with whom you wanted to end every late night— all jumping and cheering and singing along with the *other* people you most wanted to invite to the party, who were tearing it up onstage. The occasional actual celebrity who dropped by often looked around and quickly calculated that it wasn't worth staying, because they weren't among their kind.

All during that enchanting time of year in New York when daylight keeps lasting longer and each night the late sunsets and warm evenings still surprise.

Like I said. Everything about it was perfect.

The final show was on a Sunday night, and after the last encores and the balloon drop left us sweaty and wrung-out, and after we clicked our iPhone cameras at the commemorative cake backstage, and after we stayed to the end of whatever final afterparty, I went home and slept a few hours, woke up around eight, showered, gulped caffeine and cereal, threw on clean jeans, a white button-down shirt, and a suit jacket, and rushed my worn-out, hungover ass out the door for a nine-o'clock meeting. It was time to get back to that other world. All that had happened over the course of the previous week was already growing lovelier in memory as I dashed down flights of stairs. But I was trying to push it aside and release the PAUSE button I'd pressed down again for a few lucky nights.

What came next never happens. Until it does.

Downstairs a bus idled at the curb. Then I saw Pat and Nick, the drummers from LCD Soundsystem and Holy Ghost!, finishing predeparture cigarettes. *Of course they're here,* I thought: James from LCD lived in my building. Our eyes met, and they cracked up and started waving and hollering and pointing at the bus.

Get on.

Get on that bus.

Come on!

Get on!

Fine!

You know you're getting on the bus.

Come on!

You're going!

Let's go!

I cracked up, too, made sounds of excuses—*reallybusy! toomuchwork! can'tgetaway!*—and went over to slap hands and hug and wish them a great tour. Tonight was Montreal, they said, and—arching eyebrows toward James's window—they were already running a little late.

As was I. So I said goodbye and took off.

Nothing happening here was that *important,* I thought as I jogged toward the subway. But that wasn't why I was staying.

They probably didn't know how hard it was for me not to get on the bus that lovely May morning. Or how badly I hoped they were serious.

They probably didn't know how desperate I was not to lose the feeling of the past few days. That I'd do almost anything to hold on to it for a little bit longer.

The only sensible thing to do was walk away. Crank up the machinery of a more practical life, the one with far fewer highs and lows. If I got on that bus, I'd never, ever want to get off.

I kept running to the L train, sweating last night's booze into my jacket, swiped my way through the turnstile, lunged into a subway car crammed with cranky rush-hour commuters, and didn't look back.

I was forty-two, and married. You can't keep running away to join the circus.

* * *

THOUGH IF YOU'RE REALLY LUCKY, I THOUGHT, ALMOST TWO years later, seven thousand miles from home in a fancy hotel, you might get to visit it again, for a little while.

Braaaaaaaaaaang.

This odd and lovely little world. Which saved me, and then broke my heart. The world I'd been so determined to forget.

Braaaaaaaaaaaaang.

But, of course, I couldn't.

Braaaaaaaaaaang.

Even though, no matter what I expected, it always let me down.

Braaaaaaaaaaang.

I mean: Really. You *motherfuckers.* All of you. I wasted *so much time.*

Braaaaaaaaaaang.

But listen to me, for just a little longer.

Before I walk away again, and probably forever, it's important that you know how grateful I was for this chance to return.

No. I am grateful this whole raggedy culture was ever possible—ever thinkable—in the first place.

How madly, and how unreasonably, I loved every minute.

Well, *almost* every minute.

Braaaaaaaaaaang.

Even if I understood all along that the hardest thing about picking up a guitar is knowing that, one day, you'll have to put it down.

Braaaaaaaaaaang.

When I'm seventy, I'll hear a snatch of some song, somewhere, and duck my head and smile. Not because I remember. Because I still know.

Braaaaaaaaaaang.

One last time. The chord dropped away to reveal pure sound: overtones mingling, vibration purring through wood.

Then there was no sound at all, and I closed and locked the case.

Acknowledgments

The absolute worst thing about many records from the eighties and nineties was the interminably long "thanks to" lists. That said: Here's an interminably long etc., etc.

This book would not exist without my agent, Wayne Kabak, and its editor, Rick Kot, thanks to a different book idea that Wayne hatched and a subsequent lunch I had with Rick at which I shared said idea. But Rick proved more interested in my old band that was reuniting after twenty-one years, and some time after the main course told me, that's your book. This book would not exist without Orestes Morfin and Sooyoung Park, nonpareil touring and drinking companions and a hell of a rhythm section. This book would not exist were it not for everyone who ever bought a record, saw a show, or uttered a kind word about any band I played in, and I am still awed and amazed that any single person ever did. On a lighter but equally important note, the *title* of this book would not exist without Ed Fotheringham, singer of the Thrown Ups, who came up with the title and lyrics for the song "Your Band Sucks."

I was enormously lucky to meet Linc Wheeler when I did. The journey to discovering the music that most excites you is even better if a close friend is with you every step of the way. Linc, you rock. Hopefully a few more people will know that now, too.

Tad Friend, an uncommonly stylish and wise writer, made this book immeasurably better with his detailed comments and suggestions. My brother, Neil Fine, was an invaluable sounding board and counselor throughout, never more than when he parachuted in for some last-minute editing that, basically, saved my sorry ass. As always, his brilliant advice was dispensed quietly, absent any drama, and with a great deal of hilarity. I'd take a bullet for Neil, but I suspect what he really wants is for me to apologize that an earlier draft of this book incorrectly characterized his athletic ability at summer camp as sub par. I'm truly sorry about that, and rest assured, Neil, I still remember your outstanding sprint that kicked off Indian Head Camp's Rope Burn in the summer of 1978.

I have been in serious bands with many people, and not all of them appear herein. I am certain I am omitting many names but the following deserve a shout-out for being there, keeping company, and shaping and sharing these experiences: Bob Bannister, Lyle Hysen, Jenna Johnson, Jordan Mamone, Eamon Martin, Dave McGurgan, Gerald Menke, Doug Scharin, Kevin Shea, Eric Topolsky, and Jeff Winterberg. And the guitarist and bassist in Ribbons of Flesh: Roger White and Doug MacLehose.

There are many others with whom I've had long ongoing conversations about music—in person, via e-mail, on listservs in the nineties, and on Facebook and elsewhere today—or people whose writing helped crystallize how I understand music. Among them: Steve Albini, Mark Arm, Richard Baluyut, Nils Bernstein, Chris Brokaw, Joe Carducci, Paula Puhak Chang, Justin Chearno, Damon Che, Byron Coley, Ian Christe, Liz Clayton, Andee Connors, Gerard Cosloy, Ana Marie Cox, Scott DeSimon, Elizabeth Elmore, John Engle, Jayson Green, Joe Gross, Allan Horrocks, Steve Immerwahr, Jimmy Johnson, Katoman, Rob Lim, Rose Marshack, Bob Massey, DJ McNany, Nick Milhiser, James Murphy, Dave Reid, Seth Sanders, Agostino Tilotta, Fred Weaver, Bob Weston, Nancy Whang, Ian Williams, Douglas Wolk, Kiki Yablon, and, of course, all the members of the secret society of Chugchanga.

The ragtag crew at WOBC ran a hell of a radio station when I attended Oberlin, among them Martha Bayne, Jolene Callen, Rachel Maceiras, John McEntire, Jim Rippie, Bryan Smith, Steve Summers, Susannah Tartan, Will Winter, Zoe Zolbrod, and the late Rick Treffinger.

Things got heated between us and Barry Hogan for a while, but without him, Bitch Magnet never would have reunited. Big thanks to him and the rest of the All Tomorrows Parties' crew that made performing at 2011's

ACKNOWLEDGMENTS

Nightmare Before Christmas such a delight, in particular Deborah Hogan and Shawn Kendrick. It is a source of some regret that some of Shaun's craziest road stories are unpublishable.

Those last Bitch Magnet tours would not have happened, nor been as fabulous an experience, without the following people: Matthew Barnhart, Diego Castillo, Kitty Chew, Joffy Cruz, Dalse, Jeremy DeVine, George Gargan and Janice Li, Hiroki and the rest of the Kaikoo staff, Katoman, Kimi Lam, John Lee, Ana Paz Lopez, Jim Merlis, Sang Ah Nam and Kiwan Sung and 3rd Line Butterfly, Nisennenmondai, Alfie Palao, Jihong Park and the entire staff at Strange Fruit, smallgang and Former Utopia, Errol Tan, Tarsius, Peter Weening, Wilderness, the stage crew at Shibuya O-Nest, those who put on our show in Cologne, and everyone who came out to see us.

I didn't write much about record stores, but their centrality to this time and this kind of story is incalculable. I learned lots from the following. Some still exist, and should you be new to this music and curious to learn more, please direct your paychecks their way: Aquarius Records, Newbury Comics, Other Music, Pier Platters, Reckless, Sounds, Twisted Village, and Venus Records. And See Hear.

My parents, Alan Fine and Karen Fine, were forever far more supportive of my musical endeavors than I could ever have hoped, whether that meant showing up to see Bitch Magnet play opening-band slots at the CBGB Record Canteen to letting us blast away in the basement while, after a long day at work, they tried to eat dinner directly above us to, well, far too much else to recount here. Thanks, Mom and Dad.

A few musicians and denizens that I knew from this time aren't around anymore. The music and joy they created will long outlive them, but the world is lessened for losing the light they shone: Jon Cook, Michael Dahlquist, Hajji Majer, Letha Rodman Melchior, Jason Noble, and Billy Ruane. Above all, Jerry Fuchs, from whom I learned so much, with whom I laughed so hard, and to whom I still have so much to say. It is impossible to convey my sadness to know that we'll never finish our conversation.

In the course of writing this book, I interviewed around sixty musicians, label heads, and booking agents. Some were subjected to innumerable follow-up questions, yet tolerated them with ridiculously good humor and in general showed themselves to be all-around excellent human beings. In particular: Lou Barlow, Boche Billions, Ken Brown, Joe Carducci, Clint

Conley, Jeremy DeVine, Anne Eickelberg, Zachary Lipez, Juan MacLean, Rose Marshack, Doug McCombs, Roger Miller, Peter Prescott, and David Yow. Others provided particularly thought-provoking or clarity-inducing comments, even though none of their quotes made it into the book: Henry Bogdan, Rebecca Gates, Michael Gerald, Emily Rieman, and Steve Turner. Somewhat relatedly, anyone needing transcription services should carve Cynthia Colonna's name into their forearm. She's fast, accurate, delightful, and, in general, all kinds of awesome. Find her at cynthiacolonna.com.

Much of this book was written at The Writers Room, the sui generis oasis in lower Manhattan. For around a year beginning in February 2013, I depended to an embarrassing degree upon its stillness, coziness, and quiet, and it never let me down. Huge thanks to Donna Brodie, Liz Sherman, and all the others that keep this space going.

Aside from being plain delightful to spend each workday with, the staff at *Inc.* were remarkably tolerant of my mood swings and occasional missed meetings and last-minute days off as this book's final deadline loomed. It is important to note that all the stuff about the weirdness associated with explaining your fucked-up bands to people at work was all written *before* I met them. Over at Viking and Penguin, Candice Gianetti provided services far beyond and saved me from several stupid mistakes; Amelia Zalcman offered wise and judicious counsel; Daniel Lagin came up with the look and feel; Diego Nunez took care of a million little details; and Sharon Gonzalez made it all happen. I'm also fortunate to work with not one but two top-notch book publicists: Meredith Burks and Gretchen Crary.

Others who helped in ways large and small: Kurt Andersen and Anne Kreamer, Gary Hoenig and Betsy Carter, Russ Reid, Michael Weiss, and the crew with whom I want to end every late night. (You know who you are.)

And last, but really first, my wife, Laurel Touby. She was there for every minute of a project that took almost four years to complete. Her patience with its demands was constant and astonishing, even during its many crunch times. Her ferocious skills at the merch table during Bitch Magnet's last round of tours helped our little circus survive until the next show, her editing pen made the final product better. Thank you, Laurel, for all of that and so much more. Had we not met, there would be no happy ending. I love you.